ISHERWOOD

Books by Jonathan Fryer

ISHERWOOD
THE GREAT WALL OF CHINA

ISHERWOOD

Jonathan Fryer

DOUBLEDAY & COMPANY, INC.
GARDEN CITY, NEW YORK
1978

Library of Congress Cataloging in Publication Data

Fryer, Jonathan.
  Isherwood.

  "The major works of Christopher Isherwood".
  Includes index.
    1. Isherwood, Christopher, 1904–   –Biography.   2. Authors, English—
20th century–Biography.
  PR6017.S5Z67   1978   823'.9'12 [B]
  Library of Congress Catalog Card Number 77-82941
  ISBN: 0-385-12608-5

The author and publisher wish to thank the following for permission
to quote copyrighted material:

  Christopher Isherwood and Jonathan Cape, Eyre Methuen, The
Hogarth Press, Faber and Faber and the Vedanta Press for quotations
from his books and plays (see pages 293–94 for full list of Isherwood
publications).

  Stephen Spender and Hamish Hamilton for World Within World.

  Salka Viertel and Holt, Rinehart and Winston for The Kindness
of Strangers.

  Chatto and Windus for the Letters of Aldous Huxley.

  Allan Wingate for Gerald Hamilton's Mr Norris and I.

  The author also wishes to thank the many people who gave him
access to Isherwood letters, especially Sir Rupert Hart-Davis (William Plomer estate), Sylvain Mangeot (Olive Mangeot estate), Alan
Clodd, John Lehmann, Edward Upward and William Caskey.

For
Jean-Luc Hucque

ISHERWOOD

INTRODUCTION

I believe that all biographers should nail their colours to the mast, even though no honest writer can hope to be entirely objective. It usually becomes apparent to the reader soon enough if an author is an admirer of his subject, or simply a critic out for blood. The writer can never be neutral about him; if he were, he would probably lack the motivation and no less the stamina to finish his book.

Immediately after leaving school in 1969 I went to Vietnam (voluntarily, unlike most young Anglo-Saxons of my age), and there became fascinated by the Orient. This passion did not abate in the least on my return to Europe, where I frequented every society or gathering even remotely connected with the Far East, and devoured any book that dealt, however briefly, with the world east of Chittagong.

The winter of 1969–70 found me in South Africa, visiting my parents, and there I indulged in my usual hobby of scouring second-hand bookshops. That part of the world, not surprisingly, was lacking in Oriental material. But in Knysna I came across a travel book on China, *Journey to a War*, by W. H. Auden and Christopher Isherwood, which not only slaked my thirst for information about the East, but also introduced me to the work of a man who was soon to become one of my favourite novelists.

Isherwood replied promptly and fully to my initial letter of adolescent enthusiasm, and a short correspondence ensued about our mutual interest in Oriental philosophy and Quakers, and our common backgrounds in the outlying areas of Manchester. The exchange of letters stopped when I went up the Mekong again, but I soon found myself going once more into Isherwood's work and life when I joined Reuters News Agency in London. There I was assigned to work on the Profile Desk, a euphemism for the obituary service, which supplied subscribers with potted biographies of an arbitrary selection of the thousand most famous people in the world. These could be used for reference purposes, or for printing *in toto* should anything disastrous happen to the subject. Thus I researched fairly deeply into the past of a variety of Oriental, artistic or literary figures such as Kuo Mo-ruo, Kang Sheng, Pierre Boulez, Hans Werner Henze, Daphne du Maurier, Gore Vidal— and Christopher Isherwood.

Reading through files of old newspaper cuttings about Isherwood made me realise how little even a self-confessed admirer knew of the man, his work in the film world, his pacifist activities or his crusading for homosexual rights. For most people, indeed, he remains Herr Issyvoo of his classic Berlin stories, yet this is only one aspect of a many-faceted and extraordinary personality.

So the idea for this book was born, the aim of it being to present a clear picture of a man who has quietly made a significant contribution to twentieth-century life. It would not have been possible to have written it without Isherwood's close and generous co-operation, for he let himself be subjected to hour upon hour of questioning during the summers of 1975 and 1976.

The prospect of writing a biography of a controversial figure was a daunting one in view of the fact that so many of the major protagonists were still alive. However, very little has had to be left out because of tact or fear of libel actions. I have been surprised by the warmth and humour shown to me during my collaboration with many of the people involved, and would especially like to thank the following for their help:

For interviews, both long and short: Don Bachardy, Michael Barrie, Alec and Dodie Beesley, James Bridges, Mrs. Ivo Bulley (nee Rosmaira Morgan Brown), William Caskey, Claud Cockburn, Henry Davidson, Brian Finney, John Gammel (Headmaster, Repton School), Jim Gates, Peter Grose (Curtis Brown Ltd., London), Felix Greene, Raymond Greene, Carolyn G. Heilbrun, David Hockney, Dr. Evelyn Hooker, Clive Johnson, Margaret (Peggy) Kiskadden, Gavin Lambert, Jack Larson, John Lehmann, Marguerite (Lamkin) Littman, Sylvain Margeot, Edward Mendelson, Jessica Mitford, John Rechy, Gottfried and Sylvia Reinhardt, William Scobie, Peter Schlesinger, Douglas Steere, James and Tania Stern, Edward and Hilda Upward, and Peter Weeks (Headmaster, St. Edmund's School, Hindhead, Surrey).

For answering specific queries by post, or with help in other ways: Sybille Bedford, David Blamires and Michael Hutchinson (Friends Homosexual Fellowship), Edwin Bronner (Haverford College Library, Pennsylvania), Alan Clodd, Michael Davie, Sir Rupert Hart-Davis, Michael di Capua (Farrar Straus & Giroux, New York), D. J. Hall, Richard Isherwood, Lincoln Kirstein, David Machin (Jonathan Cape Ltd., London), Stathis Orphanos, Roger Pemberton and Alice Prochaska (National Portrait Gallery, London), Dame Marie Rambert, Catherine Rodriguez-Nieto (Berkeley, California), Canon Charles Smyth, Natasha and Stephen Spender, Jack Sutters and Laurama Pixton (AFSC), Rex Warner, Lesley Webster (Friends House Library, London), and Geoffrey Woodhead and R. I. Page (Corpus Christi College, Cambridge).

For the provision of welcome, quiet accommodation and writing facilities: Tony Sarver and Linda Shortland.

For help with the photographs and a thousand and one small things which enabled the book to be finished on time: Jean-Luc Hucque.

PART ONE
England

1

Christopher William Bradshaw Isherwood was born shortly before midnight on Friday, August 26, 1904, in his parents' home at Wyberslegh Hall in High Lane, Cheshire, about twelve miles south-east of Manchester. His mother, Kathleen, found the experience neither enjoyable nor exhilarating, and needed chloroform to bear the pain, but later she sensed the pride in her husband Frank's eyes and rejoiced in their new bond of parenthood. She smiled at the thought that her baby looked positively Japanese, with his broad slit-eyes, and dozed off fitfully after handing the screaming bundle to a nurse, hired for the period of her confinement.

Before breakfast the following morning Frank went over to nearby Marple Hall, where his parents lived in some style, to convey the news. His father, celebrating his own birthday that day, ordered the flag to be raised above the house to broadcast the happy tidings of a grandson and heir. For years afterwards he and Christopher would have an "official" joint birthday on August 27.

In early Edwardian England a baby was born with the advantages, responsibilities and problems of his family's class to a degree largely unknown in our present age of greater social mobility. The infant Christopher's world was one of provincial upper-middle-class respectability, in which affluence was enjoyed but which lacked the extravagance and ostentation of great wealth. Correct behaviour and form were very important, though the individual members of the Bradshaw-Isherwood family were not without their little eccentricities: both of Christopher's parents showed a certain originality by being competent amateur artists.

Frank and Kathleen had not decided in advance what the child should be called. They had reduced the choice to Louis (in homage to Robert Louis Stevenson who shared, with Robert Browning, Frank's great esteem), or Alexander (after a family friend), or the recurring family names John, William and Henry. A couple of obscurer relatives had been called Christopher, but essentially this was a name which appealed to Kathleen's ear. After a few days, Frank's elder brother, Henry—who had agreed to be the child's godfather—pressed the couple to a decision, since he wanted to have a silver christening mug engraved. Christopher William it therefore became, Frank often calling the child William, in memory of a very dear friend, Captain William Bradshaw (no relation), who was killed in the Boer War.

Although Wyberslegh Hall was Christopher's home, Marple was very much the centre of the Bradshaw-Isherwoods' family life, and the boy spent much of his time there. Marple Hall was a large, impressive, red sandstone building, one of the most imposing houses in the area, romantically covered in climbing ivy, and representative of that especially English sort of jumbled architecture that contributes to the charm of so many country houses. The original E-shaped Elizabethan mansion had frequently been added to and altered. Some of the old mullioned windows had been replaced by larger ones, while others had been bricked up in the eighteenth century to avoid window taxes. A well-stocked garden provided colour for most of the year, though the Hall's sheltered location among wooded hills on the edge of the Peak District meant that the interior of the house was often gloomy through lack of direct sunlight. The richly coloured stained-glass windows in the flagstoned entrance hall only emphasised the subdued atmosphere, as did the heavy, dark furniture, the sombre suits of armour and the walls hung with formal portraits of ancestors of the Bradshaw and Isherwood families who had been united in marriage in the eighteenth century. Their coats of arms had been painted on the oak-panelled walls and embroidered on the chairs of the library, which was lined with morocco-bound tomes which nobody read. Flemish tapestries graced the dining-room, while over the sideboard hung a forbidding painting of Queen Elizabeth I, at the sight of which Christopher's grandmother would mutter under her breath "Justice without Mercy!" like some ritualistic incantation. In such surroundings it was impossible to ignore the weight of English history.

Kathleen was acutely conscious of the gentility of the family into which she had married, and made considerable researches into its past. This proved to be far more rewarding than that of her own, which smelt all too strongly of Trade. By nature a diarist and hoarder of memories, she preserved her findings, viewing her researches not only as an amusement but also as a useful legacy for Christopher. It would be seventy years before Christopher recognised and acknowledged how valuable her work had been.

Uncle Henry, being the eldest male of his generation, had been groomed as heir to the not inconsiderable property, and enjoyed his position to the full. He seemed most unlikely to marry, though, and probably several members of the family were aware that his interests lay far more in the direction of men than women. It seemed obvious to all that Christopher would eventually inherit both the property and the family tradition. Thus, while still a child, Christopher became thoroughly conversant with his background, and often acted as a guide to visiting friends or callers at Marple Hall, solemnly rattling off a long spiel full of historical detail and anecdote. Later, however, he was to revolt against this tradition and berate Kathleen for what he called her Cult of the Past. Between them, the march of progress, financial difficulty and Christopher's indifference were to lead literally to the fall of Marple Hall.

The origins of both Marple and Wyberslegh Halls went back to the end of the fifteenth century, but it was in 1606 (exactly three hundred years before Kathleen started to write an illustrated history for Christopher) that the Bradshaw family bought Marple and Wyberslegh from their previous owners. They had already been tenants of the two houses for several years, and John Bradshaw, once famous for signing King Charles I's death warrant, was almost certainly born in the so-called Bradshaw Room of Marple Hall in 1602. He was christened in Stockport, the nearest sizeable town, and opposite his name in the parish register someone had written the single word "traitor." Tradition has it that as a boy, John (Jack) Bradshaw engraved a verse on a tombstone in Macclesfield churchyard saying:

> My brother Henry must heir the land
> My brother Frank must be at his command
> Whilst I, poor Jack, shall do that
> Which all the world will wonder at.

No one in 1906 could ignore the coincidence that the three Bradshaw-Isherwood brothers of their generation were also called Henry, Frank and Jack, and that their roles in life were those of heir, soldier and lawyer.

John Bradshaw, the regicide, had by early middle age become Chief Justice of Chester, the county capital, and was politically a republican. At that time he was a strong supporter of Oliver Cromwell, whose Parliament had recently won the Civil War, located the fugitive King Charles in Scotland and imprisoned him. When, in 1648, Parliament decided to try the King for treason, they had difficulty in finding members of the legal profession who would be willing to take part in a process which appeared to them illegal. John Bradshaw had no such qualms, though he did not attend the first sessions of the Commission established by Cromwell to conduct the trial. However, Bradshaw was nominated Lord President of the High Court *in absentia*, and did take the chair in a travesty of a trial in January 1649, during which the King bravely refused to recognise the authority of the court, his dignified obstinacy making the prosecution lose its calm on several occasions. Judge Bradshaw, aware that the trial was far from universally approved, took precautions against a possible assassin's hand by wearing a hat lined with metal plates.

Bradshaw expelled the unrepentant monarch from the court three times before he came to the inevitable moment when he passed the sentence of death upon Charles, denying him the right to speak at this stage in retribution for the King's earlier refusal to co-operate. Bradshaw's role in the affair made him a controversial figure, but among his supporters was the poet John Milton. The latter, who was Cromwell's secretary and apparently a relative of Bradshaw's by marriage, praised the judge's integrity and erudition. Bradshaw was rewarded by Parliament with a generous income, derived from the Council of State and Attorney-General of Cheshire and North Wales, though later he came into conflict with Cromwell and history was less generous to him, generally treating the trial as perfidious, and Bradshaw's role in it as ignoble. Three centuries later, the adolescent Christopher basked in the reflected light of his distinguished if somewhat disreputable predecessor, and recounted the story to school friends with relish. It is possible that this personal connection with England's past was one reason why he went on to choose history as his academic speciality.

Some years later, when Christopher was putting his personality under analysis, he decided that he could justify his reverence for Judge Bradshaw, even though he was an ancestor (thus to be loathed along with the rest of the family and the Establishment), because Bradshaw was actually an *anti*-ancestor. For, by revering a man like Bradshaw, who was condemned by history, he was flaunting the Enemy in a staid society which, he felt, he had to attack at every opportunity lest he be seduced into accepting it. Christopher also drew great comfort from the fact that some of his much less famous forebears had been distinctly odd and occasionally mad. He was delighted to learn that two contemporary relatives of his had been charged in court with being wandering lunatics, and at one time he was fond of portraying others in his family as being barely restrained from the direst crimes. The sense of the macabre or bizarre, so common in young children, grew rather than lessened in Christopher as he matured, and recurs through his conversation and written work, from the earliest schoolboy stories to his recent film about Frankenstein.

Kathleen was not the only relative by marriage who had paid undue interest to the family's past. Christopher's great-great-grandmother, Elizabeth, had gone so far as to construct a weird *tableau vivant* in a small upstairs room in Marple Hall which she dubbed King Charles's Closet. Inside was a kneeling wooden figure, purporting to be the sovereign, clothed with armour taken from the Hall's liberal supply, bewigged with her own hair which had been cut off when she had had a fever, shod in leather boots made by the local shoemaker and positioned as though he were reading his death warrant, propped up on a small table in front of him. Elizabeth's husband was heartily ashamed of this exhibition, but felt powerless to do anything more than remonstrate with her.

Judge Bradshaw's brother was also involved in anti-loyalist activities, and had served on the 1651 court martial of the Earl of Derby, an act for which he went unpunished when he was summoned before the House of Lords after the Restoration of 1660. This brother supervised the remodelling of Marple Hall around the same time, little realising that the male descendants for whom he was preparing would have died out by 1735. The estates passed to the sister of the last male heir, a certain Mary Bradshaw who had married twice into Trade, her second husband being a felt-maker named Isherwood from Bolton in Lancashire. Never again until our times was the family to gain any special distinction or notoriety. As was customary in England when property passed through a female line, Mary's family name was retained on her marriage, so that the couple had the double-barrelled surname of Bradhaw-Isherwood. Christopher quickly dropped the Bradshaw part and completed this modification in 1946, when he became an American citizen, removing both William and Bradshaw and thus legally becoming plain Christopher Isherwood.

Christopher was quite fascinated by his paternal grandfather, whose air of benign decrepitude pervaded Marple Hall. The victim of a stroke at an early age, John Isherwood had to retire from the Army after only four years of service, at the age of twenty-one. After that, he did little except administer the estates and occasionally officiate as a Justice of the Peace in local cases of petty criminality. He was already well into his sixties when Christopher was born, and with old age had lost any inhibitions he might once have had, or any embarrassment about his infirmity. He had a peculiar habit of leaving all his wine, cognac and other drinks at table until the end of the meal, when he would drink them up one after the other. Afterwards, he would mount the stairs with some difficulty and fall asleep in an armchair, sometimes relieving himself in the seat. To lessen the problem of his incontinence, he attached himself to a concealed urine bottle, which had a tendency to detach itself, filling the air with a warm musty smell. This, far from disgusting Christopher, appealed to him, reminding him of wet hay in a stable.

As time went on, John Isherwood's speech became more and

more blurred, until he was often unintelligible to the unaccustomed listener. He would also sit smiling to himself as if amused at some private joke. He enjoyed smoking, scattering ash wherever he went, and had a passion for mystery and detective novels, which he bought with his tobacco at the stationers in the village. Every morning he would be driven down into Marple to do his little shopping errands, or to chat with the local tradesmen, many of whom referred to him as "The Squire," to Kathleen's delight. Christopher later portrayed his grandfather with affectionate candour (which some of his relatives interpreted as ungrateful cruelty) as Mr. Vernon in *The Memorial.* In that novel he describes how the old man's false teeth would fall out during meal-times, causing him to laugh openly, but never make any attempt to hide or apologise for the resultant mess. On such occasions Kathleen would act as if nothing had happened, for to recognise his most blatant physical catastrophes would be to detract from her cherished image of Mr. Isherwood the Squire, to whom the villagers should show all respect.

Granny Isherwood (Elizabeth) was a more obviously pitiful creature in Christopher's eyes: a shrivelled, deathly pale old lady who struggled against a failing memory and fussed continually about the trivialities of everyday life or over the comfort of her guests. She had a particularly irritating habit of dithering around people while they were trying to read, full of concern lest they were ruining their eyes by sitting in poor light. She made a strange buzzing noise as she wandered round the big old house, preoccupied with small anxieties. Like most grandchildren, Christopher was too young to establish a proper relationship with his grandparents. Kathleen tried, but felt rebuffed. Having a particularly close tie with her own mother, who lived in the south, Kathleen found it especially hard to accept the fact that Elizabeth Isherwood seemed so distant. Indeed, at times she felt the whole Isherwood family to be incapable of deep personal affection.

Although Marple Hall had a very important effect upon Christopher's childhood, he of course spent most of his first years at his own home, Wyberslegh, three miles away. Frank and Kathleen had been living there for only eighteen months when Christopher was born. For the previous eighty years Frank's family had rented out the Hall to farmers, since the family had not needed it for their own use. When Frank and Kathleen were planning to get married, John Isherwood had the house fixed up so that it was divided into two sections, the tenant family living in the rear part. Frank and Kathleen moved there after a very brief honeymoon in Cambridge in March 1903. Relations with the farmers at the back were not good.

Wyberslegh Hall (which, unlike Marple, is still standing) is located on hilly ground, though hidden from the road, above the small village of High Lane, between Disley and Marple. The main road from Manchester to Buxton runs through High Lane, and even in the early 1900s a few enterprising suburban commuters had moved into the parish from the rapidly growing industrial conurbation of Manchester. The Isherwoods viewed this invasion with little pleasure. Curiously, apart from a few visits to concerts or the Whitworth Gallery, Frank and Kathleen seem to have made very little attempt to get to know the better side of the grimy Mancunian scene, so vividly described in Neville Cardus' *Autobiography* and in Dodie Smith's delightful volume of reminiscences, *Look Back with Love*. Kathleen, while deeply fond of her adopted country homes, inevitably looked south for cultural and nostalgic inspiration, and Christopher was quickly to come to know London far better than he ever knew Manchester.

Wyberslegh stands between the city and the still-empty hills of Derbyshire, observing both worlds. Isherwood has described its atmosphere vividly in *Kathleen and Frank*:

> The sense of weather is overwhelming. Every view is a watercolour, dripping with melancholy. The desolation of the nearby city seems to relate naturally to the desolation of the moorland. One may call this a suburb, implying that it has been tamed, but the dominant impression is of wildness. These bleak hills may be much less than mountains, but how hugely they impose their presence! (p. 179.)

The gloomy environment of his childhood also had a surreal touch in the form of an air-vent from a railway tunnel which would periodically send puffs of smoke up into the air as if some underground monster were stirring.

Wyberslegh Hall is considerably smaller than was Marple. Almost symmetrical from the front, it resembles a miniature castle, topped with crow-steps—ornamental projections resembling battlements. The front door with its cold, straight lines is flanked by windows set curiously high in the wall. Grassy banks run away from the central doorway. Like many stone houses in the area, it has a bleak atmosphere in the winter, though Christopher found it homely and cheerful. Dampness has always been a problem.

Kathleen had fallen in love with Wyberslegh at first sight, feeling that she had been there in some previous existence. She lived in constant apprehension of the day when she and Frank might have to relinquish the house. Since the late summer of 1902 Frank had been adjutant of the Fourth Volunteer Battalion of the Cheshire Regiment, based at Stockport. He had left his regiment in order to have this local posting, where he could offer Kathleen a decent home, despite his meagre salary. His financial position was eased by an allowance from John Isherwood, but by the terms of the family settlement John had only a life interest in the estate. As heir, the eldest son, Henry, had to approve any further settlement that John might make on other members of the family, including his renovation of Wyberslegh and its loan to Frank and Kathleen.

Frank was far from enchanted with his Stockport job, and had told Kathleen shortly before Christopher's birth that he would be inclined to resign were it not for the fact that this would undoubtedly lead to their having to relinquish Wyberslegh.

Frank Isherwood had been to Sandhurst and as a professional soldier had joined his father's old regiment, the York and Lancaster, in 1892. When he met Kathleen three years later he was already a lieutenant, and by the time Christopher was born he had risen to the rank of captain. A compact, attractive man with fairish hair, a fine moustache and light-blue eyes, he was far from being a typical military-career man. With great effort, he trained himself to become a competent water-colourist. He loved music, played the piano with some ability, and would happily seize on any opportunity to play duets. He adored acting, often taking comic female roles in revues, where his uninhibited clowning was put to good use. In social intercourse, however, Frank tended to be shy and punctilious. He always behaved with the utmost decorum towards his father-in-law, even during the latter's most infuriating moments, though his letters to Kathleen are quite open about his irritation with her "D.O.D." (Dear Old Dad).

Frank read quite a lot, though his taste in novels was rather conservative. His non-fiction diet included works on Oriental society, Buddhism and theosophy, perhaps partly encouraged by his brother Henry's trips to Japan and other far-off lands. He was attracted to Eastern religions because of their emphasis on self-effort and silent meditation, and had very little respect for organised religion as represented by the Church of England and its rather heavy, formal services. Kathleen foolishly attempted to make him share her reverence for the established Church and all that it stood for, and this sometimes led to family rows. The Church of England fitted into her view of things, and she loyally defended it against its mortal enemy, the Roman Catholic Church. She had a particular dislike for Catholic converts (who included Henry Bradshaw-Isherwood and, later, his sister Mary), referring to them as "perverts." Both Christopher and his younger brother, Richard, were to follow in Frank's footsteps as far as religion was concerned. Rejecting Establishment Christianity, Christopher was to follow a road which led through agnosticism and the Quakers to the Indian philosophy of Vedanta. Richard became a Rosicrucian.

Frank was a keen athlete and kept his body in fine physical shape. Christopher's first erotic image was an early view of his father stripped almost naked, doing vigorous exercises. Christopher inherited this concern for physical fitness, and they shared a taste for wrestling and other horse-play. Frank had abundant energy, frequently striding across the local countryside on brisk hikes, totally undeterred by inclement weather. He bicycled to work, even when it was pouring with rain, and was always keen for a game of tennis or hockey or a round of golf. In his less boisterous moods, he would be content to spend an evening knitting.

Despite some unconventional interests, Frank was a conscientious soldier, even if he declared frequently that he hated guns because of the bang they made. Before his marriage, he had served two tours of duty in South Africa, which only helped to confirm his Toryism. He was made uncomfortable by radical or bohemian attitudes, and by the manners of the working class. It is difficult to imagine him accepting with equanimity Christopher's development, had he lived to see it.

Both Frank and Kathleen took the institutions of marriage and parenthood very seriously. Kathleen came from a more solidly bourgeois background than did Frank. She was the daughter of Frederick and Emily Machell-Smith and until the age of sixteen had lived in the Suffolk town of Bury St. Edmunds, where her father ran a wine business. In later life, Fred Machell-Smith behaved with all the gravity of a practical business man, suspicious of everyone, especially anyone interested in his only daughter. Although he doubtlessly loved Kathleen, he caused great misery to her as well as to Frank by his protracted opposition to their marriage on tenuously material grounds. Like many mature men in dealings with their offspring, he seemed to have forgotten the feelings and dreams of his own youth. At seventeen he had run away from home, getting as far as Australia, where he worked on a sheep-farm and as a policeman. At that time he was handsome, spirited and capable of violent emotions. On his return to a settled life in England he became irritable, pompous, dogmatic and selfish, though he did maintain a then-original interest: photography. Often moody, he was nevertheless capable of displaying affection and skittishness towards Kathleen (sometimes, for example, he would jump out at her from behind curtains), and she felt great loyalty towards him, for all the obstacles he put in her path. Frederick's cantankerousness was not aided by the frequent discomfort he suffered from a bladder problem. Christopher never knew Frederick, since Mr. Machell-Smith refused to have anything to do with the baby and he died in late 1905.

Kathleen's mother, Emily, was a woman of considerable force and character—she needed to be to cope with her husband. Her letters show her to have been not only domineering but also alert and occasionally playful, adept at bridging the generation gap between herself and Kathleen. Emily remained elegant and beautiful right up to her death at the age of eighty-four. One outstanding characteristic of hers was the fact that she was frequently and sometimes spectacularly ill. She did everything with great style. Christopher remembers her as the epitome of a *grande dame*. Her illnesses had enabled her to gain her objective of moving away from the country into London, where she could indulge her passion for the theatre. Sarah Bernhardt was her idol.

Kathleen was devoted to her "Dearest Mama," and one of her

greatest concerns about getting married was her fear that it would come between her and Emily. It is quite easy to picture Kathleen as a middle-aged spinster, looking after her invalid mother, had her future spouse not guaranteed that he would respect the mother-and-daughter relationship. As it was, Frank had little choice but to accept the situation, assuring Kathleen that marriage would not disrupt her filial relations. True to form, Emily arrived to join the newly-weds on the second day of their honeymoon.

Emily came from a remarkable family, the Greenes, whose exploits have still not been fully recorded. The Greene family was, and still is, an enormous one. Among its members still alive are the novelist Graham Greene and his cousin, the sinologist and television film-maker Felix Greene. Agatha Greene was chosen as Christopher's godmother, though neither she nor Henry Isherwood were present at the christening.

Emily's brother was Walter Greene, who had a brewery (which is still in the family), and was thus in the same line of business as Frederick Machell-Smith. Walter Greene made a considerable success out of his life, launching himself into politics and later gaining a baronetcy. While Kathleen was a girl, he was already living in a large country house with spacious grounds called Nether Hall, where he entertained generously. The Machell-Smiths were frequent guests there, and Kathleen developed an early passion for country-house life, with its seemingly endless cavalcade of balls, parties, picnics, shoots and other genteel amusements. Otherwise, Kathleen's early life had followed the usual middle-class pattern of parlour games, walks, German lessons and mind-improving lectures, mild flirtation, good works for the deserving poor and amateur painting. However, she had also helped her mother prepare a book. Published in 1893 and called *Our Rambles in Old London*, this was a light guide to walks for gentlefolk in the city. Kathleen and Emily also visited the Continent together several times, though one has the impression that Kathleen did not really approve of most foreigners, especially the Germans, whose language she considered hideous.

In London the Machell-Smiths lived in South Kensington, then as now a bastion of middle-class respectability, with its rows of attractive white-painted houses. Before her marriage Kathleen took full advantage of the whirling social life offered by the capital, as well as its wide range of cultural pleasures. During their courtship Frank and Kathleen frequently visited the National Gallery in Trafalgar Square, where they would spend time copying paintings and discussing the merits or defects of various works of art. Little did they realise that years later their elder son would have an exhibition devoted to him and his friends in the portrait wing of the building!

Although she grew up in the south, Kathleen was already familiar with Frank's part of the world before their wedding, for she often stayed with family friends in Cheadle, Cheshire.

Kathleen was nearly thirty-six when Christopher was born, though often her behaviour was that of a much younger woman. Reading her diaries of the period,* with the prejudices of post-war egalitarianism, the impression Kathleen gives so often is of an unrepentant snob, immature in her appreciation of the world, spoilt, apron-clinging and blighted by a patronising attitude towards her fellow humans that was far more typical of the nineteenth than of the twentieth century. She had a blind affection for the Royal Family and a reverence for a bygone social order in which everyone knew his place, which must have struck even some of her contemporaries as archaic. The pages of her diary are full of pretentious portent concerning Christopher's birth as she notes the propitious births of two other babies: the heirs of the thrones of Russia and Italy! However, people who knew Kathleen well have testified to her general air of dignity, attentiveness and measured charm. However obvious her faults may have been, she also possessed sterling qualities, notably her loyalty to both her sons, who became involved in various escapades which must have offended the very fibre of her being.

With great pride, Kathleen charted the course of young Christopher's life in an illustrated handwritten manuscript entitled "The Baby's Progress." This was carried on right through Christopher's schooldays, the very last entry being in 1928, on the publication of his first novel, *All the Conspirators*. Kathleen's book is full of the usual observations which strike parents as being of monumental importance at the time. Thus it is noted trium-

* Quoted extensively in Christopher Isherwood's *Kathleen and Frank* (1971).

phantly that Christopher was walking shakily alone at fourteen and a half months, having bypassed the crawling stage. Kathleen's drawings and contemporary photographs show Christopher to have been dressed up in the then typical frilly baby dresses, with large hats to keep off the sun in summer, graduating to plush suits with lace collars (such as one still sees in stage versions of Frances Hodgson Burnett's *Little Lord Fauntleroy*) and the ubiquitous mock-sailor suits.

After some initial difficulty, Kathleen found a nurse for Christopher, a young woman from Suffolk called Annie Avis, who was to stay with the family for more than forty years in various roles. Christopher became very fond of "Nanny," and was more able than other members of the family to put up with her constant grumbling and other foibles, such as her later belief (and success) in having accidents every February. Nanny relieved Kathleen of all the tiresome everyday chores involved in bringing up a child, thereby gaining his affection and trust, sometimes at her mistress's expense. Christopher would tease Nanny unmercifully, and in truculent moods would boss her around; yet it was to Nanny, and not to Kathleen, that he confided many of his childhood secrets. When he had nightmares, or just felt scared of the dark, as quite often happened, it was Nanny for whom he screamed. She told him stories, relayed some of the doings of her family and friends and taught him nursery songs. He has likened their relationship to that of a white child in the old American South with his coloured Mammy.*

Frank was a great raconteur, who charmed his son with imaginative tales, and drew cartoons for him on the backs of duplicates of official army receipts. Frank taught Christopher to see art as play, removing the unnecessary solemnity of drawing, music or literature which makes culture so unpalatable for many children. Christopher would listen to Frank playing Chopin and feel it as a living thing, or sense the sheer fun of piano duets when Frank and his brother Jack were sitting down together. As the boy grew older, Frank would thrill him with the stories of Sherlock Holmes. Conan Doyle, with his calm acceptance of the lurid, undoubtedly

* *Kathleen and Frank*, p. 198.

had a very deep subliminal influence on Isherwood's earliest writings.

There was much for a young child to explore at Wyberslegh and Marple. Nanny would take Christopher to look at the animals, or else he could play in the barn. The kitchens, servants' quarters and outhouses held all sorts of mysteries. Christopher recalls the excitement of visiting the generator at Marple, where electricity was installed just a few months after his birth, and which the gardener had to set in motion by climbing on to an enormous flywheel, starting it with the weight of his body, then leaping off before he could be mangled by the kick-back.

Christopher would follow the housemaids around Marple Hall while they were doing their cleaning. He clambered over the furniture and the stairways, poking into every corner, fingering the books and the antiques, smelling the odours of the house, trying not to slip on the polished floors, or watch the tapestries being thrashed with a carpet-beater on the front lawn each spring. Cook would let him help her in the kitchen; then when his interest in rolling pastry flagged, he could climb up to the top of the house, to the attics, a fantastic world peopled by mysterious beings or presences who lived among the old trunks and discarded furnishings. In his imagination, this world was transformed into the domain of Beatrix Potter's semi-human animals, which might be expected to materialise at any moment, seen by his eyes only. (One of Beatrix Potter's stories, "The Roly-Poly Pudding," was a cult book of his, the author's landscapes being easily transferable to the Marple setting.)

A vivid imagination could dream up all kinds of horrors in the attics. Most scaring of all the dark corners was the Glory Hole, a narrow shaft which plunged all the way down from the attics into the cellars. The family talked of it as an *oubliette*, into which prisoners could be thrown to rot, unknown to the outside world.

Naturally, in view of the house's association with Judge John Bradshaw, Marple Hall was meant to be haunted by King Charles I who, as royal executees are wont to do, wandered around the building with his head under his arm. No one actually claimed to have seen him, nor the ghost of a relative who went mad when she witnessed the murder of a suspected enemy staying at the Hall during the Civil War and who was reputed to haunt the so-called

Lady Wood below the terrace. But Isherwood stands by the story of another more persistent visitor from the Other Side. While Frank and Kathleen were visiting Oxford with Emily in the summer of 1907, Nurse Avis took Christopher to stay at Marple. Christopher slept in a large north-eastern room, full of heavy Victorian furniture, which had been nominated as the nursery. While there, he awoke nightly to confront a sour-faced, muzzy old woman, whom he described in detail to his credulous Nanny. She saw nothing, but felt a peculiar presence in the room, and sometimes woke up in a sweat. When she and Christopher went back early to Wyberslegh they recounted the story to Frank and Kathleen. A few weeks later, Christopher's parents went away again, this time to Spain, and once more he was taken to Marple, where he was put in the same room. On the evening of October 29, the adults downstairs were alarmed by a shuffling noise and deep sighing out on the terrace. A moment later, Christopher's voice was heard from the ante-room of the servants' hall calling for Nanny. When she ran to fetch him, he told her that Frank (who was of course in Spain) had come into his room, switched on the lights and carried him downstairs. When Nanny carried the boy back up to his room, she found the door jammed shut. A light shone through the crack under the door, and she thought she could distinguish a shadow moving about inside. Jack Isherwood, who was visiting Marple with some friends, was summoned from the drawing-room. When he tried to force the nursery door he found it blocked by a chair placed between it and a chest of drawers. On finally getting into the room, the assembled adults found no trace of anyone.

These doings, like the previous experience, were reported back to Frank and Kathleen when they returned to England, and most of the family were convinced that something inexplicable had happened. They related it to the story of Moll of Brabyns, an eighteenth-century ancestor of theirs who was dispossessed of Marple Hall when the husband of her childless marriage died, and the property passed to her brother-in-law. She was reputed to have resented the loss of Marple so bitterly that she came back to haunt it. John Isherwood's aunts were reported to have seen her in the early nineteenth century, and it was felt that the ghost had been reactivated when Kathleen had taken down a picture of

Moll of Brabyns which hung over the staircase, with the intention of copying it. At the time the maids declared that Moll hated anyone touching the picture, and that there had always been weird knockings and creaking when it was removed for dusting during each spring cleaning.

The most plausible explanation for Christopher's visitation, if one scoffs at the ghostly interpretation, would be a conspiracy among the servants: an extremely elaborate practical joke to "prove" the validity of the maids' premonitions. But that would have presupposed a clever disguise by some accomplice to convince young Christopher that he was Frank. One truly strange aspect of the whole episode is that the family's acceptance of the occurrence as genuine did not stop them putting Christopher back into the same room that Christmas. However, when Christopher's younger brother, Richard, reported seeing the same old woman in the room several years later, Kathleen hastily removed him. Unhappily for the continuity of the story, Richard confessed to Christopher years later that it was not an old woman he had seen but a headless tailor's dummy, but that he had not dared to tell his mother so.

From time to time, to get a breath of bracing fresh air, the family would go away to the seaside for holidays, though Frank was not always able to absent himself from the Volunteers to accompany them. A favourite place was Penmaenmawr, in Conway Bay, from which you can see Puffin Isle on a clear day. North Wales was easy to reach from Cheshire, and Kathleen could indulge her fondness for sketching; even if sometimes the sea breeze did terrible things to her drawing pad. Often, though, Frank and Kathleen would go away without the child, either together or separately, leaving Christopher in Nanny's capable hands. Emily was a frequent guest and travelling companion. She had been at Wyberslegh for Christopher's birth, and the Isherwoods saw even more of her after Frederick's death. Posthumously, Mr. Machell-Smith added more bitterness to his tally: at the height of his opposition to Kathleen's marriage he had cut her out of his will, and never altered it despite intimation that he would do so. Emily moved out of the old South Kensington flat and into one just a stone's throw away from London's theatreland in Buckingham Street, at the side of Charing Cross Station, where, stretched out on a chaise-longue in Dusean grandeur, she would receive her various guests.

In early October 1907, between Christopher's two encounters with the Marple apparition, came a most unexpected piece of family news, which was to change his future outlook. Uncle Henry announced he was getting married. The young lady in question, Muriel Bagshawe, turned out to be a delightful creature, sympathetic in manner and with an assured private income of £5,000 a year. Kathleen, who had every reason to resent the intrusion of this agent of Christopher's disinheritance, in fact took an instant liking to her, and wondered how anyone could have been so silly as not to realise that Henry, like all men, needed a woman in his life. Henry had last seen his bride-to-be three years previously in Egypt, where he had proposed unsuccessfully (a fact he had not confided to his family). Miss Bagshawe had had a belated change of heart, and in 1907 proposed back, successfully. They were married in London at the end of November, Christopher attending with Nanny, John and Frank Isherwood. Frank and Kathleen were in Spain at the time. Henry added Muriel's name to his own, finding nothing ridiculous about his new triple-barrelled surname—Bradshaw-Isherwood-Bagshawe.

Henry and Muriel gave a large dinner party at Marple Hall when they returned from a continental honeymoon in January 1908. Christopher (aged three and a half) amused some of the guests in a side-room by giving a precocious speech beginning: "Ladies and Gentlemen, I rise on this auspicious occasion. . . ." Frank and Kathleen gave great offence by not being present at the dinner, preferring to stay over at a friend's house-party near Macclesfield, and adding insult to injury by arriving back home the morning after the newly-weds' dinner.

Frank, however, was preoccupied with more urgent worries than trying to smooth his brother's ruffled feathers. His Stockport adjutancy was coming to an end, and he was to rejoin his old regiment in York. He spent some time on the other side of the Pennines house-hunting before settling on a cottage in the village of Strensall, a few miles north of York. Kathleen viewed the move from Wyberslegh with as much enthusiasm as she would a funeral, remarking ominously in her diary: "It seems like the passing away of Romance and Youth!"

Kathleen never took to Strensall during the family's brief stay there. For Christopher, it was just another stage in the widening of his horizons. Grandfather Isherwood came over on a visit in May 1908 and took him to York Minster, one of Britain's most impressive churches, to see the very flag he had carried for the regiment when he was a raw young officer.

Shortly afterwards, Christopher was taken to stay at Nether Hall with Great Uncle Walter Greene, who amused the child with his eccentric practical jokes, the most sophisticated of which was a stuffed rabbit that a concealed gamekeeper would drag across the lawn on a wire. This was usually timed for the hour when the house-guests assembled for tea, whereupon Walter would cry, "There's that confounded rabbit again!" race into the gunroom with male guests and blaze away with various firearms from the windows. Christopher liked him enormously, and in later life retained a taste for pranks which struck some of his friends as childish. Many years after his visits to Nether Hall, for example, the playwright Dodie Smith arrived home one day in America to find to her horror that Christopher and some friends had thrown her garden furniture into the swimming-pool for "a lark."

In November 1908 the little family was on the move again, this time southwards to Aldershot, England's largest military base. There they inhabited a house called Frimley Lodge. But Christmas that year was spent at Marple, where Christopher got to know his Toogood cousins, children of Frank's younger sister, Esther, who had married a personable young Church of England minister in a match much disapproved of by the family. He was also taken to see Uncle Henry and Aunt Muriel, who had infuriated Frank and Kathleen by arranging an alteration of the settlement on the estate: now a daughter of Henry's could inherit, not just a son, as had been specified before. Such precautions, as it turned out, did not deny Christopher the property, since Henry's marriage was without issue, and in many ways a failure.

By the time Christopher was four and a half he was already playing toy theatricals of a rudimentary kind, using china animals and other ornaments as his dramatis personae. One of his earliest

toy theatres was built from an old shoebox, with cut-out paper
figures drawn and made by Frank, representing the execution of
Anne Boleyn on Tower Green. Empty Quaker Oats packets
ended up the same way, and the countless hours playing with toy
theatres are among Isherwood's happiest childhood memories. He
avidly scanned his parents' magazines for pictures of plays, and
was often happier in his private world of theatre than when he
joined other children for games.

Christopher would often play at dressing up, Kathleen inventing various situations which they could enact. She taught him
how to dance the Sir Roger de Coverley so that they could pretend to be at a ball. Like many little boys, Christopher found his
mother's clothes far more interesting than his father's, and Kathleen did nothing to stop the child kitting himself out in her finery.
Indeed she enjoyed the game, draping him with her silk petticoats
or furs, and showing him how to clasp her "switch," a hairpiece
made from her own hair which could be worn to give body to
some of the more elaborately fashionable coiffures.

Less pleasant experiences included the noisy military manoeu-
vres around Aldershot, as well as the more usual hazards of
bee-stings, falls, cuts and rowdy playmates. Bonfire Night 1909
(an occasion for far more enjoyable bangs than those made by the
Aldershot guns) was spent at Marple, where Christopher dressed
up as Guy Fawkes and rode on a pony specially hired by his grandfather. The following day, Kathleen records in her diary, Christopher dictated a story to her, entitled "The Adventures of
Mummy and Daddy," though its contents seem to have been
chiefly about himself.

Back at Aldershot there was great excitement when Christopher
saw his first aeroplane in May 1910; nearby Farnborough was a
pioneering base for airborne activity. At this time, the Isherwoods
were also seeing more of Frank's younger brother, Jack, who had
recently moved to Shere after a fairly bohemian life in London
among writers, artists and musicians. An extremely competent
musician himself, Jack Isherwood was a close friend of the composer Cyril Scott, whose autobiography *My Years of Indiscretion*
recounts their delving into various esoteric philosophical and
health practices, such as hatha yoga, spiritualism, vegetarianism
and cold-water cures. Jack kept himself healthy by cleaning his

system out once a week with a stomach pump. Christopher grew up with an intense admiration for his handsome, reckless young uncle, with his rich sense of humour and zest for life, though Jack's recklessness was actually veneered over a solid foundation, that of a steady job as a government lawyer. Christopher dreamed of emulating Jack's life. Considering that both Frank and Jack took an interest in Oriental religions, it is not so surprising that Christopher Isherwood turned to Vedanta.

Kathleen encouraged Christopher to share her pleasure in writing, producing with him a tiny hand-made book called "The History of My Friends," written during the winter of 1910–11, and giving little intimation of things to come.

In December 1910 Frank started giving Christopher elementary French lessons. Frank and Kathleen, like many of their class, sometimes talked French at table, so that the servants would not understand what they were saying. Nevertheless, Kathleen's grammar was frequently lamentable. French was just beginning to come back into fashion in England (Lytton Strachey's *Landmarks in French Literature* would appear in 1912), replacing German, the favourite foreign language of the Victorian age. French was thus Christopher's first foreign tongue, which he improved at school and in France, but as a young man he grew to hate French and ended up with a mental block about it which often left him speechless when he was expected to communicate with a francophone.

Frank aided Christopher's reading progress by producing a daily illustrated journal for him called "The Toy-Drawer Times." This appeared for nearly four years, until Christopher went away to school, by which time it had evolved into a comic strip. Cherishing these sessions with his father, Christopher remembers Frank as a wonderful man. He was not at all put off by his father's occasional outbursts of temper. If Christopher was being singularly dull with a lesson, Frank might fly into a rage and shake him until his teeth rattled, but paradoxically Christopher found this sensation rather pleasant.

Isherwood sites his first auto-erotic experience as taking place at Frimley Lodge. Sexual fantasies led to masturbation, one of his vivid dreams being of himself lying wounded on a battlefield, his clothes half torn off, while a woman gently administered to him. His homo-erotic fantasies developed later.

In May 1911 Christopher went off to school for the first time, to a one-hour-a-day institution of the kind that would normally be called a dame-school, except that this one was run by a man, Mr. Penrose. In it, five little boys were taught the Three R's. According to Kathleen, Christopher already wrote very nicely, but was rather behindhand at reading, despite his father's efforts. His parents continued to provide the rest of his education at home, Kathleen pandering to his passion for the theatre by reading to him from that indispensable volume for children, Charles and Mary Lamb's *Tales from Shakespeare*. Sometimes Christopher would bring home one of his classmates. Kathleen always allowed him to bring friends home, and both she and Nanny turned a blind eye to whatever was going on with some of these friends in years to come.

Frank was aware that being an army wife did not really suit Kathleen, and he tried on several occasions to find some appropriate job in civilian life which would enable him to resign his commission. Hoping to get settled nearer his home (perhaps even at Kathleen's beloved Wyberslegh), he tried for a place with the Cheshire Constabulary, but was turned down. Whatever Frank's qualities were, he was not adept at impressing prospective employers. Although he joked about the possibility of scraping a living as an artist (one of his pictures of South Africa had sold for ten shillings), he knew that Kathleen was not made for such a life, particularly now she was pregnant again.

Kathleen viewed the prospect of another child with some apprehension. She was nearly forty-four years old, and Christopher's delivery seven years previously had not been easy. To make matters worse, Frank's regiment was due for transfer to Limerick, in Ireland, in late September, when the baby was due. Frank's efforts to delay this posting were fruitless at first. He had just been promoted to the rank of major, and his commanding officer insisted upon having a major with him on the spot from the beginning. No standby or replacement at that time seemed feasible. Frank consulted Emily about his dilemma. She recommended that he retire from the Army while he was still young enough to find decent civilian employment. Accordingly, he sent in his papers, but served through the bitter month of August 1911, when a transport strike led to widespread civil unrest and confrontation between workers and the Army. Frank's loyalty was firmly behind the cause of authority. If you gave the agitators an inch, they would take a mile.

In between the encounters with the restless working class, Frank soothed his worries by writing stories for Christopher. In mid-September he attended a farewell dinner given by his regiment, and signed on at an art class in Reading while awaiting further developments.

Christopher, meanwhile, was getting very excited at the prospect of a new baby arriving, though no one thought it proper to enlighten him as to how this miracle would come about. On October 1 the doctor duly "brought" him a baby brother, Richard. Delighted with the little creature, Christopher took advantage of Richard's first airing in the garden by decorating him with flowers as though he were a Hindu shrine.

The War Office refused to accept Frank's retirement unless he agreed to enter the Militia for five years, which was clearly impossible if he were to adopt a new full-time profession. However, another major had been found to accompany the regiment for its first few weeks in Ireland, and now at least the baby had been safely delivered, and Kathleen seemed to be recovering quickly. Frank persisted as far as he could in his attempt to leave the Army, but the War Office made it quite clear that his release could not be granted. So he went on ahead to Limerick, and immediately wrote to reassure Kathleen that it was not nearly as bad as they had feared.

In early December Kathleen took Christopher to London on a visit to Emily, who treated him with his first visit to a theatre. The occasion was a variety show at the Coliseum, a spectacular production during which a real motor-car and a coach with live horses appeared on the stage. While in London Christopher was also able to see some of the Christmas displays in the big department stores along Oxford Street, a wonderland of ingenious models and miniature historic tableaux, depicting such scenes as London during the sixteenth century and the frozen Thames crisscrossed by moving sedan chairs and coaches.

Christmas itself was once more spent at Marple, where John and Elizabeth Isherwood were able to inspect their new grandchild. Christopher's Christmas present that year was guaranteed to please: a sophisticated toy theatre made in Germany or Switzerland, with cardboard figures representing the romantic figures of some mighty Teutonic drama. It had two standard sets: a banqueting-hall scene and a clearing in a pine forest. Their gloom and Christopher's temperament naturally led to Wagnerian stage productions, full of eerie shadows cast by candles placed in the wings. Frank taught him how to simulate lightning by blowing rosin through a tube in a candle-flame. There were thunderstorms in every play.

Kathleen and the children, with Nanny as ever in attendance, left Cheshire on New Year's Day 1912, then suffered a choppy crossing on the ferry to Ireland, where they were met by Frank at the dock in Kingstown, just south of Dublin. After a night in a hotel they proceeded to Limerick, where Kathleen started a weary house-hunt. The seventeenth place visited, Roden House, was just what she had been looking for. It was a sizeable dwelling, protected from the bustle of the town by high walls covered in creeper. A long glass veranda ran the length of the house, while upstairs there was a maze of little passages and doorways. From some of the windows the barracks could be seen, as well as a large technical school. The garden contained some quaint box-bordered beds and an apple tree favoured by passing birds. Ornamental urns grandiosely topped the crumbling pillars which supported the iron gate.

Christopher started school almost immediately, being one of several little boys registered at the local girls high school. He did well at this school, and enjoyed it. Saturdays and Sundays were free, so he could accompany his mother on her explorations around the town. On Sundays, after church, they could go to the old-fashioned market hall, with its Doric pillars, where they could see merchants and colourful farmers' wives, in their characteristic head-scarves, leading donkey cars. Pleasant walks took them quickly out of town to meadows, where they could look back to the cathedral towers dominating the little city.

Far from being abated by this contact with new worlds, Christopher's passion for toy dramatics began to take on truly epic proportions. In June 1912 he announced a Shakespeare week, reading extracts from the Bard's works, liberally edited, with various china animals interpreting the roles. A rabbit was cast as Lady Macbeth. Notices announcing the current production were pinned to the nursery door, and his parents and Nanny were expected to attend every performance, which they faithfully did. Fortunately, even *Macbeth* only lasted fifteen minutes in Christopher's version—poetry and other superfluous matter were expurgated to reveal the essential framework of treachery and carnage, with appropriate sound effects. He took these dramatics extremely seriously, and was deeply offended if anyone laughed in the wrong place. His parents indulged him up to a point, but sometimes Frank lost his temper at Christopher's exhibitionism. On occasion, Kathleen would blush with shame at his displays in public, though fortunately most people seemed to find his juvenile lack of self-consciousness quite appealing.

Frank was naturally pleased that to some extent his son was following in his footsteps. Until the move to Limerick Christopher had not been allowed to stay up to see Frank in one of his amateur dramatic shows, but by now he wanted to be an actor, like his father. He even wrote his first "play," which took the form of a melodramatic scene in which a woman read a letter telling her of her son's death, after which she fell into a swoon. As Sarah Bernhardt (familiar through the theatre magazines and family stories) was his idol, Christopher wrote his play in French, entitling it *La Lettre*. It was banned one memorable day after he marched into a room full of guests and gave an impromptu performance without permission.

Frank spent much of his day at the barracks with his men, and sometimes Kathleen would take Christopher to the parade-ground to watch them drilling. In the evening at home Frank would loosen his uniform and chew on his pipe, suddenly transformed from the correct officer into a homely figure who could easily be persuaded to do some doodles on the spot, or to recount adventure stories.

Life was not all fun and games at Limerick. In the eyes of the Irish Republicans the British Army was an occupying force denying their right to independence. Tension could be felt despite surface calm. Even the children seemed infected, and Kathleen complained in her diary: "The Irish seem *hopelessly* lawless, and murders are overlooked in a way to make an Englishwoman's blood boil." She called in the police to see about ragamuffins who ran up and banged on her front door, or sneaked into the house to steal fruit or flowers. In keeping with the practice of other Army families, she had to tell Christopher which children were considered "safe" to play with. Catholic children would shout "Dirty Protestant!" at him as he walked down the street.

When in his late twenties Christopher analysed the political background to that period of his life, he placed himself firmly on the side of those who had condemned British involvement. Similarly, he opposed the Raj in India. In relation to both situations he sometimes used terminology which has given the impression that he is or was committed more firmly to left-wing groups than has been the case.

In the autumn of 1912 rioting in Limerick led to the smashing of shop windows and other destruction. The (Protestant) archdeacon was chased out of his house by the mob and cut about the face. Peace was only restored by the intervention of Catholic priests. Until the Easter Rising of 1916, though, such blatant violence was relatively limited, and it does not seem to have bothered Christopher one jot. While at Limerick he "took the hostility of the street boys for granted, as a part of daily life, along with the caressing foreign charm of their eyes and voices, the music of their accent, the filth of the picturesque lane and the stink of sewage in its puddles and gutters."*

For his eighth birthday Christopher was given a magic lantern by his father, another source of great delight. He was reading Johann Rudolf Wyss's *Swiss Family Robinson* at that time, and enacted castaway scenes among the refuse of the Technical School with a bossy little girl called Mirabel, whom Kathleen thought odious. Old doors served as imaginary rafts, and together they would rush at phantom wild animals which they hunted for their evening meal.

In late September 1912 Christopher was taken to the cinema for the first time, so beginning a love which was to surpass that of the theatre and become one of the most important aspects of his

* *Kathleen and Frank*, p. 269.

life. The silent movie-makers had already learnt the art of winning faithful young audiences by producing adventure serials that
went on month after month. Often, to economise, bits of footage
would reappear at different stages of these marathons, and the
plots were rarely imaginative, relying more on brash excitement.
Nevertheless Christopher, like the majority of audiences, was
enthralled, just as a later generation of children sat transfixed before the new invention of television. Apart from the serials, there
were newsreels, the more patriotic ones about the British Royal
Family sometimes soliciting howls or whistles from the Limerick
audience, and feature films, which introduced Christopher to the
Keystone Kops, Dorothy and Lillian Gish and Mabel Normand.

The family went on leave to England at the end of November
1912, not returning to Ireland until early February of the following year. Frank and Kathleen travelled around the country, but
Christopher, Richard and Nanny were installed in Marple Hall
for over two months. Aunty Moey (Mary), the nearest in age to
Frank of the Isherwood family, was also there. She wrote children's books, but was much less fun as a child's companion than
might have been expected. Her books, like herself, were of high
moral tone, published by the Society for the Promoting of Christian Knowledge. She was a sick woman, with a melancholy temperament, and rather masculine in appearance. She remained a
spinster to her death. Unfortunately for Christopher, Richard was
still too much of a baby to be a playmate, and the brothers were
not to get to know one another well until much later on in their
lives.

Back in Ireland Christopher was given a change of school, ostensibly to give him the chance to be with more boys. Still, there
were only seven pupils in the school, one or two of whom were
girls. At Miss Burns's school, however, he was able to get a taste
of the ups and downs of friendships, to scuffle with other boys,
and be scolded for his weak arithmetic. Kathleen read Kipling's
Child's History of England with him, and he was learning to play
the piano. But 1913 was a restless year. Kathleen was twice called
over to England to tend to Emily in one of her protracted
illnesses, and in early August, when Frank had to go on manoeu-
vres, she went again with the children, taking them to Marple.

Kathleen felt a growing political tension when they got back to

Ireland that autumn. Probably the deteriorating situation was one reason why his parents decided that Christopher should be sent away to school in England, which was in any case common practice among Army families. The children would get a better education than was considered available in Ireland, and would be educated in preparation for the inevitable day when the family returned to their own country. So, when the Isherwoods made their traditional Christmas pilgrimage to Marple in 1913, they took advantage of their visit to look round a few preparatory schools. They finally chose St. Edmund's School in Hindhead, Surrey, which was run by relatives of theirs, Cyril Morgan-Brown and his sister Mona (Monica). Christopher, made conscious by the prospect of boarding-school that he was growing up, declared at Christmas that he no longer needed Nanny to sleep with him at night, and decamped into Frank's dressing-room armed with an electric torch, a supply of books and a clock.

Christmas 1913 was exactly as tradition dictated: thick snow enabled Christopher to enjoy tobogganing around the Hall, and he informed his parents that it was the nicest Christmas he could remember. The midday family dinner, after church, consisted of the time-worn menu of roast turkey, a blazing plum pudding and champagne. Christopher played with his presents: an electric dynamo, a Meccano set, and a box of conjuring tricks. Whatever fears anyone present might have had about the future of Ireland, no one could have predicted that this Christmas would mark the end of an era, that within months half of Europe would be at war, and that the family would be struck by a tragedy of irrevocable importance.

2

Christopher left Ireland for his boarding-school on April 23, 1914, accompanied by Kathleen. After a couple of days at Marple they went down to London for a week's stay with Emily at her maisonette in Buckingham Street. Emily's home took on the role it was to have throughout Christopher's schooldays—as a holiday base-camp, from which to make forays into the exciting city, with its theatres, cinemas, bookshops and other entertainments. Christopher loved the flat, decorated in a traditional manner, yet feminine with pale marble, alabaster, gilt frames and pink and sky-blue fabrics. The walls were almost obscured by Emily's collection of water-colours and etchings, many of foreign places, which aroused in Christopher a sense of wanderlust. Laid out in an alcove would be Emily herself, protected from draughts by a series of screens, and swathed in furs and perfume, while in front of her on a table stood a bottle of champagne or vials of the homeopathic medicines in which she was a staunch believer. Kathleen took Christopher to see Granville Barker's production of Shakespeare's A *Midsummer Night's Dream*, which impressed him with its gold make-up and fairy costumes. He also visited Madame Tussaud's waxworks, the National History Museum, Regent's Park Zoo and Hendon Aerodrome.

On May Day Cyril Morgan-Brown was at Waterloo Station to escort a group of boys to St. Edmund's. He struck Kathleen as being dazed and incapable, and did indeed have a dreamy disposition which made him subject to ragging behind his back at school. Only three days later, Mona Morgan-Brown wrote to Kathleen to reassure her that Christopher was settling in well, and that she was keeping an eye on him. "He seems a very jolly little chap and one feels very friendlily disposed towards him, over and above the fact that he is a relation."* Kathleen went for a visit a few days later, just to make sure.

St. Edmund's School was a late-Victorian country house, near the village of Hindhead, on the London to Portsmouth Road. It was set in expansive, hilly grounds that were a wilderness of trees, gorse bushes and long grass. Isherwood once described it with characteristic subjectivity as: ". . . an aggressive gabled building in the early Edwardian style, about the size of a private hotel. The brickwork is varied here and there with sham frontings of criss-crossed stucco. In the foreground is a plantation of dwarf conifers, such as are almost always to be seen in the grounds of better-class lunatic asylums."†

George Bernard Shaw had lived in the house for a few months, in 1899, just prior to its conversion into a school. St. Edmund's had been founded a generation earlier in Norfolk by the Reverend John Morgan-Brown, Cyril's father. In deference to the school's origins divinity played an important part in the curriculum, and there were compulsory chapel services twice a day, as well as private prayers. Latin and Greek were stressed, as were mathematics and French. English literature was expected to be picked up *en passant* during history and geography lessons. Music was also represented, and a grand piano dominated the school's spacious drawing-room. The music mistress was a young woman who was going deaf and who rapped pupils' knuckles with a large red pencil when they made mistakes, though some people wondered how she could tell. In the twenty-nine acres of grounds there were ample sports facilities, as well as plots for gardening, a carpentry shop, and an outdoor swimming-pool where the boys swam naked.

* Letter dated May 4, 1914, quoted in *Kathleen and Frank*, p. 284.
† Quoted in Christopher Isherwood, *Exhumations* (1966), p. 194.

The headmaster, Cyril Morgan-Brown, nicknamed "Ciddy" by the boys, was a shambling man with grey hair and a large floppy moustache. He had once been handsome, but had of late gone to seed, and did nothing to lend himself the dignified air befitting a headmaster. Visiting parents who caught fleeting glimpses of him usually thought he was the odd-job man. Nonetheless, he was a brilliant classical scholar whose principles were those of a Victorian gentleman. He tried to impress upon his wards the importance of honesty, forthrightness, thoroughness and perseverance, and seemed to think Christopher a bit of a funk and a show-off. The boy had cultivated a precise, know-all, supercilious tone of voice which could be extremely irritating. Moreover, he chattered incessantly, frequently looked bored and inattentive, was sure to be among the noisiest boys when it came to scuffling or tearing round the corridors, yet demonstrated a contempt for team sports.

Cyril's daughter, Miss Rosa (Rosamira) Morgan-Brown, also taught at the school. She was an attractive, energetic young woman, who once lost her temper at Christopher's attitude and gave him a resounding slap. From this he deduced that she did not like him, a harsh judgement which, when she read it fifty-seven years later in *The Times Saturday Review*, prompted her to write him a kindly reproach, pointing out that she had had happy memories of his time there. Gallantly, he recanted. "As for the slap," he wrote, "I am sure it did nothing but good!"* The other relative on the staff, Mona, left the school after Christopher's first term.

It was possibly not a good idea to send Christopher to a school run by relatives, however kind they might have been. Blood ties put an undue strain on the natural pupil-teacher relationship. The teacher is frightened of seeming to show favouritism, yet has to avoid being too cold lest the boy writes complaining letters back to his parents, thus causing a family row. The boy himself is often regarded with distrust by his schoolfellows because of his connection with the authorities. Kathleen came to regret her decision to send Christopher to St. Edmund's, and grew actively to dislike both Cyril and Rosa. Probably her judgement coloured Christopher's memories.

* Quoted in *W. H. Auden: A Tribute* (1975), ed. Stephen Spender, p. 32.

Among the other members of staff was Ivor Sant, another fine academic, who would often be in charge of the boys on their Sunday walks. He won favour with Christopher by admitting to a liking for the theatre, and would feed his appetite for stories about Sarah Bernhardt. Mr. Sant was also in charge of games, and despaired at Christopher's pathetic performance on the cricket and football fields. However, Christopher loved the physical excitement of wrestling, and even enjoyed being knocked around in boxing. In contrast there was nothing sensual about cricket; the hard ball hurt his hand when he caught it.

Christopher settled in quickly at St. Edmund's. His letters home, written under supervision at a Sunday ritual, for which suggestions of news were written up on the blackboard, show no undue strains. His clowning helped avoid the unpopularity that might have resulted from his affectations, and he began to make friends, most of whom naturally came from the same sort of favoured background as himself. The Morgan-Browns did all they could to make the school a happy one, wherever possible giving individual attention to the fifty or so boys (supplemented by a couple of girl day-pupils from the village). Although the educational emphasis was on producing obedient, upright, God-fearing youths, there was plenty of time for adventure and fun. The locale of the school had been especially chosen for the beautiful, wild surrounding countryside, which gave the boys the opportunity for thrilling walks. Returning from these without dirtying the school uniform of dark trousers with jacket and Eton collar was a major problem. Newspapers once proudly recorded how boys of St. Edmund's had put out a brush-fire in the nearby Devil's Punchbowl. They neglected to mention that it was the boys who had started it.

Special religious days or holidays were usually an excuse for an outing or a special treat. On Shrove Tuesday there would be "progressive" games, while on Ascension Day all the boys would go off on a picnic. At the beginning of the Michaelmas term a blackberry picnic would take place, where there would be great rivalry between the different "firms" (tight groups of school friends) to see who could pick the most. Jam was made from the pickings, strictly labelled, so that the "firms" who picked the most fruit also got the most jam.

Kathleen came over to England to fetch Christopher when the summer holidays began at the end of July. No sooner had they returned to Limerick, however, when mobilisation commenced. The following day, August 5, war was declared. The Church proclaimed that God was on England's side, and the Dean at Limerick Cathedral cheerily informed his congregation of soldiers that their widows would be looked after. He called at the Isherwood house the next day to say how sad it was that perhaps half of the men who had been in the cathedral that Sunday would never come back. He was right.

Frank left for England on August 14. Christopher was not of an age to understand fully what was happening, so while his mother fretted, he went off to the cinema or played with horrid Mirabel. Everything was very confused in those first days of the war. Soon Frank, who had been stationed comfortably at Cambridge, decided it was unlikely he would be sent immediately to the Continent, so he asked Kathleen to join him there. Nanny and the children travelled with her as far as Crewe, and then they went on to Marple. On September 7 Frank received his orders to leave for France. Kathleen went up to Marple to be with the children. Empty cottages were being prepared in the village for the first consignment of Belgian refugees. Christopher returned to school, where later that month Kathleen visited him with Emily, hiring rooms in the nearby village of Grayshott. John Isherwood wrote saying that the family was welcome to consider Marple as its base, as there was no point in returning to Ireland. Kathleen took Christopher on a drive by way of Frensham, where the common was already occupied by tents and soldiers, most dressed in old-fashioned scarlet jackets as the supply of khaki had run out.

The war was a permanent presence during Christopher's time at St. Edmund's, though at first not a tragic one. Frank wrote cheery letters to him from France, saying how pretty the guns looked when they were fired at the German aeroplanes which "fly about the shells in a very daring way." Frank sat in his trench knitting, to the amusement of his men. His letters made frequent reference to a dream that became a common one among those at the front: maybe we'll be home for Christmas.

As the war progressed the army camp on the common near Christopher's school grew immense. Many of the soldiers were Canadians, who were loved by the boys because they handed out cigarette cards. The boys at St. Edmund's were crazy about cigarette cards, and Christopher was no exception. Of course it was possible to obtain a complete set of these cards, one of which was given away free in each packet of cigarettes, just by sending off a shilling or two to the cigarette company, but that would have been cheating. Complete sets had to be obtained by legitimate means, including the swapping of duplicates. Inevitably, some cards were much rarer than others, and to acquire a complete set became an obsession which could dominate a boy's thoughts for weeks. Isherwood captures this mood brilliantly in a short story entitled "Gems of Belgian Architecture," written in 1927 and reproduced in *Exhumations,* which also gives a good idea of the peculiar slang prevalent at the school.

Frank's regiment had its first taste of open fighting in mid-October 1914, suffering heavy casualties in an attack on Radinghem. Frank began to experience the common sensation of not being affected by the horrors around him, not because of callousness, but as a means of psychological self-defence. As the nights grew colder he wrapped his head up in old socks, and used coats belonging to fallen men.

At school, one or two black arm-bands appeared. Boys wearing them were treated with great respect, even if most of the pupils were too young fully to understand grief. A boy in an arm-band would not be ragged so much. If he felt like joining in the fun, all he had to do was to take off the arm-band. One child, suffering from loneliness, pretended his father had been killed, to gain sympathy and attention. When his lie was uncovered, he was pitched into a gorse bush, a common punishment meted out by the boys for any serious infringement of their private code. When another was taken out of class one day to be informed of his brother's death, he was thronged by friends who asked eagerly: "Did you blub much?" Cyril Morgan-Brown gave rousing speeches about the honourable actions going on in Europe in defence of Decency. Towards the end of November Frank was granted ten days' leave, during which he visited St. Edmund's to see Christopher, who was very pleased to be able to display his father as a major.

On December 21 Kathleen met Christopher at Waterloo, then travelled with him to Marple, where John and Elizabeth Isherwood were celebrating their golden wedding anniversary. The family tried to make Christmas as joyful as they could in Frank's absence. Meanwhile, in France, the Allied and German soldiers fraternised with each other, and group photographs were taken, making a mockery of the whole affair.

In London, towards the end of his holidays, Christopher went to dinner with his Uncle Henry, all dressed up in a white piqué waistcoat, Eton jacket and collar. The following day his Uncle Jack appeared, and took him off to a restaurant and to the theatre. Ciddy and the boys were waiting for him at Waterloo on January 27.

Frank was made a lieutenant-colonel in the King's Honours List in February 1915. A few days later he was back in England on leave. As usual, he and Kathleen visited Christopher, who was limping badly, and had his ankle bound up. He had suffered chronically for some years from a mysterious leg ailment, which might have been a rheumatic reaction to changing weather conditions, or cramp or simply growing pains. Kathleen had discovered that the most effective cure was to wrap the leg tightly with a woolen scarf. They had lunch together, then went for a drive.

Frank had to return to France on March 1, the same day Christopher went down with measles. The disease was running through the school like wildfire, so that a fortnight later the Morgan-Browns called in a specialist to help direct the cure. Christopher meanwhile had developed a touch of pneumonia. Kathleen had been warned to stay away, as measles can be quite serious for adults, but on March 20 she went to the school to find him weak but pleased to see her, and being fed only on liquid foods. He had lost a lot of weight. On March 31 he was transferred, all wrapped up in blankets, from school to Ventor, in the Isle of Wight, where Kathleen was then staying. The sea air proved therapeutic and he grew stronger. On April 9 Kathleen broke out with a measles rash—only Christopher, the doctor and a help were allowed to see her. Fortunately, it was a very mild dose.

Frank speculated by post whether it would not be a good idea to move Christopher to a day-school:

> The whole point of sending him to school was to flatten him out, so to speak, and to make him like other boys and, when all is said and done, I don't know that it is at all desirable or necessary, and I for one would much rather have him as he is. He has tried the experiment and we know that he can hold his own and he could retire with all the honours of war to a day school, if we ever had the chance of sending him to one. But at present it seems rather impossible.*

Isherwood has speculated on many occasions whether sending him to a day-school, or even better a co-educational day-school, would have helped to orientate him sexually towards women. Whatever the answer to that might be, it is worth noting the Isherwoods' conventional desire to "flatten out" their child, to make him like everyone else. Fortunately, even the public-school system allows a pupil with artistic sensibility to retain his individuality.

Christopher should have returned to St. Edmund's on May 3 but he was still not fit enough. He had lumbago in his back, and both his legs were stiff. The pain moved to his big toe, and the doctor ordered him back to bed. Kathleen's concern was increased by her fears for Frank, now at Ypres, where casualty figures were mounting by the thousand. On May 8 the York and Lancaster Regiment was ordered to retake some trenches lost during the night. From there they pushed ahead in an evening attack on the German positions. In that attack practically every officer present was put out of action. Frank was posted as missing.

A few days later Kathleen received a telegram from the War Office telling her that her husband was believed wounded, which initiated a long and fruitless search on her part to acquire more information. Conflicting rumours from soldiers on leave or in hospitals only increased her anxiety, as each new story was proved to be false. For six weeks she followed every possible line of enquiry in London, while Christopher and Richard remained happily with their grandparents at Marple. At the end of June the British Red

---

* Letter dated April 9, 1915, quoted in *Kathleen and Frank*, p. 284.

Cross wrote to say that Frank's identity disc had been found, after which all real hope for Frank's safety evaporated. John Isherwood offered Kathleen the opportunity of moving back into Wyberslegh Hall, whose tenant had recently died, but Kathleen felt that she could not bear to live there without Frank, and subsequently spent much time with Emily.

Throughout the summer of 1915 Kathleen journeyed between London and Marple with Christopher. Her diary records that she found his sweet disposition a great comfort, while he was still too young to feel the full force of the tragedy. In mid-September, after nearly six months without proper schooling, Christopher returned to St. Edmund's, to be confronted with a new image of his father: the dead soldier hero. From the boys came initial half-comprehending sympathy, while the staff were full of extravagant condolence mixed with lectures about the pride which he should be feeling in his father's noble end. Sometimes they would reduce the boy to tears with their reprimands for not living up to Frank's example.

Frank's posthumous role in Christopher's consciousness did not fade with time. Instead it grew in the boy's formative years, becoming a source of great mental conflict. Gradually he developed an acute adolescent disrespect for the Establishment, as represented not only by the school authorities and the Church, but by adults in general. As he had only happy memories of his father, it came to disturb him greatly that he was so lauded by the very elements of society which he despised. He was eventually able to reconcile this dichotomy to some extent by deciding that Frank was essentially an anti-hero, who could therefore be admired without any qualms. He seized on the reported detail that Frank died in battle with only a walking stick in his hand as evidence of his father's anti-heroism. Whether Christopher's judgement would have been so kind if Frank had lived is quite another matter. Kathleen, who survived him, was doomed to years of contempt for the sin of being a parent and widow cherishing her recollection of times past. Ironically, Frank had foreseen such a development, evident in a letter to Kathleen dated September 7, 1905: "I am rather disgusted with [Samuel Butler's] *The Way of All Flesh*. He is so frightfully down on parents, and I look at dear innocent William [Christopher] and wonder if we shall hit it off so badly, and if he too will one day 'find his parents out and never forgive them' as Oscar Wilde says. I think very few people do ever really forgive their parents!"*

The time away from books did not seem to have hindered Christopher's academic progress, though school reports for the Michaelmas term of 1915 complain of inattentiveness and complacency. Not all news from school was bad, however. Christopher got an honourable mention for an unspecified entry in the annual "holiday competition" arranged at the beginning of that term, of which the best submissions were later exhibited in the school's drawing-room. In the same competition the following year he received a first-class award for a carefully kept journal illustrated with postcards and photographs. This was a predecessor of a faithfully kept diary of great length and frankness which, if published, could well become Isherwood's most celebrated work.

Among the new intake at St. Edmund's in 1915 was a grubby little boy named Wystan Auden, aged eight, who was accompanied by his elder brother, John. There was no reason why Christopher should have had anything to do with a new boy in view of their difference in age and standing in the school, but W. H. Auden as a child was sufficiently extraordinary to draw the attention of older schoolfellows without exciting their wrath. However, he and Christopher probably did not really get to know each other until Christopher's last year at the school, 1917–18.

Called Dodo Minor for no better reason than that Dodo was the nickname of John Auden and referred to his somewhat bird-like appearance, Wystan was a very precocious child. His father was Schools' Medical Officer for Birmingham, and lectured at the university of that city, being a competent classicist and antiquarian in his spare time. Wystan had Icelandic ancestry, and possessed a temperament and way of expressing himself which reeked of the dark grandeur and symbolism of the sagas. On arrival at school he is reputed to have declared that he was looking forward to the experience as it would give him the chance of studying the different psychological types represented there.

Wystan had the good fortune to come from a home where intellectual pursuits were enjoyed to the full. There were plentiful

* *Kathleen and Frank*, p. 204.

books in the house, and music was a common pastime. He had the even better fortune of landing squarely on his feet at prep school. Rosamira Morgan-Brown took an immediate liking to him, and he to her, while amongst the boys he made friends easily. Sharing Christopher's dislike of sport, Wystan made up for this defect in the eyes of his schoolmates by his ability to entertain and shock. He played the piano with great gusto, heavily but quite well. He dazzled people with the extent of his general knowledge, especially of esoteric subjects, and even at this tender age delivered pronouncements with terrifying finality.

In his early autobiographical work *Lions and Shadows*, Isherwood recalls Auden (Hugh Weston) as "a sturdy, podgy little boy, whose normal expression was the misleadingly ferocious frown common to people with very short sight. Both the brothers had hair like bleached straw and thick coarse-looking, curiously white flesh, as though every drop of blood had been pumped out of their bodies."* Large red ears flapped out over the sides of his Eton collar.

The boy who was to become a celebrated poet wanted at that time to become a mining engineer. His playbox was full of fat geology handbooks borrowed from his father's library, and his conversation reflected half-assimilated scientific knowledge gained from these and from John Auden, who was to achieve distinction as a geologist. Portentously, Wystan would come out with long Latin names, horribly mispronounced but nonetheless very impressive. Even more appealing to his contemporaries' natural hunger for worldliness were his hints of secrets of shattering import. He had found the key to the locked bookcase in which Dr. Auden kept his German illustrated anatomical manuals, so that Wystan, in a garden of innocence, was able to give favoured beings, such as Christopher, their first lessons in sex. He would draw explicit diagrams on a blackboard, extemporising those facts he did not know for sure, pointing out details with his stubby, ink-stained, nail-bitten hands. He enjoyed the status of a kind of witch-doctor.

At St. Edmund's, though his contact with Wystan was rather limited, Christopher did co-operate with Auden's best friend at school, Harold Llewellyn Smith, in planning a long historical

* *Lions and Shadows* (1938; 1953), p. 181. This and subsequent page references are to the Methuen edition of 1953.

novel, most of the work for which was carried out surreptitiously on the cricket field, where they should have been giving their attention to playing the game. The setting for the novel was clearly taken from Marple Hall, and Harold Llewellyn Smith still remembers Isherwood's "luscious" description of tapestried galleries where suits of armour alternated with shelves of leather-bound books "inlaid with great lozenges of velvet."

The Morgan-Browns had written to Kathleen and Frank when Christopher first went to the school that he was "not very communicative about Divinity," an understatement considering Christopher's early dismissal of the Anglican Church as a possible spiritual home. Nevertheless, he subsequently won the school divinity prize several times. He and Wystan had many religious arguments in the dormitory, Wystan defending the High Anglicanism inherited from his mother. Using typical hyperbole, he ranted against those churches in which there were no sculptured crosses, but merely painted ones behind the altar, for which sacrilege the church should be burnt and the vicar thrown in prison.

Wystan really made his mark on the school at the Field Day in the Devil's Punchbowl in the Easter term of 1917 (when Christopher, incidentally, won the third form prize). Boys at the school were drilled with artificial rifles and shown the rudiments of warfare, though this field exercise must have seemed a mere romp to most of them. Wystan (Corporal Auden junior) was given the No. 1 machine-gun, to cover his forces retreat, but:

. . . machine gun fire did not seem to be forthcoming . . . (as) Corpl. Auden (junior) was engaged on his own. . . . Corpl. Auden (senior) then turned up and asked for advice. Corpl. Auden (junior) replied that the machine-gun was going to retire, and could he hold out a bit longer until he had reached the top and cover his retreat. This was done, and then they both turned their attention to the enemy's advance, and during the charge the Corporal gave them a good deal of lead, but was unable to stop them. Of Lance.-Corpl. Loring there is little to be said except that he gallantly slaughtered (or tried to slaughter) all enemy troops that he could see.*

* The St. Edmund's School Chronicle (June 1917), pp. 53–55.

To encourage a healthy war spirit, the boys were asked to write belligerent poems, one of which Christopher produced in April 1917:

With Apologies to Lewis Carroll

"You are old, Father William," the Crown Prince said,
"And your hair has become very white,
And yet you incessantly can't go to bed,
Do you think at your age it is right?"

"In my youth," Kaiser William replied to his son,
"I slept every night without pain,
But now that I think of the crimes that we've done
I shall never slumber again."

"You are old," said the youth as I mentioned before,
"And have grown just a trifle too fat,
Yet you kicked old Von Tirpitz right out of the door,
Pray what is the reason for that!"

"In my youth," said the sage, as he shook his grey locks
"I kept all my limbs very supple
By use of these hate pills, one pfenning a box,
Allow me to sell you a couple."

"You are old," said the youth, "and your jaws are too weak
For anything tougher than suet,
Yet you finished the war bread they baked here last week,
Pray how did you manage to do it?"

"In my youth," said the Kaiser, "I once loved to roar
And sing hymns of hate at my wife,
And the muscular strength that it gave to my jaws
Has lasted the rest of my life!"

"You are old," said the youth, "One would hardly suppose
That your eye was as steady as ever,
Yet you balanced a sausage right up on your nose;
What makes you so awfully clever?"

"I have answered three question, and that is enough!"
Said his father, "Don't give yourself airs,
Do you think I can listen all day to such stuff?
Be off, or I'll throw you downstairs."

In the holidays, Christopher often saw Emily, who showed no sign of losing her vitality despite advancing age. When the Germans made occasional daylight raids over London, she would position herself in a deckchair on the roof of her flat in Buckingham Street, and watch the spectacle through a pair of opera glasses.

Christopher left St. Edmund's as the Great War drew to its bloody close in late 1918. It was decided that he should go on to Repton, which had been his Uncle Jack's public school, situated just a few miles outside Derby. Had Kathleen wished to keep her son's education in family hands, she could have done so by sending him to Berkhamsted School, where Charles Henry Greene was headmaster, and both Graham Greene and Felix Greene pupils. In fact, Richard Isherwood was to go to Berkhamsted in the autumn of 1919.

In January 1919 Christopher went to Repton. The school still dominates the tiny village, the main street leading through an arch into the school grounds, where a variety of dark stone buildings reflect the different architectural styles employed in its gradual construction. The oldest building is The Priory, built in 1172, the school itself being founded in 1557 by Sir John Port of Etwall. By Christopher's time it catered for about four hundred boys, giving them what was called a rounded education, including large doses of sport and Anglicanism. Most of the headmasters had an ecclesiastical background which continued into their later lives. In 1919 the headmaster was Geoffrey Fisher, who was also housemaster of Hall, which was Christopher's house. In the public-school system the house has a crucial significance, for it is the centre of a boy's social life, and its conditions can make his schooldays a delight or a misery. The Hall, with the headmaster in charge, had a rather special role at Repton but not a particularly disagreeable one. Dr. Fisher was a strict disciplinarian, but at the same time a kind man with a pleasant wife. He had a well-developed sense of humour, and was very down-to-earth and businesslike. Like his predecessor, William Temple, Fisher went on to become Archbishop of Canterbury.

About eighteen months before Christopher's arrival at Repton the school had been rocked by a showdown between Fisher and a young master, Victor Gollancz. Gollancz had been assigned to the school in 1916 as a form of wartime service, his eyesight being below the standard required for duty in France. He outraged conservative members of staff by his "pink" views, culminating in a publication written with a history master, David Somervell, called *A Public School Looks at the World*, under which title was written: "published by members of Repton School." After a heated debate, the two masters found themselves dismissed. Gollancz was posted to Singapore, and went on to have a very successful career in publishing. He left the school with a significant legacy, a discussion group for sixth-formers which sometimes received important outside speakers, called the Civics Class. According to its constitution, this class was founded in the belief that "each man ought to learn Civics as a part of his education, so that he may be competent to bear his sense of responsibility as being an integral part of an Empire; the improvement of whose organisation becomes daily more imperative." Despite the apparent jingoism of that description, the class led to a greater awareness of events in the world outside. Discontinued on Gollancz's demise, it was resuscitated in the Michaelmas term of 1920, and speakers that school year included Gilbert Murray lecturing on the League of Nations, Canon Temple on the Workers' Educational Association and the school's own G. B. Smith on "The Co-operative Movement and Unemployment." Thus Repton could be called a fairly middle-of-the-road public school in character, with a certain progressive section which owed its existence to Gollancz's influence.

Already fourteen when he came to Repton, Christopher missed out on the trials of being a very young boy in such an institution. Fagging was still in practice but he was fortunate in that his fagmaster was the happy-go-lucky head of the house, who treated him with great kindness and helped him to become absorbed into the community. The usual public-school separation of age groups was avoided by a system of shared studies of between four and six boys of different ages. This in theory helped the younger boys to overcome their awe of their seniors and inculcated a sense of responsibility in the older ones. The boys slept in utilitarian dormitories on iron beds. Before the installation of full plumbing, the smaller boys would be sent downstairs to fetch water for washing in the morning. The toilets, arranged in a long row, were doorless. Clothes were kept on large wooden shelves in a separate room.

At first sight, Hall seems a maze of corridors and little stairways, the building having grown slowly around an old tower overlooking an ox-bow lake. Other windows, grilled to protect them from balls and other missiles, look down on a sports yard, while on another side are the playing fields, the pavilion and the "Grubber," a tuckshop where boys can buy chocolate and other treats. School food at the end of the First World War was not very appetising.

Boys below the sixth form were not allowed to fraternise with boys from other houses. This was to discourage the development of "unhealthy relationships" which might elude the watchful eye of the housemaster. As in most public schools then and now, adolescent homosexuality was quite common, though Christopher had no physical experience of it while at school. His "affairs" were simply of the heart and in fantasy. This is perhaps rather odd in view of the comments of the poet Vernon Watkins, two years Christopher's junior at Repton, who told his biographer that he had saved himself from homosexual assault from other boys at school by the strength of his stomach muscles.* Christopher had a series of crushes at school and during the holidays, one being a long-legged blond hockey player in Cheshire, whom he incorporated into a fantasy in which he was Heathcliffe (he had just been reading Emily Brontë's *Wuthering Heights*) and the boy Catherine Linton. On holiday at Marple Christopher could indulge his fantasy all the more as the local scenery evoked Brontë country very faithfully. He rode his bicycle over the wild, hilly countryside "dreaming of death and despair and hopeless love."†

Christopher was producing poems of his own at this period, one of which was written one afternoon after a field exercise with the Officers' Training Corps, a school military training scheme which still blights many public schools. He composed the poem in his

---

* Roland Mathias, *Vernon Watkins* (1974).
† *Kathleen and Frank*, p. 179.

head during training the exercise, then scribbled it down furiously when he returned to his study, before even taking a shower. His title for it, "Mapperly Plains," was, he thought, romantic sounding. He had come across the name following a balloon race, in which a hot air balloon released small balloons which had a postcard attached with their name and address written on the back. The card asked the finder of the balloon to write to the contestant, with details of where it had landed, the prize going to the person whose balloon had travelled the farthest. Mapperly Plains was one of the locations mentioned on a returned postcard, and Christopher filed the name away in his mind for further use. Years afterwards he discovered Mapperly Plains was an unexceptional suburb of Nottingham. The poem itself is a competent romantic piece in three stanzas, which appeared in an anthology of Public School Verse published in 1923, and was reprinted in *Exhumations*. Other poems of his were published in school magazines, but he did not write very many, and he is amused to find himself still referred to sometimes as a poet on the strength of those which survive.

Despite his increasing distaste for established religion Christopher was confirmed into the Anglican Church while at school, not having the necessary will-power to resist the process, though he did not go through the experience without considerable soul-searching. His religious supervisor happily steered him across the troubled waters of spiritual anxiety, and through the ceremony. Soon afterwards, Christopher realised that it had been a shameful surrender to the will and norms of the establishment.

Life at Repton took on a new dimension for Christopher when he entered the sixth form in 1920–21. This was largely owing to two people: his history teacher, G. B. Smith, and a fellow history student, Edward Upward. Graham Smith had arrived at Repton in 1919, and took to his task with great confidence. He was in many ways an ideal schoolmaster, and stayed at Repton for seven years before accepting the post of headmaster at Sedbergh School.

Smith was a small man in stature, with reddish receding hair, and suffered from a slight but not ugly speech defect. He was a keen musician, and held musical evenings in the house he had had built at Repton. A confirmed bachelor, he was thought by the masters at school to be a very entertaining fellow, and an ideal travelling companion. Isherwood once described his manner thus:

> Almost everything Mr. Holmes [Smith] did or said contrib-
> uted to a deliberate effect: he had the technique of a first-
> class clergyman or actor. But unlike most clergymen, he was
> entirely open and shameless about his methods. Having
> achieved his object—which was always, in one way or an-
> other, to startle, shock, flatter, lure or scare us for a few mo-
> ments out of our schoolboy conservatism or prejudice—he
> would explain to us gleefully just how this particular trap,
> bait or bomb had been prepared.*

His teaching method was wildly unconventional for the period. He would launch into outrageous generalisations about history, to encourage a boy to shoot them down, and to know *why* they should be shot down. He got to know each pupil's special likes and interests, foibles and weaknesses, and then played on them to shake him out of the state of boredom which is at the root of so much apathetic adolescent behaviour. Not all the boys responded as favourably to Mr. Smith as did Christopher. Some found the man's sense of humour, with its curious dry mixture of academic wit and ruthless cut-and-thrust, disconcerting. G. B. Smith did not hide the fact that he appreciated those who in their turn appreci-ated his attempts to teach them a love of history. To those who put no effort into learning he could exhibit a devastating iciness.

From early 1921, when Christopher was assigned to the history sixth, G. B. Smith directed all his studies except divinity and a lit-tle classics. Henry Davidson, a young master at Repton in Isher-wood's day, recalled in an interview that his colleagues "realised Bradshaw-Isherwood was clever, but no outstanding personality." Christopher was considered as potentially good Oxbridge material, so it was decided to enter him for a Cambridge History Award, the examinations for which would be held at the end of the Michaelmas term of 1921. Repton had much closer links with Cambridge than with Oxford and G. B. Smith himself was a Cambridge man (King's).

The most striking classmate in the history sixth was Edward Upward, born in Essex, but from a family which had been con-

* *Lions and Shadows*, p. 10.

nected with the Isle of Wight since the time of Charles I. He was a member of Latham, a different school house to Isherwood's. In *Lions and Shadows* he is called Allen Chalmers. Isherwood chose the pseudonym with happy disregard for the fact that there *was* a Chalmers among Upward's contemporaries at Latham, a boy who later changed his name by Royal Licence to John Rutherford, going on to become a barrister and Member of Parliament.

Edward Upward, a year older than Christopher, was a compact, intense-looking youth, with the kind of romantic attractiveness and idealism which immediately appealed to Christopher, who determined from the start to get to know him well. Normally quiet and broodingly contemplative, Upward (it was then customary for even quite close friends to call each other by their surname) would sometimes burst out with a tirade against some particularly unjust aspect of the school, to which he invariably referred as Hell. He had never ceased to loathe the school. Christopher found his attitude of defiance courageous and enthralling, and was impressed that Upward had escaped confirmation by confidently declaring himself to be an agnostic. Slowly, under Upward's influence, Christopher reappraised his own attitude to life, and to this day Isherwood considers Upward the ultimate arbiter of his actions and writings. G. B. Smith became aware of the closeness of their friendship, and dubbed them the Mutual Admiration Society.

This important friendship was influential to both parties. Upward was often shaken out of his disillusionment by Christopher's enthusiasm for things and people, and he loved Christopher's habit of building up his friends and acquaintances, exaggerating their traits to the borders of caricature, which they would then sometimes try to live up to. Upward, now known for his novels, was writing poetry at Repton, some of which was published in the school magazine. He won the Howes Verse Prize for 1920–21 for a work entitled *The Surrender of the German Fleet at Scapa Flow*, full of romantic imagery and intimations of quasi-mystical doom. G. B. Smith could not have approved of Upward's contempt for the school, yet he encouraged him to develop his imagination, to write down his thoughts, and accepted even the most florid flights of imagination in Upward's essays without sarcasm.

Most of the writing went on in the library, a haven at Repton, where silence and privacy were hard to come by. It was a large, comfortable room, thickly carpeted and equipped with inviting easy chairs. Here it was possible to work at leisure with almost no interference from the masters, though sometimes a boy who dozed off might find himself rudely awakened by a sharp nudge from Dr. Fisher, who happened to be passing through. Both Christopher and Edward Upward spent countless hours in the library, dipping at random into books, studying, or writing.

The most prolific writer at the school was Hector Wintle, who, like Christopher, had lost his father. His uncle, the distinguished Harley Street specialist Mackenzie Wintle, acted as his guardian. Overweight and amiable, Hector Wintle willingly shared his considerable literary output with other library users, unlike Edward Upward, who only let a very privileged few see his unprinted work. Wintle was a prose writer whose juvenile products were infinitely worse than the novels he wrote in later life. During 1921 he was working on a long and involved novel called *Donald Stanton*, which Christopher and others would dissect with great glee, pouncing on each *double entendre* or descriptive absurdity. Wintle never shirked from this criticism, continuing to write and ever eager for comments.

Although the other budding man of letters at Repton, Vernon Watkins, was in Christopher's house, Christopher had almost no contact with him, and when asked to contribute to a Watkins memorial volume in 1968 he found he could remember nothing at all about him. Edward Upward's brother, Mervyn, who was also at Repton, knew Watkins better. Being twice the size of the other houses, Hall was less intimate. Boys were divided into two groups by the initial of the surname: A-K and L-Z.

The year 1921 brought two important changes to Christopher's family life. In March his grandmother Elizabeth died; while in the autumn Kathleen rented a house in London—36 St. Mary Abbots Terrace, Kensington—which became Christopher's new home base for several years. Kathleen knew that she could no longer count on Marple as an adopted home, as John Isherwood was far from well. Emily moved in with Kathleen and Nurse Avis. She had left her Buckingham Street flat on doctor's orders, as the tall stone staircase there was a strain on her heart.

In December Christopher and Edward travelled to Cambridge

together for the scholarship examinations. By now they were talking their own private language, which derived most of its inspiration from Edward, who had persuaded Christopher to identify himself completely with the opposition to The Others, The Enemy, Them. The journey was seen as the beginning of an adventure into The Enemy's territory; the gloom of the Fenland in winter suited their fantasies perfectly. As the train pulled into Cambridge station, Edward declared solemnly: "Arrival at the Country of the Dead."

Cambridge itself seemed destined to promote their fantasy. Their minds still full of the atmosphere of Beatrix Potter and Conan Doyle, they revelled in the dark mystery of the icy fog swirling off the Fens; the blurring street-lamps which greeted them when they emerged from days in the examination halls; the formless shadows of Gothic buildings, and gowned students who appeared briefly on bicycles through the gloom. To confound their belief that people would be out to attack them, everyone in the university was as helpful and welcoming as possible. They were housed in rooms belonging to undergraduates down on vacation, and were woken in the morning by a college servant bringing a cup of tea. Comfortable sitting-rooms and superb libraries full of exquisite and valuable tomes were put at their disposal. Good wine was freely available, and the food was considerably better than the grub at school. Determined that their fiction of the conspiracy of The Enemy should not be thwarted by this show of generosity, they sternly declared to each other that it was all an extravagant bribe, which they must strongly resist. They swore eternal fidelity to their cause. Entirely wrapped up in their dreams, their friendship and the business of taking examinations, they had very little to do with anyone else there.

When the results came out they found that they had both done well. Edward had won a scholarship, while Christopher had earned an exhibition (financially a less valuable award). But as Christopher was only seventeen, it was thought that it would be better for him to stay on another year at St. Edmund's, at the end of which he could always sit the examination again and try to upgrade his award. He was not happy at the prospect, especially as Edward would be going up to Corpus Christi College, Cambridge, in October. Edward left Repton after the examinations, spending a large part of 1922 in Rouen, France, learning French *en pension*.

Life in the history sixth was not the same without Edward, yet Christopher was not such an alien in the final year as he implied later. He got on well with the other boys, among whom was Geoffrey Kingsford, a jolly boy from Edward's old house, Latham. Kingsford also studied history under G. B. Smith, and went on to become an architect.

Richard Isherwood was getting on less well at Berkhamsted, where he had established a reputation as a highly sensitive and most unusual boy. He was much closer to his mother than was Christopher, who was beginning to find St. Mary Abbots Terrace, with its female triarchy of Emily, Kathleen and Nurse Avis, rather claustrophobic. Christopher seized at the opportunity of joining a small school party, led by G. B. Smith, which was going to the French Alps for a walking holiday. He was filled with excitement at the prospect of his first trip abroad, as the scenes in Emily's pictures passed through his mind. His pleasure was capped by the knowledge that he would see Edward again, as the party had scheduled to stop at Rouen. Geoffrey Kingsford was also in the group.

At the beginning of August they caught a ferry from Southampton to Le Havre, where Christopher was shocked by the post-war shabbiness and the poor food. As he confessed in *Lions and Shadows:* "I was very pink and young and English, and quite prepared for a Continent complete with poisonous drains, roast frogs, bed-bugs and vice." Edward was at Rouen Station to meet the group, calm and diffident, while Christopher buzzed with excitement. Edward had grown a moustache and was smoking a pipe, which became an essential prop for his successful wistful-poet image. He had found himself in his element in Rouen, revelling in the romantic world of Flaubert and Maupassant, liberated from the oppressive conventions of England, and not deeply enough involved in French society to feel the weight of *its* conventions.

If Edward had succeeded in making himself look like Christopher's idea of a Montmartre poet, G. B. Smith had become a parody of an Englishman abroad, his tubby little form bundled in loud pepper-and-salt tweeds, topped with a cloth cap. The motley band went on to Paris, making a whistle-stop tour of the sights, during which Edward denounced Les Invalides as a Shrine of War. Christopher was rather impressed by it, but he was not going to admit it. He had not yet achieved Edward's total rejection of the Establishment, but felt he was well on the way to doing so. Sadly, the travel diary kept by Christopher on this trip reveals nothing of the complex thoughts going on inside his head.

From Paris they caught an overnight train to Aix-les-Bains, travelling third-class on wooden seats, surrounded by Frenchmen who made themselves completely at home in the carriage in a way that was a revelation to Christopher. The following day the party moved on to Annecy, taking a trip on the lake. Edward spoke enthusiastically of Baudelaire, whose *Fleurs du Mal* he had just read. Christopher rushed to the nearest bookshop to buy a copy, thus beginning a great esteem for the poet whose *Journaux Intimes* he would one day translate.

Christopher found the alpine scenery of the walking tour stunning, but again complied with Edward's pronouncement that mountains should be consigned "to the great rubbish-heap of objects and ideas admired by our adversaries."

G. B. Smith, anxious that the tour be both amusing and instructive, let the boys drink, even to excess. Christopher, imitating Edward, tried a pipe, and was sick. His digestion, after several days of French food, gave way completely, and he remembers little else about the three days spent in Paris on the return journey, apart from a visit to the opera to see Wagner's *Die Walküre*, during which he fell asleep.

Back in London Christopher was ill for some weeks, while Kathleen coped in the resigned manner of someone used to invalids all her life. Her experiences with Emily had made her efficient as a home nurse, but had killed her capacity for effusive sympathy. This failing infuriated Christopher, who would have enjoyed a more dramatic reaction.

During the Michaelmas term of 1922 Christopher became literary editor of the school magazine, wrote a few poems, and produced a paper for the Repton Literary Society on "Chivalry in English Literature." He had a study of his own in which to conduct this activity, and two fags to keep it clean. He had something of a crush on one, appropriately named Darling, but this did not stop him caning the boy for losing his football boots one day. In general, he treated his fags far worse than he had been treated in his first term. Christopher also took part in the school Debating Society, passionately defending a motion deploring patriotism, and he attended the Civics Class, where G. B. Smith was giving a series of lectures on war. The subject was one which came up again and again in adults' conversation. Boys of Christopher's age had to come to terms with the fact that they had not been quite old enough to take part in it, and that their immediate seniors had done so and had often died—allegedly for them.

Edward wrote regularly from Cambridge, describing it as even more hellish than school. He was now thoroughly disgusted with his chosen subject, history, which in university lectures was no longer the fun it had been with G. B. Smith. He felt the lecturers became submerged in their quest for precise detail, losing any overall view of events. They almost never made the students laugh. In other people's eyes, the Cambridge history faculty had a high reputation, and Corpus Christi had the advantages of having a first-rate mind in Kenneth Pickthorn (later a baronet and Conservative Member of Parliament for Carlton), but nevertheless it was condemned out of hand by Upward. Unfortunately, many of the best lectures were held in the early morning, and Edward could not be bothered to get up in time for them. It was anyway still a gentlemanly tradition at Oxbridge in the 1920s not to do any work.

Christopher duly went up to Cambridge in December for the scholarship examinations. He heard a few days later that he had won the best scholarship of his year at Corpus Christi. To celebrate, G. B. Smith invited him to his house on the last day of the school term, getting him slightly drunk on claret. There Christopher confided to Mr. Smith that he did not wish to study history at all, but English. Smith reacted sensibly, suggesting that Christopher read history until part one of the Tripos examinations, then switched to English for Finals (which is what Edward Upward did). Warned by Edward what to expect of Cambridge history, however, Christopher decided to attempt the change as soon as possible. He wrote to the college tutor, William Spens, explaining why he wished to change faculties, but received a polite reply to the effect that Pickthorn could not sanction such an action, although they could discuss the matter again after part one of the Tripos. Spens was not happy at the prospect of losing what promised to be his best history student of that year and possibly thought Christopher's wish was just an immature whim which would disappear when he got to university and buckled down to the course. It is an acknowledged fact that undergraduates who change courses early on often ask to change back shortly afterwards. Spens unfortunately weakened any good impression he might have made on Christopher by mentioning the duty the boy had to the tradition of the college in taking a responsible attitude towards his studies and his position as a scholar.

Christopher spent some of the intervening time getting to know London better, but he also followed in Edward's footsteps by going to Rouen to improve his French. He stayed in the same *pension*, Le Vert Logis, in the resonantly named Impasse des Arquebusiers, where horse-drawn wine-drays would clatter by in the morning to deliver merchandise to the nearby wine-merchants. The *pension* was run by a small, precise schoolmaster, Mr. Morel, from the local lycée. Madame Morel was of peasant stock, and was aided in the housework by two slavish maids. She told Christopher that Edward had been a most exemplary lodger. In fact, Edward had once caused great offence by not practising the French habit of shaking hands with everyone, but his mother had sent Madame Morel a handsome present to thank her for looking after him, so his minor misdemeanours had been overlooked.

Christopher kept in constant touch with Edward, and a letter which survives from this period gives a good idea of the stage of development their private language and imagery had reached. Like most of Isherwood's early letters it is undated, but Upward identifies it as June 1923. The writing is already tiny and precise, but there is a clear opening and an end. Soon, in their correspondence they would dispense entirely with the necessity for a conventional format:

> The time is passing more and more rapidly and the Vert Logis is always as house of shadows. Only green remains, colour of Lust and of the thievish worms who steal down marvellous stairways through our bowels. . . . I am glad you have abandoned women. There is no really pure love like the

passion for a child. The flame still burns brightly before Darling's altar. . . . I am in high favour with my family for the moment, not having seen them for three months. The epitaphs on Laily are superb. . . . These are the best I can manage on the spur of the moment:

> Laily is dead—and many a don might weep
>   That so much ordure should be put to sleep
> Did not the jolly worm cry from his bed
>   The teeming Laily—"Laily is not dead!"

> Now the wise man, made infinitely wise
>   Is raised in glory far beyond the skies
> He fawns on Beaver,* and devises most
>   Discreet attentions to the Holy Ghost.

"Laily," also known as "The Worm," was a rather confused imaginary being in their growing canon, a don who was their special enemy, or a swot; a bookworm who was nonetheless eager to be accepted by the body of students, and so professed an enthusiasm for sports. The name is derived from a couplet from an old ballad—"and she has made me the laily worm/That lies at the fit o' the tree"—and means "Loathly." In *Lions and Shadows*, for dramatic tidiness, Isherwood intimates that the construction of their later elaborate fantasies, centred on the Cambridge works, was begun after he went up to university, but this is not true. The obsession with death and worms is quite typical of their letters and conversations at the time.

Christopher returned to England in early July 1923 and did a couple of weeks' library duty at Repton. Edward joined him there for the second week, during which they continued producing doggerel as well as some more serious creations. Christopher had already started work on the first of many drafts of an abortive novel. Edward was still writing poetry, and Christopher had had a "vision" on his first trip to France that Upward would become the poet of their generation, a realisation that had made him nearly burst into tears with excitement and pride.

* In the slang of the period, a man with a beard, i.e., Christ.

3

"Every biographer knows that the undergraduate years are, or were, the most important, the most 'formative' to use an up-to-date expression, in a man's life—that is of a man who enjoyed the fortune of having been educated at Oxford or Cambridge."

Clive Bell's generalisation in his book *Old Friends* is undoubtedly true in most instances, but in Christopher's case it was not at Cambridge that he bloomed. His most important friendships had been, or were to be, made elsewhere, and he never fitted into the university environment, nor truly profited from it. It is tempting to point out that creative life among the undergraduates at Cambridge was at a low ebb. The brilliant days of Lytton Strachey, Maynard Keynes and other budding Bloomsburyites had passed. Without a doubt, in the 1920s Oxford was the centre of creative and social brilliance, counting among its number Harold Acton, Brian Howard, Peter Quennell, Evelyn Waugh and his cousin Claud Cockburn. But that cannot explain Christopher's Cambridge débâcle; his problems there were entirely personal.

Corpus Christi is one of the smallest of Cambridge colleges. Founded in the fourteenth century as a college only for priests, it remained a strongly religious college for most of its history. Great changes had taken place around 1906–7, when the range of some of the subjects offered was considerably widened, and some tal-

ented new blood joined the resident teaching staff. It retained an
aura of political conservatism, but its predominantly religious colouring changed from Evangelist to moderate Anglo-Catholic.*
Typical of the new mood were the Master (Principal), Dr. Pearce
(the future Bishop of Derby), the theologian, Edwyn Hoskyns,
and Christopher's tutor, Kenneth Pickthorn. It had undergone up-
heavals during the Great War, like the other Oxbridge colleges,
but by Christopher's time had settled down again. It was small
enough for everyone to know each other, and for no one to escape
the eagle eye of the community.

Christopher had second-floor rooms on the same staircase as
Edward's, but he thought that his sitting-room had the atmosphere of a dentist's waiting-room, and preferred to spend his time
in Edward's cosier quarters. There he became familiar with Edward's copies of Katherine Mansfield, Walt Whitman, Edgar
Allan Poe, Baudelaire, Flaubert and others. The usual state of
chaotic muddle in Edward's rooms was a great contrast to Christopher's, the surgical appearance of which was exaggerated by his
fanatical tidiness. Every tiny object had its proper place, and Edward would tease him by moving things. Christopher used to be
particularly upset when Edward scattered ash in his grate; while
Edward, who believed Christopher should not worry about such
things, did not refrain from his habit, watching with amusement
as Christopher invariably whisked out a brush and pan to sweep
up after him.

Christopher's early tutorials with Kenneth Pickthorn were not a
success. A brilliant man still in his twenties, with a handsome,
finely chiselled face, Pickthorn did not suffer sham gladly. Confronted with Christopher's first showy but inept essay, he became
increasingly fidgety, finally strumming on the mantelpiece with
his fingers. When Christopher had finished, and awaited a tirade,
Pickthorn said crushingly: "I'll say this for you—it's not the work
of an entirely uneducated fool. Look here, Isherwood, don't you
yourself agree that it's all tripe?"

Isherwood remembers the almost masochistic pleasure he felt
during some of these encounters, yet Pickthorn was a most sympathetic man. Aware that Edward Upward was totally disenchanted

---

* Brian Little, *The Colleges of Cambridge* (1973).

with his work, Pickthorn once asked Upward if studying history seemed worse than working in a bank. Pickthorn was less effective when lecturing than in tutorials, and it was in the lecture-halls that Christopher realised he could not cope with the course unless he was prepared to do a great deal of detailed study. He could not concentrate on what was being said and, instead of taking notes, daydreamed. Racked by guilt afterwards, he would borrow other people's notes to copy, but after a while he ceased to do so. He was quite unable to exert the same discipline he showed in keeping his rooms tidy to his studies. Possibly his excessive tidiness was a subconscious recompense for not working. There is no better incentive for washing up accumulated coffee cups than an awkward essay which needs writing.

Edward had found a new and even more convincing objection to lectures: in his view the dons showed no humanity in their approach to history, no passion for lost causes, no anger at the brutality and futility of man's actions. Edward was developing a strong social consciousness, though still criticising politics and ridiculing the politicos at university. He also objected to many of Christopher's friends, for Christopher had got involved in the social niceties of tea-parties in people's rooms, squash games and general banter or ragging. He came from a good family and a reasonable school, he was amusing and idle and thus had several qualities to make him popular. Edward, who was shy and had no interest in the people Christopher saw, began to voice his disgust. Christopher in turn was growing to dislike the back-slapping hearties who sometimes congregated around Edward (who played football) talking loudly about sport and girls, and drinking beer. They therefore agreed to enjoy their friends apart, while preserving their own closer comradeship and fantasy world which, though it was only a part of their university lives, was from a literary point of view the most interesting.

Walking through the streets of Cambridge they kept up their game of conspiracy against The Enemy, discerning spies among waiters or shop-assistants. One evening they happened to turn into an unfamiliar alley, at the end of which was a small old door let into a high stone wall. Edward announced that it was the doorway into the "Other Town." The Other Town became an escape world parallel to their mundane college life. Over the coming months they worked together to describe this mythical place (almost a dimension), and to define its vocabulary. They revelled in the possibilities of the English language. The Other Town was redolent with Gothic imagery, peopled by good eccentric beings or fantastic creatures, forces drawn from the writings of Poe, Conan Doyle and the drawings of Albrecht Dürer. Such artists were aligned with Christopher and Edward against the great "blague" of Cambridge. Their favourite writers were also made cohorts, notably Wilfred Owen, Katherine Mansfield and Emily Brontë, a trio to whom they referred affectionately as Wilfred, Kathy and Emmy. Edward horrified Christopher by suggesting that Shakespeare was also a good thing. Having brushed aside his earlier passion for the bard's works, Christopher had consigned Shakespeare to the same fate as the Alps, disgraced because of its universal approbation. At Edward's insistence, however, he went away and reread Shakespeare, then returned with the judgement that Edward was right.

They kept a diary of their imaginary lives, calling themselves "Hynd" (Upward) and "Starn" (Isherwood). They wrote humorous and often lewd verses about Laily and other enemies, such as Edward's: "About the middle of the night a thing with fins,/Came to reprove the Tutor for his sins. . . ." For Christopher's benefit, Edward would sometimes insert homosexual references, especially in his later stories.

Christopher was also working hard on a novel, *Lions and Shadows*, the title being from C. E. Montague's *Fiery Particles* ("arrant lovers of living, mighty hunter of lions or shadows"). When the novel floundered he put the title into cold storage until fourteen years later, he resurrected it for his autobiographical work, dramatised in the form of a novel. In the earlier work the hero, a preparatory school pupil when the Armistice is signed, is due to enter the public school Rugtonstead (a clumsy compound of Rugby, Repton and Berkhamsted) in 1919 when he is struck by rheumatic fever—a dramatic detail borrowed from Hector Wintle's life. The story embodies Christopher's reflections on his time, real and imagined, at Repton. Later he wrote:

I built up the daydream of an heroic school career in which the central figure, the dream I, was an austere young prefect,

called upon unexpectedly to captain a "bad" house, surrounded by sneering critics and open enemies, fighting
slackness, moral rottenness, grimly repressing his own romantic feelings towards a younger boy, and finally triumphing
over all his obstacles, passing the test, emerging—a Man.*

The test became one of Christopher's preoccupations, this need
to prove himself obviously indicating an inner insecurity. Isherwood has tried to explain this on many occasions by diagnosing a
sense of guilt in his generation for being too young to take part
in the war, thus missing out on the supreme Test. A similar feeling has been recorded by other writers, such as George Orwell,
who wrote in his essay "My Country Right of Left": "As the war
fell back into the past, my particular generation, those who had
been 'just too young', became conscious of the vastness of the experience they had missed. You felt yourself a little less than a
man, because you had missed it."

The War Test had obvious parallels with a need to prove one's
masculinity, to show that one was not impotent—or homosexual.
Conscious of his small stature and ambivalent sexual orientation,
Christopher exercised in secret with a chest-expander. A virgin
when he arrived in Cambridge, he can have had no doubts about
his sexual inclinations, yet he made no attempt to satisfy them.
When he did finally have his first sexual experience, with another
student from Corpus, it was the other boy who took the initiative,
locking the door and sitting himself down on Christopher's lap, so
that there would be no chance of escape.

The novel progressed smoothly, elegantly outlining the mental
anguish and deceptions of the hero in his attempts to compensate
for not going through the test without losing face. Edward read
parts of it, and encouraged Christopher to persist with the work.

During the Christmas vacation they continued to enlarge the
literature of their fantasies. Christopher sent Edward verses of a
Latin Mass, signing the accompanying note "Yours in Darkness,
Christopher." Unabated, the charade went on when they resumed
college in January.

Christopher and Edward saw several other Old Reptonians who

* *Lions and Shadows*, p. 78.

were up at Cambridge, especially Christopher Orpen, who had been in Edward's house and who went to Corpus at the same time as Christopher. Orpen was the son of a very reverend, and related to Sir William Orpen, but he had turned out to be completely wild. A favourite trick of his was to swing out of his window in his gown, terrifying passers-by. Fond of practical jokes, he once slowly untied a parcel at the college dining-table, under the close scrutiny of his fellow diners, to reveal a bloody cock's head. Orpen and Upward invented a clever card-trick, using discreet signals by means of smoking a pipe in a certain way. They passed this off as a spiritualistic phenomenon. Christopher was foxed but, suspecting a hoax, one day demanded that Edward leave the room while he chose a card—little realising that the pipe signals could be seen through the keyhole of the bedroom door.

Geoffrey Kingsford was also at Cambridge (at Magdelene College). It was he who helped Christopher choose a motor-cycle in the spring, a powerful 1924 model AJS. The machine both terrified and thrilled Christopher; it was the Test on Wheels. He dared not ride it often in the narrow, crowded streets of the town, but wheeled it around, pretending that it had broken down. Following a couple of minor accidents, he sold it only a few months after buying it.

A major friendship started at university with Roger Burford, who had recently founded the Cambridge Film Club. Christopher soon became an enthusiastic member. Edward laughed at Christopher's indiscriminate love of the movies, which Christopher himself put down to a fascination for the outward appearance of people. One of the first guest speakers at the Film Club was the producer George Pearson, who invited the club's members to visit his studios in Islington. Christopher followed up the offer in the Easter vacation, travelling with a very handsome young fellow student, Pembroke Stephens. A scene representing the Savoy Hotel on Armistice Night was being shot, and the two young men found themselves being coerced into being extras. Christopher was dressed up as a midshipman, and spent the day dancing round and round, while other extras pelted his group with balloons and streamers. Take after take was shot, during which the studios were filled with a cacophony of shouted directions while an interminable fox-trot was played by an orchestra. He was paid one pound four shillings for the day's work, which ended at 10 P.M., and did not feel encouraged to pursue an acting career. He was not even visible on the finished film. Pembroke Stephens, however, was seized upon by the casting director, and a few months later successfully played a major role in a film called *Satan's Sister*, shot in the West Indies, in which he acted the part of an English undergraduate hero.

Subsequently, Stephens crossed Christopher's path on several occasions. He was a fine and aggressive reporter in Germany in the 1930s, and was expelled by the Nazis for tracking down and reporting on concentration camps. Later he was in China during the Sino-Japanese War (as was Isherwood), being killed by Japanese machine-gun fire while covering a battle from a watch-tower in the neutral international settlement of Shanghai.

Christopher wrote in a letter to Edward that vacation, dated April 7, 1924:

> Here I am in the midst of dreams and magical faint extasies. Trees full of angels at Peckham couldn't have thrilled Mr. Blake so much. . . . Who says dissenters aren't mystics? The symbols of the Hostel surround me, but I was unprepared for my brother's exclamation, on looking out at the street from the sitting-room window: "There's a light blue horse!"
>
> I have introduced Mr. Gunball to the family, under a decent veil of piety, and his saga is a constant source of amusement to Wintle, who made the shrewd comment that we are indebted to Alice in Wonderland. . . . The Slug's Jesus is crucified on Crouch End, and the hot-gospeller bittern bears witness at Balham. I see a two-decker tram, full of pianos, heading for Java; sixteen cormorants praying at St. Paul's for pardons for the Pekinese Pope and an enormous cortege of rabbits bearing tailor's dummies interminably toward a mausoleum of pumice-stone. . . .
>
> Yours, till we meet in Pintu's Spinkey,
> Christopher

It is worth bearing in mind that at this time neither of them knew of the existence of the Surrealists on the other side of the Channel. The Hostel mentioned in the letter is the "Rats Hostel." It is typical of a certain atmosphere, a genre, a special brand of medie-

val surrealism which they had made their own. Gunball is one of
their slowly accumulated characters and will be discussed later.

On May 9, 1924, Grandfather Isherwood died. Uncle Henry
had moved into Marple Hall some while before when he and
Muriel had separated. The Hall was revitalised by his presence,
the air being full of incense which he burned in the fireplace, and
the library converted into a sitting-room filled with little knick-
knacks and photographs of society ladies. Before long, however,
the call of the big city became too much, and he took a flat in London where there was easier access to the guardsmen whom he
fancied.

During the summer term 1924 Edward and Christopher saw
less of each other. Edward was working hard, not only for part
one of the Tripos which was now before him, but also in writing a
poem which he intended to enter for the Chancellor's Medal, the
university's most prestigious literary prize—the subject being Buddha. In the examination he gained a miserable third, and changed
faculties. But he won the Chancellor's Medal. During this time
his joint creations with Christopher naturally suffered but in any
case summer had transformed Cambridge into a warm, sunny
town, in which long afternoons could be spent punting along the
Backs. The creations of their dark fantasies went into a summer
hibernation.

Christopher was also working for exams in June (perversely
called "Mays"), of no importance for the final degree, but a useful
gauge of a student's progress. He cannot have been entirely idle,
as he emerged with a creditable IIi—to his surprise and the college's disappointment. Whatever his attitude to studies might be,
they had hoped for better things.

In the long vacation Christopher saw a great deal of Hector
Wintle in London. Hector lived in North Kensington, in a
gloomy basement decorated with photographs of film stars. Of all
the portraits in *Lions and Shadows*, probably Hector Wintle's is
the most accurate. He had not gone to university from Repton,
but attended a crammer's with the aim of entering a London
medical school and eventually becoming a doctor, like his guardian. His heart was not in the work, however, as he believed his true
vocation to be that of a successful novelist, fêted by society, and
in particular by beautiful women. He had abandoned *Donald*

Stanton, but was progressing well with another novel. Hector's friends were amused by his soulful amorous exploits, and monitored the progress of the carefully planned but often unsuccessful advances he made to various girls. He was short and stout, but always immaculately groomed, and had cultivated a suavity which coexisted incongruously with his general pessimism and unhappiness about the world and his future. Isherwood wrote that with Hector (Philip Linsley):

> I felt always perfectly at home. His endless succession of little chills, twinges of rheumatism, worries about his health (twice, already, he had been seriously ill with rheumatic fever) were, somehow, very endearing. He understood perfectly my complex about "War" and "The Test." He himself did exercises night and morning: he was terribly concerned at the prospect of becoming fat. . . . He was generous and absurdly extravagant with his small allowance—and quite rightly, for the least whiff of luxury gave him pleasure out of all proportion to its cost.*

Christopher's financial position was better than Hector's. His eighty pounds' scholarship at Cambridge was worth a considerable amount in 1924, and while in London he was able to stay at his mother's house. Provision had been made by John Isherwood for the family in the event of Frank's death.

Christopher and Hector loved to walk the streets together, particularly in the shabbier parts of London. Christopher found this contact with reality sexually stimulating. Having initiated Hector into his fantasy world, they were able to continue the sort of imaginative and ridiculous conversations which Christopher had had with Edward at Cambridge. Hector's taste for the absurd and the grotesque was almost equal to theirs, and in that respect he provided an excellent holiday substitute for Edward. He and Christopher frequently went to the 1924 Wembley Exhibition, where they rode the Big Dipper, reading aloud from a newspaper as they wooshed up and down.

Around this time Christopher started to write a journal of his life, largely inspired by the *Diary of a Disappointed Man,* a then

* Ibid., p. 94.

popular book by Barbellion (Bruce Cummings), which had been published in 1919, the year Cummings died of disseminated sclerosis. Christopher's diary was full of despair and self-pity. Through this medium, he was able to describe and develop the personality of a sensitive *littérateur*, alienated from the great outside world by his unique perception of its sordid futility. Illness seemed an essential factor in maintaining this pose, and since there was now very little physically wrong with him, apart from some dental trouble, Christopher gave full vent to his latent hypochondria.

Back at Corpus, Edward was full of enthusiasm to continue the Hynd and Starn stories. A fresh element to his fantasies had been added by his new college rooms, which were said to be haunted, though neither of the friends ever saw anything to support the legend. During the vacation Edward had clarified the rather muddled overall concept of their private world by deciding that the Other Town was not an alternative existence in Cambridge but a village, far away, lost among rolling downs, by the Atlantic Ocean. To emphasise its deathly dankness, the village was named Mortmere.

Several of the stories written about the village of Mortmere by the two young men in the mid-1920s are still in existence, Upward possessing several short manuscripts neatly written out in Isherwood's precise hand. Upward resisted Isherwood's attempts to have some of these published later, though the longest and most sophisticated of all, *The Railway Accident*, was eventually published in 1969. It was written entirely by Upward in 1927, Isherwood having lost interest by then.

Mortmere was a convenient vessel into which they could pour their own peculiar brand of political and sexual anarchy. The Church was a natural target for parody, though the amount of space given to vicars, choirboys and vergers is an acknowledgement of the rich fictional material and atmosphere offered by ecclesiastical ritual, as well as the homosexual undertones of some religious ceremonies for those with a mind for them. Mortmere's vicar, the Reverend Welken, had pushed ritual beyond the realm of magic. A widower who had been guilty of sexual offences with a choirboy, he indulged in "angel-manufacture" in the belfry, an unusual form of alchemy demanding repetition of the act of buggery. Welken was also a devilishly skilful amateur conjurer. His best friend was Gunball, a hedonist, drunkard and liar. He was blighted by frequent visions of two-headed monsters, ghouls, torrents of human blood and fearful astronomical happenings—all of which phenomena Edward excelled in describing. Indeed, without much stretch of the imagination, these two principal figures of the Mortmere stories can be seen as outrageously inaccurate caricatures of their authors.

As well as containing liberal doses of the supernatural and the perverse, the stories have all the qualities of good tales of mystery and suspense. One, the *Javanese Sapphires*, is a surreal parody of Sherlock Holmes, in which a seemingly impossible crime is executed by a trained snake who enters Gunball's house by way of the plumbing, and swallows some valuable sapphires before making his escape. Unfortunately, the plot backfires when the snake is unable to regurgitate the gems, and slowly digests them.

While at university, Christopher and Edward often talked of writing a full-length book about Mortmere, but never did. The project repeatedly got lost in flights of imagination when they tried to discuss definite plans. The book

> . . . was to be illustrated . . . with real oil paintings, brasses, carvings in ivory or wood; fireworks would explode to emphasise important points in the narrative; a tiny gramophone sewn into the cover would accompany the descriptive passages with emotional airs; all the dialogue would be actually spoken; the different pages would smell appropriately, according to their subject-matter, of grave-clothes, manure, delicious food, burning hair, chloroform or expensive scent. All copies would be distributed free. Our friends would find, attached to the last page, a pocket containing banknotes and jewels; our enemies, on reaching the end of the book, would be shot dead by a revolver concealed in the binding.*

Nothing less would do.

Christopher was unable to keep the world of Mortmere a secret. Telling his family in London about it had proved harmless, but indiscreetly he took Vernon Watkins into his confidence. The stu-

* Ibid., p. 114.

dent in turn shared the stories with a don, who pronounced them childish, as indeed they were. Edward was appalled at Christopher's treachery.

Undoubtedly the value of the Mortmere stories lies in the opportunity they gave their creators to write out their discontent, to rebel against the prudery and conventions of their times. Their literary interest lies in the fact that, imaginatively speaking, they are considerably more extravagant than any of Isherwood's published novels.

On November 10, 1924, Emily died of pneumonia. Christopher travelled up to London for the funeral and cremation at Golders Green. The ceremony struck him as dismal and untheatrical. Later he accompanied Kathleen to Brompton Cemetery to visit Frank's grave.

The Michaelmas term ended with a bumper dinner at Corpus, after which everyone got very drunk. Christopher enthusiastically took part in a butter fight, which virtually wrecked Edward's rooms.

During the vacation Christopher went roller-skating almost every day with Hector Wintle. Hector was a great expert, and would invite strange women on to the rink to dance, confident of his skill. He even dreamed of abandoning medicine to become a professional skating instructor.

The novel *Lions and Shadows* was finished on January 7, 1925. Christopher took the completed manuscript along to the Irish novelist and translator Ethel Mayne, who had been a great friend of Frank Isherwood's before his marriage. Frank had met her in the late 1890s, during early posting in Ireland, and had nicknamed her Venus. She was witty and self-assured, and occasionally coarse. Kathleen was shocked by the fact that she smoked. Christopher found her fascinating and enjoyed her conversation, highlighted by French phrases, which struck him as being reminiscent of Henry James. She moved to London, where she became well known in literary circles. She had promised Christopher she would show his manuscript to her publishers if she liked it. She did not like it. She recommended him to put it away in a drawer and forget about it. But, she said, if he really wanted to write, he would go on writing, no matter what anyone said.

Back at college Christopher read *Lions and Shadows* out loud to Edward. It was well over a hundred thousand words long, so that although he started in the early evening, he did not finish it until the following morning. Edward, exhausted, enthused politely, but a couple of days later admitted that he, too, did not think it was very good. Christopher was already convinced—and was the first to admit—that it was in many ways a poor imitation of Compton Mackenzie and Hugh Walpole, expressed in tortuously emotional language.

Edward was bitterly disappointed at having changed to reading English at Cambridge. All too often literary texts were treated like corpses on the dissecting-table. All passion or romanticism was lost in the don's technique of nit-picking textual analysis. The one exception to this rule was the young I. A. Richards, who was giving a series of lectures on modern poetry, which both Edward and Christopher attended. Despite his funny little voice, Ivor Richards held their attention as no other lecturer had managed to do. He opened their eyes to what was going on outside their limited field of vision. "To us," Isherwood was later to write, "he was infinitely more than a brilliant new literary critic: he was our guide, our evangelist, who revealed to us, in a series of lightning flashes, the entire expanse of the Modern World."[*] He convinced them that it was necessary to heed Katherine Mansfield's injunction to be a part of life. They began to see their Mortmere stories for what they were: a private indulgence. Edward reacted by losing his faith in himself as a poet, and subsequently turned to prose. He was often troubled and irritable, and the two friends started to get on each other's nerves.

Richards fired them with his enthusiasm for T. S. Eliot, whom he saw as a crucial voice of the post-war scene who had "given a perfect emotive description of a state of mind which is probably inevitable for a while for all meditative people."[†] He believed that Eliot would be *the one hope* for the then brand-new English Tripos. "I was then just beginning to lecture for it. And I was soon full of dreams of somehow winkling Eliot out of his bank and annexing him to Cambridge."[‡] According to Richards, *The*

---

[*] Ibid., p. 121.
[†] *Science and Poetry* (1926), pp. 64–65.
[‡] I. A. Richards, notes for a talk at the Institute of Contemporary Arts, London, June 29, 1965.

Waste Land was a major testament of the times. Edward and Christopher, who had hitherto deliberately ignored Eliot's work because of its popularity among the "in" crowd at Cambridge, now fell upon it voraciously.

Richards did much more than introduce them to new poets. He annihilated their innocent, arrogant rejection of work being done in other fields, notably in psychology. When they condescended to read Freud (whose *Introduction to Psycho-analysis* was published in English in 1922), it was as if a floodgate had been opened. Isherwood now feels Sigmund Freud was responsible for the greatest literary event of his time. Through Freud, Christopher and his peers accepted the belief that their parents were responsible for absolutely everything. "It was all their fault, and we would *never* forgive!"* The parents' crime was doubled because they failed to recognise that a psychological revolution had taken place. Christopher quickly developed a clear image of his mother as being a thoroughly menacing presence.

In February 1925 Christopher started a new novel, called *Christopher Garland*. The plot, with obvious references to his own experience, tells of a young Cambridge undergraduate with literary pretensions who finds the university utterly stultifying.

> In the vacation, the young man, cut off from his friends by his preceptions but not yet fully initiate, drifts into a dismal struggle with the personality of the aunt with whom he lives. A love affair with a friend's fiancée brings him to himself, and, with its renunciation, he enters upon a period, if not of peace, at least of courage and assurance for the future.†

In this story Christopher Isherwood tried to come to terms with his role as an artist in society, but "as I still imagined that 'being an artist' was a kind of neurotic alternative to being an ordinary human man, it is hardly surprising that my ideas got a little mixed."

Among the first-year students at Corpus that year was Meredith Worth, an Old Reptonian from Christopher's house, who founded a literary society at college. Christopher was in on this at the be-

* Isherwood, in a lecture at Berkeley University, April 23, 1963.
† *Lions and Shadows*.

ginning, and both he and Edward read papers to the society. Christopher also continued to attend Film Club meetings, and argued at length about the merits of film with Roger Burford and other members. Roger was talking of finding a job with a film studio, and Christopher envied him this imminent independence. The fact that he would not be free of the university for a whole year began to depress him. His new history tutor was less demanding than Pickthorn, and Christopher got by with the minimum of work, often just copying out Edward's essays from the year before.

The approach of the Tripos examinations in June did not prove any particular incentive for study. Guilty panic made Christopher work for two days, then he sank back into apathy, convinced that it was too late for him to do enough work to give an acceptable performance. One evening in April, while on a walk with Edward, he decided quite suddenly that the only proper course of action was that he should get himself sent down—to finish Cambridge not with a whimper of academic mediocrity but a bang of defiance. Plotting his own demise became the ultimate Test of the Mortmere consciousness, a gesture against The Enemy which was no mere private fantasy but very much part of Life, liable to affect the whole of Christopher's future. They worked out the most effective course of action which would lead to certain banishment from the university: a thrust at the system itself by mocking its sacred symbol, the examinations. Christopher sold all his history textbooks, with the exception of Bishop William Stubbs's *The Constitutional History of England,* which he dropped ritualistically into the river Cam.

As spring turned into summer, Christopher and Edward spent their time punting up the Backs, listening to Beethoven and Schubert on Edward's portable Gramophone and telling each other funny stories. Christopher threw himself into the pleasures of Cambridge in the sun, visited friends, walked and talked, but let no one but Edward into his secret. Hector Wintle came up to Cambridge for a visit and read them passages from his latest work in progress, a novel set in his home territory of North Kensington, "eighty thousand words of middle-class gloom." Edward became excited as the fatal day approached, while Christopher, whatever sick feeling he had in the pit of the stomach, knew that now it really *was* too late to do anything about it.

Oxbridge examinations are usually swift and intensive with three or four days of papers, morning and afternoon. While Christopher's classmates busily wrote down everything that they knew about the defeat of King Charles, he composed whatever came into his head. What he produced was not much of a testimony to his literary abilities. Unwilling or unable to write anything at all interesting, or even genuinely funny, he filled his papers with short satirical passages, third-rate verse and a few mild jabs aimed at the imbecility of some of the questions, leaving himself plenty of time in which to make a copy of his answers for Edward's benefit. Between examinations he read the answers to his friend, who pranced about with glee. The process continued right through the exams, as Christopher gave no sign either to the invigilators or to the other candidates that he was doing anything other than faithfully answering the papers. Later, without fuss, he packed his bags and returned to London to wait for the bombshell.

A week later a telegram arrived from his tutor recalling him immediately to Cambridge. In a manner that was at once kindly, but obviously pained, he asked Christopher if there were any extenuating circumstances for his unusual behaviour. Christopher had no excuse, but sat in silence, feeling rather stupid. The tutor shrugged his shoulders, shook Christopher's hand and wished him luck. The college authorities were furious, and Kenneth Pickthorn never forgave him. To save him the ugly process of expulsion, Christopher's tutor suggested he remove his name from the college books, which he did. His two years at the university were officially wiped out.

4

In later life Isherwood felt heartily ashamed of what he had done. Edward Upward went through pangs of remorse for not attempting to stop him; indeed for encouraging his foolhardiness. He wonders if Christopher would have gone on to become a don had he stayed on and been allowed to study English. Or would he have become a schoolmaster, as Upward did? The prospect terrified Christopher at the time. Finally, Isherwood made a return trip to Cambridge to make his peace with the college, and his name was written back into the records.

Christopher's action was a cruel blow for Kathleen. She had always dreamed that Christopher would become a don, preferably at Oxford. Having had no warning about the depth of his discontent, she was even more upset. But she was not the sort of parent to slam the door in his face for such irresponsibility, so he became a more permanent member of the St. Mary Abbots Terrace household. Kathleen, toughened by the deaths of her husband, parents and in-laws, and without brothers or sisters, was determined to stand by her sons, whatever they did. Maybe because of their lack of inhibition about what they said to her, she had become virtually unshockable. Christopher filled his conversations with quotes from ribald student talk and some of the fruitier parts of the Mortmere stories. As an example of her surprising liberality in such areas, when she was doing jury service around this time she helped dismiss a charge against a man who had put his hand up the skirt of a lady on a bus.

Christopher felt an immediate sense of relief in his new freedom. On holiday in the Isle of Wight he wrote to Edward on July 1:

> A Saint-Blaise, à la Zuecca,
> Nous étions bien là.
>
> In other words, this is pure heaven. I am sitting on a veranda whose roof is curiously curved with wooden struts like the bottom of a rowing boat. . . . One can walk down to the beach and back in two minutes debating the next paragraph —equivalent, in fact, to those journeys to the Corpus rears. . . . Last night I hired a canoe, and went right out to sea. It was utterly calm. . . .
>
> They are all here. I met Gunball stalking under the cliffs with a gun over his shoulder, a curious three-pronged spike projecting from the barrel. We embraced with tears. . . . No writing done, thank God.
>
>   Your bemused friend, Christopher

The writing is almost illegible without a magnifying glass, having shrunk to minute proportions. A psychiatrist later told Isherwood that it indicated a desire to disappear completely.

Christopher had come to appreciate the Isle of Wight when he visited it as a child, but in the twenties it became a refuge from his everyday life, and he made several visits, either alone or with Edward Upward, and most of his other major friends visited him there. He lodged in a typical guesthouse in Freshwater Bay, called Marine Villa, whose landlady, Miss Johnson, smoked like a chimney but left him perfectly alone.

In August 1925 he celebrated his twenty-first birthday. Even if the dark cloud of Cambridge still hung over his head at home, he was determined to enjoy himself, and blew his Post Office savings (£150) on a large second-hand car. This car provided a release from some of his more pressing worries, such as how he was going to make a living. He had gone for an interview at a film studio, but there was no opening for him there. He had a small allowance, thanks to the generosity of his family, but it was not enough on which to lead the life of a young man-about-town. He did, however, persuade his Uncle Henry that it would be a good idea for him to enjoy now some of the money which he was due to inherit later. Henry seemed to appreciate this direct approach, and was well aware that he had been equally calculating in his own relationship with his father. Christopher determined to foster his relationship with his uncle, choosing to overlook some of Henry's more patronising attitudes to the world at large, while Kathleen continued to receive the full brunt of his criticisms.

Henry had such a selfish, outdated view of things that Christopher felt able to laugh off most of his uncle's prejudices. He even spoke like a caricature, dropping the final "g" when he used words like "huntin'" and "shootin'," being unable to roll his "r" so that he always said "fwightfully," and punctuating his conversation with expletives such as "Don't you know." By this time he was in his late fifties, but still considered himself dashing. He played his role of the wealthy uncle with great panache, illustrating his talks with sweeping gestures and displaying his *objets d'art* and good wines with pride, while a smiling Italian valet served the meals. Henry and Christopher's *tête-à-têtes* became considerably intimate later when Christopher admitted his own homosexuality. Henry loved to hear about Christopher's adventures. He would then tell the young man about his own experiences with guardsmen or other members of the lower orders. Like many homosexuals of his class, Henry was sexually interested in rough, working-class youths whose social origins he despised. He was a shameless snob, and rather foppish, but was physically attracted to brute masculinity to such an extent that he once paid a man not to wash for a week. After his acts of lust, Henry would trot off to a priest to confess. Unfortunately he was not one hundred per cent reliable, and on several occasions during the 1920s and 1930s Christopher's monthly allowance did not arrive.

Christopher happened upon his first job by accident. He was generous with his car, and often took his friends for rides, so that he was not surprised one day when an old school friend, Eric Falk, asked him if they could go together to the house of a young boy, Sylvain Mangeot, who was laid up with a bad knee and who would appreciate being taken out for a run. The Mangeots lived in a mews in Chelsea. Sylvain's mother, Olive, was one of the very first women to realise the desirability of these formerly ignored garages and servant's quarters, though her initial motive had been to provide her musician husband with a place to practise where he would not disturb the neighbours. Olive was English, but her husband André was French. Apart from Sylvain, then aged eleven, they had another son, Fowke, who was a year older. Christopher fell instantly in love with the family, who seemed to be living just the sort of intimate artistic life that appealed to him and which he would like to emulate. The house was in a cheerful state of disorder, the complete opposite to Christopher's own room at home, and it conveyed to him the impression of being a warm, friendly household of individuals living in mutual respect and intent upon their work.

André Mangeot, thin, sunburnt and forty, won Christopher's immediate approval by accepting without question his motives for leaving Cambridge. He enquired about Christopher's future plans, and by the end of the afternoon had hired the young man as his secretary—at the salary of one pound a week. Kathleen was not very impressed by the wages, but Christopher was thrilled with the job—which struck Hector Wintle and his other close friends as being wildly romantic. Christopher flushed with pride when he saw his own name printed at the top of new stationery ordered for the string quartet of which André Mangeot was the leader. The other members of the quartet were Boris Pecker (second violin), a very sociable and amusing man of Russian-Jewish origin, whose family were furriers in the East End of London; Harry Berly (viola), who liked fast cars and penny dreadfuls, and was a first-rate jazz player; and a very serious-minded young cellist, John Barbirolli, who learnt musical scores off by heart, and dreamed of becoming a conductor, as of course he did, rocketing to fame as resident conductor of the Hallé Orchestra.

Olive Mangeot was dark and elegant, eminently cultivated, understanding and charming. At first Christopher was shy of her, but later she became his confidante, the first of several. She was a calming influence in an otherwise frantically active environment. The family and musicians were totally enthusiastic about their work, and were also keen on sports, while Olive was only too happy to sit down and put her feet up. She became a sort of honorary mother to Christopher, who wrote to her as "My darling Mop," signing himself "Your loving eldest."

Of the two boys, Sylvain was the closer to Christopher. An intelligent, artistic child, then at preparatory school, he worked with Christopher on a little book of anthropomorphised animals called *People You Ought to Know*. The book contains thirty drawings (by Sylvain) and amusingly relevant verses by Christopher, which often have gently satirical references to members of the family. Christopher seems to have rattled off the whole series in a couple of days, which was quite an achievement. One, "The Common Cormorant," was published in *Exhumations*. Here is another:

> A common error about the shark
> Is that its bite's worse than its bark
> But, as I have too often found,
> The truth is just the other way round. . . .
> Imagine a giant knife and fork
> Scratching a plate the size of New York,
> Or the way a slate pencil squeaks and rubs
> When the slate is bigger than Wormwood Scrubs,
> Or an organ played by paralysed cats,
> Or a gong being struck with cricket bats
> By a party of drunk and angry bears,
> Imagine an elephant in tears,
> Imagine me singing the whole of Tanhaüser,
> And you get some idea of the wonderful noise a
> Shark can make when it's really cross
> To hear that Australia won the toss.

Christopher's relationship with the family became very possessive. He was jealous of their friends, and recalls looking enviously through their old photograph albums, thinking of all the years of their life in which he had not shared. Touched by their apparent innocence, he wanted to try and cut them off from the dangers of the outside world, and be acknowledged by them as part of the family. He invented work, in order to have an excuse to stay longer than his official hours; while on Sundays, when he had to stay at home or be with other friends, he often felt lonely and bored.

An important member of the household was Hilda, the cook—a large strong-willed woman with a thick Suffolk accent. She gave nicknames to everybody, referring to André Mangeot as the Guv'nor, Christopher as the Secretary or, if she was being sarcastic, the *Darling* Secretary. Wystan Auden, who later frequented the house, was known as the Nurse, while Edward Upward (for some reason disliked) was the Purple Rat.

On Sundays Christopher would often go to see Edward at his home in Essex. At the time of Christopher's Cambridge disaster, Edward had graduated with a Second in English. They were still thinking a great deal about the Mortmere stories, and they had decided that Hynd and Starn, their *alter egos* of earlier fantasies, should be introduced into the Mortmere tales as external observers, or rather as one observer, "Hearn." The nature of Hearn posed numerous problems, however. Initially, they conceived of him as a neurotic young man who arrives in Mortmere to recover from a nervous breakdown, but they soon realised that too much of the reader's attention would be focused on Hearn and not on the fantastic characters of the village. The problem then seemed insoluble, but later Isherwood *did* find a solution, in the relationship between the self-effacing narrator of the Berlin stories and the principal "stars."

Shortly before Christmas a friend brought Wystan Auden to Christopher's for tea. At first sight, Wystan did not seem to have changed much, except in size, from the way Christopher remembered him at St. Edmund's. Despite his expensive clothes, he was still grubby and unkempt, and Christopher was quick to notice the broken shoe-laces, the socks tumbled round the deathly white ankles, the nicotine stains mixed with ink on his hands.

In the six years since their last meeting, Wystan had attended Gresham's School in Holt, and had won an exhibition in natural sciences to Christ Church, Oxford ("The House"), which he entered in October 1925. He had started smoking a pipe, and demonstrated a lack of concern for material possessions, including books, which scandalised Christopher, who watched with horror as Wystan casually flicked through some of his most precious volumes, then dropped them unceremoniously face down on the floor.

After an initial display of bad manners, sometimes adopted by

Auden as a cover for his shyness, he and Christopher started exchanging memories and jokes about St. Edmund's. Then, casually, Wystan told Christopher that he had started to write poetry. Christopher was very surprised, as Auden had had no such inclinations at school. Wystan promised to send him some examples of his work. Sure enough, a few days later, a packet of poems arrived, showing the clear influence of Thomas Hardy, Edward Thomas and Robert Frost. The handwriting was so atrocious that whole lines were indecipherable. Wystan's accompanying note requested Christopher's comments, but sadly Isherwood's reply is not extant, as Auden threw away all his mail. Isherwood was not the only person whose judgement was being solicited at this time. The artist and stage designer Robert Medley, who had been at Gresham's with Wystan, remembers being sent some of the same poems that Christopher received.

In January 1926 Edward Upward took a job as a private tutor near St. Ives, in Cornwall. He wrote long, imaginative letters to Christopher, evoking the doom of shipwrecks, and dissecting every particle of the absurdity and loathsomeness of the local inhabitants. Having been convinced by Christopher that he should be a prose-writer, not a poet, Edward naturally started writing a novel, called *The Market Town*.

Christopher took a break from his work with the Mangeot Quartet at Easter, to go and visit Edward. In his suitcase he carried the first six chapters of a new novel, entitled *The Summer at the House*. After Cambridge, he had abandoned writing entirely for several months, and he was not happy with the way things were going with the new awakening. Fortunately, he was able to abandon the new book with a clear conscience, because Edward had exciting news that changed their whole outlook to writing, and which made *The Summer at the House* redundant. Edward had been reading E. M. Forster's *Howards End*, and had been struck by a massive realisation:

> Forster's the only one who understands what the modern
> novel ought to be. . . . Our frightful mistake was that we
> believed in tragedy: the point is, tragedy's quite impossi-
> ble nowadays. . . . We ought to aim at being comic
> writers. . . . The whole of Forster's technique is based on the

tea-table: instead of trying to screw all his scenes up to the highest possible pitch, he tones them down until they sound like mothers'-meeting gossip. . . . In fact, there's actually *less* emphasis laid on the big scenes than on the unimportant ones: that's what's so utterly terrific. It's the completely new kind of accentuation—like a person talking a different language.*

Forster thus became their mentor. Considering the respect which they accorded to this new literary scale of values, it is easy to understand why Virginia Woolf should also have gained their profound admiration. Henry James was especially savoured for a favourite line: "The whole thing was to be the death of one or the other of them, but they never spoke of it at tea."

From Cornwall, the friends went by boat to the Scilly Isles, where Christopher turned the soil for his new novel, which was to be entitled *Seascape with Figures*. On walks through the island's superb flower gardens, and in pubs swigging beer, Edward and Christopher discussed the novel's melodramatic plot. The two central characters were a medical student (Hector Wintle was destined to appear in Christopher's first novel, whatever it was) and a would-be painter and writer. The artist persuades the medical student to leave home; then they go to stay in the Scilly Isles, where both form an attachment with a fourteen-year-old girl. A posh Cambridge hearty, also on the island, takes the girl climbing, and she falls to her death. Complicated circumstances in London lead to the murder of the hearty by the medical student, with a poker. All was to be tea-tabled, and subtly comic, though the denouement should be pure farce.

One morning in May, back in London, Christopher discovered that the threatened General Strike had actually happened, despite its being pronounced impossible by most of his acquaintances. Kathleen, looking brighter than ever at the breakfast-table that morning, briskly declared her opposition to the strike. Olive Mangeot (the future secretary of the Chelsea branch of the Communist Party!) wondered aloud why the workers had to do such an "uncosy" thing. Hector Wintle signed up the first day as a con-

* Isherwood paraphrasing Chalmers (Upward) in *Lions and Shadows*, p. 173.

ductor on the Underground, one of an army of volunteers who
kept the public transport going, after a fashion. Undergraduates
came up from Oxford and Cambridge to do their bit, treating the
whole thing as a romp, though several ugly confrontations with
strikers occurred. Among Christopher's literary contemporaries
the young Rex Warner drove a tram in Hull, while his Oxford
house-mate Cecil Day Lewis roundly condemned the blacklegs
and drove cars on liaison work for the TUC. Christopher himself
did not know what to do. He could not write to Edward for advice, as the postal service was disrupted. Should he support the
strikers, or do something for the Country, as his mother's friends
put it? Finally, he volunteered for service, asking for the most unpleasant task available. He was assigned to the sewage department, but before he could start work the strike was over.

Having utterly failed that political test, Christopher went to the
Isle of Wight again in July, this time taking Wystan Auden along
with him. Wystan was dressed in dirty grey flannels, with a black
evening bow-tie, and a large black felt hat, which drew immediate
attention to him. Christopher was profoundly embarrassed by the
sniggers this attire drew from the locals, while Wystan himself
brushed aside their mirth by declaring: "Laughter is the first sign
of sexual attraction."*

The effect the two young men had on each other was crucial to
the development of both of them. Wystan, then only nineteen
years old, was undergoing a constant intellectual ferment, and
used Christopher as a guinea-pig for some of his new ideas. He
had overthrown his previous literary models, and now loudly declaimed the brilliance of T. S. Eliot who was, like all Auden's en-
thusiasms, the *only* possible thing, my dear. The dogmatic utter-
ances which have since become legendary were already present in
his conversation. Having recently devoured Freud, Jung and the
writings of various anthropologists, he littered his talk with esoteric words and related jargon, sometimes chosen as much for
their sound as for their meaning. Christopher had an impression
that Wystan was experimenting as he talked, seemingly oblivious
of the effect that his loud and pretentious undergraduate mono-
logues had on passers-by, but in fact well aware of his power to

* *Lions and Shadows*, p. 188.

shock, particularly a comparative innocent like Christopher. Astounded and fascinated, Christopher listened to the diatribes, blushing bright red with shame when Wystan nearly had them thrown out of the local pub for giving a recitation of some of the juicier items of English verse, and stared in disbelief as Wystan burnt a hole in his overcoat with a lighted cigar.

Soon they became lovers, in the loosest sense of the word. For ten years or so they went to bed together when the occasion arose, but they did not consider themselves emotionally tied to each other. Their physical relationship was a kind of retarded public-school dalliance, and both were to enjoy relationships with other men over the years to come.

According to Robert Medley, Wystan was well aware of his own sexual preferences while at Gresham's School. He had a showdown with his father about it after Dr. Auden discovered some poems by Wystan, betraying a sexual appreciation of Medley by the school swimming-pool. Dr. Auden had suggested that such emotions, although not uncommon in adolescence, were not a very good idea for adult life, but Wystan was unimpressed. His acceptance of his homosexuality and the frankness of the tales he told of his sexual adventures took Christopher's breath away. Ironically, their position was reversed in later life when Isherwood became completely adjusted to his own homosexuality. Undoubtedly, their mutual homosexuality, which was missing in Christopher's relationship with Edward Upward or Hector Wintle, was an added factor in their friendship. The latter friends respected Christopher's homosexuality just as he respected their interest in women, but he felt that neither side could fully comprehend the other.

Wystan considered nothing forbidden territory for his probing interest. Spotting a dark hairy spot on Christopher's shoulder, of which Christopher was highly self-conscious, he prodded it with a stubby finger. Despite this rude acceptance of the blemish, Christopher did not lose his complex about his acne until the extraordinary psychologist John Layard, about 1930, showed him how un-ugly it was by kissing it.

Although Wystan frequently complained of the cold, he did not like direct sunlight, and would draw the curtains of his room during the daytime, preferring to work with a table lamp. At night he would pile overcoats, carpets and anything else available on to his bed, as he liked to be weighed down. He smoked a pipe incessantly ("Insufficient weaning. I must have something to *suck*"), scattering ash everywhere. He thumped out hymn tunes on the piano at Marine Villa, and drank endless cups of tea. He wore extravagant hats, which Christopher tried to brush off as an Oxford affectation. The objects of Wystan's enthusiasm and criticism changed frequently. So, too, did his studies; he abandoned science at Christ Church, spent a brief transitory period reading politics, philosophy and economics, and finally he settled in the English faculty, where he was very fortunate to have as his tutor the young Nevill Coghill, who became a valued friend.

Christopher was surprised and flattered to see how much influence he was having on Wystan's writing. If he disliked a word or a line from a poem, Wystan would cut it out:

If, on the other hand, I had praised a line in a poem otherwise condemned, then that line would reappear in a new poem. And if I didn't like this poem, either, but admired a second line, then both the lines would appear in a third poem, and so on—until a poem had been evolved which was a little anthology of my favourite lines, strung together without even an attempt to make connected sense. For this reason, most of Weston's [Auden's] work at that period was extraordinarily obscure.*

Needless to say, not all of Wystan's poems at this time were such hybrids. Often Christopher would enthuse about a poem *in toto*, and it was saved. He was beginning to accept Wystan as the poet of his generation; the Mutual Admiration Society had grown.

Wystan introduced Christopher to the world of Icelandic sagas, letting him read copies of *Grettir* and *Burnt Njal* that he had brought to the island. The heroic warriors' behaviour and language struck Christopher as being similar to that of the boys at St. Edmund's, which led to the construction of "school-sagas" with Wystan, who fell into the spirit of the game. Out of this grew the story "Gems of Belgian Architecture," written by Christopher about a year later, and a short verse play, *Paid on Both Sides*, by

* Ibid., pp. 190–91.

Auden, in which the two worlds of Norse legends and preparatory school are interwoven.

In August, Edward and Christopher went back to the Haute-Savoie region of France, to try to do justice to the alpine scenery which they had scoffed at on their school trip. The tour was plagued by small misfortunes about hotel-rooms, and Edward frequently moaned that he wanted to go home. They had a small tiff when Christopher hit a sore spot by declaring: "You'll only write one slim book of verse. You're far too fastidious!" However, that was soon past, and they laughed together about the idea of a Life-and-Death Kit, the Life part being French letters or some other sexual aid, the Death part being a revolver. Soon, though, they did decide to go their own ways, Christopher choosing to search for a boy he had seen in company with a guardian or some other older man.

The two trips, with Wystan and Edward, deeply disturbed Christopher. Back in London he no longer felt able to live out his existence happily working with the Mangeots or larking about with Hector Wintle. Not yet ready for another dose of Wystan's brutal instant analysis, he went away to a cottage in Wales to sort out his true feelings about his own homosexuality and his plans for the future. He started reading Proust, a most counterproductive exercise in the long run, as he was horrified by the portrait of the ageing homosexual.

Christopher's depression, far from lifting, became more unbearable, so that after only four days he returned to London, bent on suicide. He bought himself a Browning automatic pistol and went to consult Hector Wintle about the best part of the anatomy at which to aim in order to ensure success. It is easy to distinguish another, perhaps subconscious, motive in this visit to Wintle: the desire to have someone try to stop him going through with the act. In this he was disappointed. Hector, a master of dramatic melancholy, clinically described exactly what he should do. He recommended sticking the gun in his mouth, correctly positioned for maximum destructive efficiency. In fact, the method was far from foolproof, as another friend of Christopher's found out. The information was duly filed away and used in the novel *The Memorial*. Some commentators have pounced on what they see as homosexual symbolism in the position of the gun. In Christopher's case, Wintle probably realised that he would not have the nerve to go through with it—and he did not, although he had gone so far as to make a will (leaving everything to Edward Upward), with a request that all his diaries and other papers be destroyed.

The next best thing to suicide, Christopher decided, was to leave home. However, this break was not the theatrical coup he had hoped for. Kathleen thought it would be rather a nice idea for him to rent a small place of his own, not too far from home, where he could concentrate better on his writing and enjoy the independence that a young man needs at twenty-two. Not being the type to take the opportunity to race off to South America or Java for adventure, though he did dream of doing so, Christopher settled on Redcliffe Road in Fulham. He felt the street to be infinitely romantic, because Katherine Mansfield had lived at Number 47 for a few months in 1918. Many of the big houses had been split up into flats and bed-sitting-rooms, occupied by various bohemian types including artists, bit-actors and students.

Christopher had renewed his acquaintance with Roger Burford, his old friend from the Cambridge Film Club (Roger East in *Lions and Shadows*). Roger had abandoned his attempts to work in films and was now earning a living by free-lance journalism. He had a furnished room in Redcliffe Road, where Christopher went to visit him, and got to know his fiancée, Stella (Polly East). Christopher liked Stella a lot, with her bubbling, uncomplicated ways. She called him "Bisherwood" (a contraction of Bradshaw-Isherwood), which Wystan Auden typically shortened to "Bish," pronounced like *biche*, the French slang-word for "lesbian." As Roger and Stella intended to get married at the end of the year, Roger had decided to give up his room, and it was this one which Christopher took over.

One consequence of his impending move was that Christopher now needed a more lucrative position than his job with the Mangeot Quartet. Having no specific qualifications, he took up teaching, or rather private tutoring. It was not very difficult to find a job as a tutor in those days, if one spoke well, had been to a public school and, better still, to Oxford or Cambridge, and Christopher contacted an agency which fixed him up with a series of pupils.

During 1926, despite his black moods and listlessness, Christopher completed his novel *Seascape with Figures*. He showed it to Ethel Mayne (Venus) for her comments, and she was far less damning about it than she had been about *Christopher Garland*. She recommended that he send it, with a few alterations, to a couple of publishers, but both of them rejected it. Edward Upward, normally appreciative of Christopher's writing, did not think much of it, so Christopher decided to put it away for possible revision the following year.

Meanwhile, another novel was born inside his head—a massive survey of the post-war generation, which would be set in London, North Wales and the Alps. Not only Hector Wintle but also Edward Upward, Wystan Auden, the Mangeots and other friends were scheduled to appear in this work, along with Christopher himself. The plot was none too clear, but the theme was, and the book was to be entitled *The North-West Passage*. The phrase was intimately connected with the Test, now more rationalised in Christopher's mind because of his having read the psychological writings of Bleuler. One of Bleuler's case histories, a homicidal paranoiac, talks of his concept of the Truly Strong Man; Christopher adopted and adapted the phrase and its antithesis, the Truly Weak Man, to describe two sorts of people. It was not always easy to distinguish the sheep from the goats, since the Truly Strong Man could not be identified by mere heroics, which could be symptomatic of the opposite extreme. T. E. Lawrence, for example, was considered by Christopher to be a Truly Weak Man who needed a dramatic show in Arabia to hide his real nature. Frank Isherwood, on the other hand, had been a Truly Strong Man, brave but disdainful of heroics. In many ways Christopher's categories fit in with Chinese philosophy, the Truly Strong Man being the Taoist sage who sees through the world's imbecility, or the Confucian *cheng-tzu* (so often misleadingly translated as "Gentleman"), with his intimate knowledge of correct behaviour, justice and humility. But Christopher had not yet delved into these works. By his definition, the Truly Strong Man was:

> . . . calm, balanced, aware of his strength . . . it is not necessary for him to try to prove to himself he is not afraid . . .

the Test exists only for the Truly Weak Man . . . so with immense daring, with an infinitely greater expenditure of nervous energy, money, time, physical and mental resources, he prefers to attempt the huge northern circuit, the laborious, terrible north-west passage, avoiding life.*

The book was never written.

Early in December 1926, Christopher went to Oxford to visit Wystan Auden, who had comfortable oak-panelled rooms in Christ Church Peck Quad. Although Wystan disdained the college social climbers, who courted the "in" group of Harold Acton, Bryan Guinness and Christopher Sykes, he did have an impressive circle of friends at Oxford, including the budding poets John Betjeman, Cecil Day Lewis, Louis MacNeice and Rex Warner, as well as the future politicians Richard Crossman and Gabriel (Bill) Carritt. He had a piano, located in a closet startlingly decorated with a red-and-black cubist mural representing a railway accident, and he would play Bach and selections from *Hymns Ancient and Modern* to illustrate points in his conversation. Christopher was treated to a torrent of Wystan's latest fads, including the German lyric poet Christian Morgenstern, Gertrude Stein and Sophie Tucker. Ballet ought, apparently, to have been banned by Act of Parliament, while the only possible form of evening entertainment was a visit to a greyhound track.

Reeling from Wystan's monologue, Christopher was taken to the George Restaurant for a splendid dinner, a gesture presumably made to impress the visitor from London; Wystan was not normally a member of the "Georgeoisie" like Alan Pryce-Jones or Mark Ogilvie-Grant, who dined there every night to the strains of a string band. From the restaurant, they went to the college Essay Club, a cockpit of undergraduate literary brawls which made Christopher feel very uncomfortable. He barely understood the abstruse paper on "The Concept of Duty," while the students brought back all-too-recent unhappy memories of his time at Cambridge.

The following day, having returned to London, Christopher developed influenza, and indeed in future managed to catch a bad cold nearly every time he saw Wystan. Wystan had no sympathy

* Ibid., pp. 208–9.

for people who moaned of their ailments, declaring: "No gentle-man should admit to sickness." He insisted that Christopher's ill-ness was psychosomatic, and referred to his friend's frequent sore throats as "liar's quinsy."

Installed in his room in Redcliffe Road, Christopher received numerous visits from Hector Wintle, the Mangeots, Roger and Stella Burford and other friends. He had little contact with Ed-ward Upward though, as witnessed by a postcard from Upward (dated March 20, 1927) inscribed with the single line: "Are you, perhaps, dead?" Christopher thrived on company, and when left alone in his room, fretted. He settled into a weekday routine of visits to the houses of his pupils, surprisingly relishing in teaching divinity.

Early that summer he returned once more to the Isle of Wight. He worked consistently on the revision of *Seascape with Figures*, showing himself capable of a discipline which has characterised his later writing method. He rose early, then worked from after breakfast until eleven, when he took a walk around Freshwater Bay, stopping to chat with the vicar, the coastguard or fishermen. From these conversations he gained snippets of fact and folklore, retained for possible use in novels. He took down notes from com-ments heard on the beach, and sent them in long letters to Ed-ward. He despised the noisy middle-class holiday-makers, who were all too clearly enjoying themselves, deciding to cast himself in the role of a permanent outsider looking in on their world with contempt. To counterbalance this detachment, he went to great pains to be on friendly terms with the local fishermen. In order to hide his upper-class Oxbridge accent, which he thought would be a barrier to comradeship with them, he adopted a Cockney accent which, once started, could not be abandoned. He spent much of his time with a ruggedly attractive seventeen-year-old fisherman, partly as an exercise in inverted social climbing and also, doubt-less, because of the boy's animal appeal. He went drinking with the boy, and the two of them took girls to the local cinema, where, after a few gins and tonics, Christopher discovered that he quite enjoyed cuddling in the back row. When some of the dates seemed to be leading all too fast towards more serious petting on the downs, he nobly passed on his girl to the ever-willing fisherman, who was all too pleased at Christopher's generosity to question it.

Christopher finished the revised version of *Seascape with Figures* in July. He had cut out the murder and pared down the whole novel to bare essentials. He had worked from the basic idea that the form of a novel should be extremely contrived, that it should be a contraption. While still respecting the mood of Forster, he derived much of his construction from detective stories and the plays of Henrik Ibsen; every word was meant to be a clue leading to some great discovery.

Edward Upward, when shown the new manuscript, announced his approval, but disliked the title. After much thought, Christopher chose one with a better ring to it, *All the Conspirators*, taken from Antony's speech over Brutus' body in the last scene of *Julius Caesar*, though with little relevance to the content of the book (it has since been taken as referring to the attitude of Isherwood, Upward and Auden to the Establishment). The theme of the book is a domestic drama in North Kensington; the subject, if not the style, owes much to Hector Wintle. Aldous Huxley's description of his own *Time Must Have a Stop*—"A curiously trivial story told in considerable detail, with a certain amount of squalor" —could be applied perfectly to *All the Conspirators*. The novel opens with Edward Upward and Hector Wintle sitting in a little hotel by the sea. They are thinly disguised as Allen Chalmers and Philip Lindsay,* and both contain elements of Christopher. Their professional roles are reversed, and in the novel Allen is the medical student. As Alan Wilde has correctly stated in his study of Isherwood's fiction, *All the Conspirators* is the angriest of Isherwood's novels. Isherwood had described its style as "trembling with aggression," a reflection of what Shelley calls the great war between the old and the young. In this war Philip's revolt is a failure, but it is just an incident on a frontier, where some shots are fired without result; the main battle goes on somewhere else. Isherwood and his characters are angry young men, but they differ from their 1950s' counterparts in that they have no clear political

---

* In *Lions and Shadows* the Hector Wintle figure becomes Philip Lindsay, as the Hogarth Press was worried that the real-life novelist Phillip Lindsay might object to his homonym.

consciousness; their vision of injustice is blurred, confused and egocentric.

All the Conspirators is an intensely private novel too. Only Christopher and his closest friends can possibly have understood all its allusions, with its clipped language, filled with phrases from their own jargon, and incidents taken from their lives. It was very useful in that it provided a vent for its author's dissatisfaction with the world of his mother and her friends. Mrs. Lindsay is the first of a series of diabolically portrayed mature women, and the most two-dimensional. Perhaps this caricature was necessary in Christopher's development, so that later he could write more objectively. Some critics, notably Carolyn Heilbrun, have discerned a misogynist attitude in this book, but this hardly seems justifiable. Philip's sister, Joan, is meant to be a sympathetic character, almost a comrade-in-arms, though her sexual attraction to Victor Page naturally compromises her position. But her characterisation is comparatively weak, and an overall impression of the females in the book is conveyed through Mrs. Lindsay and her ineffective companion Miss Durrant (her name being a subconscious borrowing from Virginia Woolf, whose influence can also be detected in the style). The women are condemned not for their sex but for their total identification with the other side, the older generation.

Christopher sent his finished manuscript to two publishers in the autumn, both of which refused it. However, he did appear in print, anonymously, soon afterwards. While he was putting the finishing touches to *All the Conspirators* Wystan Auden and Cecil Day Lewis, who were on holiday in the Lake District, editing a volume of 1927 *Oxford Poetry*, decided to include in it a poem of Isherwood's, "Souvenir des Vacances," but obviously could not reveal the identity of the author as he was no longer an undergraduate nor had he ever been at Oxford.

At the end of the summer Christopher moved out of his Redcliffe Road digs and went back home. His landlady had proved impossibly incompetent, screaming babies kept him from work and sleep, Irish neighbours had stolen his Gramophone and his finances were strained. He found that Kathleen had entered a new phase in her Cult of the Past. On July 25 a gate was dedicated at Ypres in memory of the 56,000 unfound and unburied British troops who had died on the Salient. Frank's name was not listed, so Kathleen wrote a letter of protest to the Imperial War Graves Commission. They replied that his death would be recorded on a similar, smaller gate at Ploegsteert, as officially he had belonged to the Second Battalion when he was killed. A haughty exchange of letters continued into 1928, when the government bureaucrats agreed to put Frank's name on both lists, if this was the only way of calming his widow.

Through the autumn and winter of 1927 Christopher continued to do some part-time tutoring, but much of his time was spent drinking and carousing with a painter friend of the Mangeots, William Lichtenberg. Gin was Christopher's favourite tipple, though William made a special cocktail from a secret recipe, two of which were enough to have Christopher wandering in a state of euphoria around the artist's studio. William played upon his friend's fascination for the supernatural by staging séances or recounting horrific stories to him. Sometimes they would race off on an impulse in William's car, once getting as far as Scotland, where Christopher wrestled with imaginary enemies on a beach after downing three-quarters of a bottle of Highland whisky.

Lichtenberg came from a cigarette-paper making family (Job) and loved experimenting to find new exciting materials for his art. He eventually built himself a beautiful home near St. Tropez where he accidently blew himself up.

Between these bouts of escapism Christopher considered the possibilities open to him. Despite Hector Wintle's stories of the unbearability of medical school, Christopher decided that medicine was a definite possibility. Edward Upward liked the idea, drawing on examples of famous writers who had chosen this profession because it gave them an ideal opportunity for making contact with eccentrics and invalids, who could then be described in great novels. Christopher's family were rather surprised by his new interest, but doubtless pleased. They arranged for him to go and see one of his numerous relatives, Raymond Greene, elder brother of the novelist Graham. Raymond Greene was then a fresh intern at Westminster Hospital, and although he has no recollection of what he said to Christopher at the time, it cannot have been too discouraging. However, there were practical reasons why Christopher would not be able to start his medical studies until the academic year began in the autumn of 1928.

Meanwhile, out of the blue, the stroke of good fortune which Christopher had been awaiting finally arrived. Jonathan Cape, the publisher, wrote to Christopher in early January asking him to come to see him about his novel. Mr. Cape received him at his office, suggesting just a few minor alterations to *All the Conspirators*, and saying that he would like to publish it in May—a speed which seems almost miraculous in this day and age. Christopher received the advance copies while on holiday with Edward Upward (who had just finished the story *The Railway Accident*). To commemorate the occasion, Edward took a snap of Christopher holding a copy, and looking very serious indeed. At the age of twenty-three, it looked as though his long dream of literary fame was at hand.

PART TWO
Europe and Beyond

5

One of Christopher's more distant relatives was the British vice-consul in the German city of Bremen, a certain Basil Fry. In the spring of 1928, while on a visit to London, Mr. Fry wrote to Kathleen and suggested that he pay her a call. Christopher found the visitor loathsome, because of patronising air and pedantically delivered classical allusions. However, when Mr. Fry casually invited Christopher to Germany for a short visit, he rose immediately to the bait. Though rarely a person to make great plans for his future, Christopher was never slow to pursue opportunities which presented themselves. Thus in May he set sail for Germany in a tramp steamer. Basil Fry had predicted that Christopher would be violently sick on the voyage, but that the journey might help make a man of him. Christopher was determined to prove Fry wrong and, armed with sea-sickness tablets, he successfully weathered the rough ride.

Shortly after his arrival in Bremen Christopher wrote to Edward from Fry's apartment at 42 Elsassestrasse:

> The city was mild, with moist fernlike trees. The houses are covered with vines and have sliding doors. Yes, after all, our later days must be spent in travel. The pleasure of sauntering along streets of ratsly [sic] lettered shops, soon to be left behind. Never to remain more than a week in any country.

Conrad was wrong—but the tramp steamer had a Chinese cook and a Welsh cabin-boy. The captain appeared drunk on the bridge as soon as we entered the Weser. His barely credible insults to important German officials on the quay. "Now then, Tirpitz—show a leg." They merely smiled. I know now which side started the War.

Proust, also, would have rewritten a volume if he'd attended the consular dinner. The ices had coloured lights inside them. There is a kind of brandy liquour [*sic*] which you drink out of a beer-mug. It makes you speak French better than English. My cousin is a prig, a fool, a neuter. Hatefully tall. His Oxford titter.

The whole town is full of boys. In their silver-braided forage-caps, mackintosh tunics and green *ingles* lace-up shirts. Wherry* would be stunned.

Don't write here. I shall be gone. Fire a shot for me at Wagram.

Marco Polo

In that letter is the birth of "Mr. Lancaster," though the story did not see the light of day until 1962, as the first part of *Down There on a Visit*. Mr. Lancaster is a fairly accurate representation of Basil Fry, though Fry did not commit suicide unlike his fictional counterpart.

Some of Fry's chilly manner might well have resulted from his father's upbringing. Dean Fry of Lincoln, to whom Graham Greene referred uncompromisingly in his autobiography, *A Sort of Life*, as "my father's sinister sadistic predecessor," was, like Greene's father, headmaster of Berkhamsted School. Dr. Fry had a reputation as a flogger, and Basil had certainly suffered at his hands. Nevertheless Basil considered such conduct quite proper, and a forbidding photograph of the dean glared at visitors to Basil Fry's drab Bremen flat.

Basil Fry himself had a head "so small it seemed feminine. He had very large ears, a broad, wet moustache, and a peevish mouth. He looked sulky, frigid, dyspeptic. His nose was long and red, with a suggestion of moisture at the end of it. . . . I reminded myself

* A Mortmere pederast.

with approval of . . . [Auden's] dicta: 'All ugly people are wicked.' "*

Having ruled out Basil Fry completely as a possible companion, Christopher turned his attention to the office-boy, a cute but reserved young man with whom he made little progress. As Christopher's letter to Edward reveals, he had an instant sexual reaction to German youth, which would be the fundamental reason for his love of the country. Basil Fry one day gave a long, reproachful lecture about the amount of corruption and moral degeneracy that there was in Germany. Berlin itself, he said, was unspeakably vile. Christopher decided therefore that, as soon as he was able, he would go there, and for a long spell.

In magazine interviews Isherwood has often told journalists that Auden was directly responsible for his going to Germany, but that is not quite borne out by the facts, as Wystan did not go to live there until the autumn of 1928, when he had left Oxford. It was surely the ten-day visit to Bremen which prompted Christopher's Germanophilia, though undoubtedly Auden's reports from Berlin during 1928–29 reconfirmed Christopher's desire to return there.

When Christopher returned to London the reviews of *All the Conspirators* were waiting for him. It was not widely noticed, and some of the critics were merciless. *Punch* declared: "Mr. Christopher Isherwood is either badly troubled with that kind of portentous solemnity which so often accompanies the mental growing pains of the very young, or else he has written his novel with his tongue in his cheek. . . . Altogether, the book leaves behind it a faintly nasty taste. . . ." A few, notably the *Manchester Guardian*, were kinder, but the book sold poorly (about three hundred copies) before being remaindered and, for the time being, forgotten. However, in 1933, Hugh Walpole described it as one of the half-dozen most unjustly neglected novels since the war. It did not find an American publisher until 1958, though it has undergone considerable critical revaluation in recent years. Cyril Connolly generously commended it in the 1950s as being "a key to Isherwood and the twenties. It is as mature, as readable, as concen-

* *Down There on a Visit.*

trated, as perceptive as anything he has written since." In 1976 it was reissued in a paperback edition.

Christopher went up to Oxford to see Wystan soon after his return to England. Wystan was in his final term at Christ Church, and was to astound his tutors by graduating with a third-class degree. In Auden's rooms one sunny afternoon Christopher met Stephen Spender for the first time. Spender had been eager to meet Isherwood for months, as Wystan had inflated his talents to unbelievable proportions. Spender wrote in his autobiography *World Within World:*

> Auden had spoken of Isherwood in a way which made me think of him as The Novelist, who applying himself with an iron will to the study of material for his work, was determined to live the life of The Ordinary Man, going to the office in the train, dancing in dance halls at seaside resorts, dressing with a studied avoidance of every kind of distinctiveness, and so on. Isherwood, according to Auden, held no opinions whatever about anything. He was wholly and simply interested in people. (p. 101.)

Isherwood had asked to meet Spender after Auden had shown him a short story based on Spender's tight friendship with a boy at a *pensionnat* in Lausanne, Switzerland. That afternoon in Oxford, Spender came into the room to find all the blinds drawn and the electric light on.

> Auden wore a green shade over his eyes, and looked like an amateur chemist. Isherwood looked like a schoolboy playing charades. . . . Auden looked up abruptly when I came in and said: "You're early. Sit down." Isherwood giggled, and while I sat down he turned to Auden and said: "But really I don't see the image of a 'frozen gull flipped down the weir': it sounds like cold storage." Auden flushed and struck out the lines with a thick lead pencil.
>
> When they had finished, Isherwood made a quite formal little speech saying he had read my manuscript, and that he regarded it as one of the most striking things he had read by a young writer for a long time.*

* Stephen Spender, *World Within World* (1951), p. 102.

It is interesting to contrast this with Isherwood's own account of his first meeting with Spender (Stephen Savage), which, in *Lions and Shadows*, he situates several weeks later, in London:

> He [Savage/Spender] burst in upon us, blushing, sniggering loudly, contriving to trip over the edge of the carpet—an immensely tall, shambling boy of nineteen, with a great scarlet poppy-face, wild frizzy hair, and eyes the violent colour of bluebells. . . . In an instant, without introductions, we were all laughing and talking at the top of our voices. (p. 281.)

They saw each other several times in London in the summer of 1928, and became close friends. Spender came from a middle-class intellectual family, and had lost both his parents by the time he went up to University College, Oxford, in 1927. His father had stood unsuccessfully as a Liberal candidate for the constituency of Bath in the General Election of 1923. Stephen was of partly Jewish origin, through his maternal grandparents, though his grandmother had joined the Quakers. His elder brother, Michael, had been at school with Wystan Auden.

Christopher was impressed by Stephen's vitality and spontaneous generosity; and often Stephen would arrive at a rendezvous bearing a carefully chosen present. His appearance was equally impressive: he towered over Christopher, and would accentuate the striking impression he made by wearing brilliant scarlet ties and other unconventional attire.

> He inhabited a world of self-created and absorbing drama, into which each new acquaintance was immediately conscripted to play a part. Savage [Spender] illuminated you like an expressionist producer, with the crudest and most eccentric of spot-lights: you were transfigured, became grandiose, sinister, brilliantly ridiculous or impossibly beautiful, in accordance with his arbitrary, prearranged conception of your role. And soon—such is the hypnotic mastery of the born *régisseur*—you began to live up to his expectations.*

Many of Christopher's friends have testified that he has often had the same effect on people himself. He has never been slow to

* *Lions and Shadows*, p. 281.

flatter where flattery was due. The similarities in Christopher's and Stephen's natures, especially with regard to other people, helped establish a rapid friendship, but also occasionally proved a basis for friction.

Wystan left for Germany in August, at first staying with a bourgeois family who hindered his desire to learn German by practising their English. Soon he moved into a working-class district, and sent Christopher enthusiastic letters about his new experiences.

Christopher began his medical studies in October at King's College, London. He had the disadvantage of approaching the subject without any previous intensive study of science, though the course did begin at a most elementary level. Most of his fellow students were several years younger than he was, fresh from school and familiar with physics, chemistry and biology. He realised very quickly that medical school was a mistake, that he did not have a true vocation to become a doctor or sufficient interest to do the enormous amount of tedious rote-learning necessary to pass the examinations. Luckily he was able to befriend a willing youth of eighteen, who steered him through the most difficult experiments and lent him his notes to copy. However, Christopher successfully passed one of the largest hurdles in a medical student's career: the first operation. Hector Wintle was working as a dresser during an operation at St. Thomas's Hospital, and Christopher arranged to go and watch. The amputation of the patient's leg seemed somehow quite unreal to him and, after an initial wave of tension, not in the least nauseating. Afterwards, he had tea with Hector in the hospital canteen, where Wintle spoke with such authority about the operation that Christopher realised that his friend had overcome his early difficulties with medicine, and was fast becoming a good doctor. Wintle went on to have many adventures as a ship's doctor—his first boat, rather auspiciously, was called *Hector*—before settling down in England as a medical officer. He published several novels, though none enjoyed a great success.

In Christopher's case, the urge to study was subjugated to his desire to write and almost as soon as he started medical school he began a new novel. *The Memorial* was to be a study of the effect of the Great War upon Christopher's generation. The theme was epic, but its treatment was to be in tea-tabled style. Every afternoon, when classes had finished, Christopher rushed home and began writing and by the end of term he had finished the first draft. In the King's College chemistry examination, meanwhile, he came at the bottom of the list.

At Christmas Wystan Auden came back to England to visit his parents, and called on Christopher. His latest enthusiasm was for the teachings of the American psychologist Homer Lane, whose disciple, John Layard, he had met in Berlin. The crux of this new teaching was that there was only one sin—disobedience to the inner law of one's own nature. Layard preached that many of man's problems were caused by the unhealthy education given to children, which tried to turn them into miniature adults. Disease was seen as an outward manifestation of inner sickness, so that cures were dependent on purifying the soul. Lane and Layard's methods of treatment were unconventional, often involving the use of shock, to give the system a jolt, to shake it out of its unhealthy ways.

Wystan, particularly attracted by Layard's contempt for obsessive hygiene, looked even shabbier than usual. He immediately made Christopher the guinea-pig for a bit of Layard-style treatment. Christopher had admitted to suffering from a sore throat, whereupon Wystan informed him he was harbouring a death-wish.

"When people are ill, they're wicked" [said Weston/Wystan]. "You must stop it. You must be pure in heart."

"What nonsense!" I retorted. "How can I stop it? There's nothing the matter with my heart. It's my tonsils."

"Your tonsils? . . . I suppose you know what *that* means?"

"Certainly. It means I've caught a chill."

"It means you've been telling lies!"*

Christopher scorned Wystan's diagnoses, but was nonetheless impressed by what he heard of Layard's teaching. Wystan had spoken to Layard about Christopher, and conveyed the assessment that Christopher could not be a completely hopeless case of a neurotic "artist" if he had shown the initiative to leave Cambridge in the way he did. Christopher was pleased. He began to

* Ibid., p. 302.

apply the new-fangled analysis to his present situation, and decided that there was only one conclusion: that he must leave medical school. He informed his mother, who implored him to stay on at least until the end of the academic year, as the fees had been paid and he might change his mind. He compromised, and agreed to hold out until the end of the Easter term. During the weeks of January and February he was merely marking time. His decision was already final, and the next stage was to make a break with his whole life up to the present. He must go away, and where else but to Berlin? There he had Wystan, and the possibility of getting to know Layard personally. Better still, Wystan had confirmed cousin Basil's dire warnings about the city; it was a homosexual's Mecca.

On March 14, 1929, Christopher boarded the Dover to Ostend ferry for the beginning of the great adventure. This trip was to be for ten days or so—Berlin on approval—but he left already sure that he would love it.

Wystan used Christopher's arrival as an excuse to start a diary, which is on occasions quite obscene and remains unpublished. One of the more printable remarks (for March 19) was that Christopher seemed so babyish with his notebook and sulks. The notebook accompanied Christopher everywhere. In it he would jot down not only his thoughts and actions, but also entire overheard conversations verbatim. He was extremely thorough in recording exactly what people had said, and quickly able to capture their mannerisms. In this respect, he was akin to a first-rate journalist. Indeed, some of his novels resemble the work of a journalist, who nonetheless cannot resist improving upon reality with a little bit of fictionalisation.

Wystan lived on Furbingerstrasse, near a brothel at the Hallesches Tor. Very soon he took Christopher along to the Cosy Corner, one of the small working-class bars patronised by homosexuals and German boy prostitutes. Many of these boys had gone into the trade for fundamentally economic reasons. It was difficult to find work in the climate of economic ruin and inflation that characterised the Weimar Republic, and they had realised that a few marks could easily be picked up from foreigners, some of whom lived like kings because of the extraordinary exchange rate of the period. German currency had stabilised by the time Christopher arrived, but it was still possible for him to have a good time. He was never wealthy in Germany, but neither was he quite as poor as some of his friends or he made out.

The Berlin boys were often looking for camaraderie as well as financial benefit in their relationships with foreigners. They sometimes became involved in relationships which were much more than commercial transactions, though little presents, such as a shirt or a tie, were anticipated and received. Many of the boys were shamelessly vain and knew that the upkeep of their bodies was a vital part of the business. They almost never considered themselves homosexual, and prided themselves on their encounters with women, often prostitutes. Indeed, in their minds, the fact that they were sexually desirable to homosexuals only proved how very masculine they were. Many were devoutly interested in physical fitness, played sports or loved to wrestle. Christopher reacted instantly to this kind of "horseplay," which brought back memories of the happier side of schooldays, with the sexual element now realised. And as he did not yet speak German, the triviality of their conversation did not bother him. Trying to make himself understood in a new language with rugged and often humorous boys seemed almost a sexual experience of its own.

Christopher had a romanticised ideal of the Blond German Boy. On this short visit to Berlin he found the incarnation of this myth almost immediately—never mind that the boy was Czech. Christopher met Berthold (or "Bubi" as he was always called) in the Cosy Corner, an unpretentious, almost homely place, often overheated by a big stove, and lacking in distinctive decoration, except for a few photographs of boxers and cyclists pinned up over the bar. Christopher later took several of his friends and acquaintances there, including the practitioner of the occult, Aleister Crowley, who declared on entering: "I haven't done anything like this since I was in Port Said." Crowley then walked up to a very tough-looking youth in an open shirt, standing by the bar, and scratched the boy's chest deeply with his nails. Only a sizeable gift of money succeeded in restraining the boy from beating him up on the spot.

Bubi was a poor German-speaking youth of independent spirit who had once been a boxer. There was a very gentle side to his na-

ture as well as the more cunning and occasionally deceitful side of
his professional character. Christopher saw him every day; apart
from making love, they did a tour of the city, visiting the zoo and
the big dipper at Luna Park, and swimming in the Wellenbad.
Wystan Auden wrote a poem about Bubi, "This Loved One,"
which begins rather cynically:

> Before this loved one
> Was that one and that one,
> A family
> And history
> And ghost's adversity
> Whose pleasing name
> Was neighbourly shame . . .

Christopher went several times to the cinema, and reacted enthusiastically to some new silent films in which there was no language barrier except in the titles. He saw Georg Pabst's *Die
Büchse der Pandora* (Pandora's Box), notable for the sensuous
performance of Louise Brooks as Lulu, the Franz Wedekind
character, who meets her fate at the hands of Jack the Ripper. He
also liked *Potomok Chinghis-Khana* (Storm over Asia), Vsevelod
Pudovkin's last great silent film about a Mongolian nomad who
rouses the masses against British oppressors.

Christopher realised his other dream, that of meeting John
Layard, though they did not become close friends until the following year when they remet in London. In the last week of March
he returned home, deeply touched by the farewell present of a
cheap gold bracelet from Bubi.

At about this time Olive Mangeot suggested that Christopher
join her and Sylvain on a trip to the South of France. In St.
Tropez they came across Anthony Gross, an exact contemporary
of Christopher's at Repton, who was now well launched on an artistic career. However, from the health point of view, the trip was
a disaster. Sylvain Mangeot contracted rheumatic fever, which left
him with a weak heart. Christopher developed a sore throat in
Marseilles, and when he returned to London fell ill with tonsil-
litis. During his convalescence Christopher dreamed of getting

back to Berlin, hoping for a deep relationship with Bubi. He started a teach-yourself crash course in German.

Through Wystan, Christopher was put in touch with a Colonel Solomon, a wealthy, rather bitter man who was paralysed from the waist down. His Russian wife, apparently a mistress of Kerensky, had founded the Blackamore Press. Wystan told the Solomons that Christopher was absolutely brilliant at French, and was there-fore just the man they needed to translate Baudelaire's *Journaux Intimes*, so they commissioned him for the job. The book ap-peared the following year (1930), with a complimentary intro-duction by T. S. Eliot, and reads well, though people whose French was more perfect than Christopher's were quick to point out various mistakes. When it was reissued a few years later he was able to make a few alterations. Christopher's most vivid mem-ory of the Solomons is that of driving around Piccadilly Circus with the colonel, who took particular delight in pointing out ho-mosexuals who loitered by the Underground station entrance, say-ing: "Look! There's another one!"

Christopher managed to return to his new spiritual and carnal home in July, joining Wystan at Rothehuette, near Königshof, where Wystan had installed himself in early June. Wystan was cohabiting with a cheerful youth called Gerhard, and shocked the local people by wrestling with the boy naked in the meadows. He was also flirting with the idea of marriage, and seems to have been engaged to a girl, possibly a nurse, around this time, Christopher urging him to abandon this foolhardiness.

Christopher had hoped that Bubi would join them, but he did not arrive. Concerned about what might have happened to the boy, Christopher travelled to Berlin and contacted a friend of Wystan's, Francis Turville-Petre, who might know of his where-abouts. Turville-Petre was a decadent young archaeologist who led a totally wild life among the city's available boys. Christopher dis-covered that Bubi had been in some sort of trouble with the police and had fled over the border into Holland, where he in-tended to embark for South America. Bubi did write to Chris-topher at his Rothehuette address, asking for money, whereupon Christopher persuaded Wystan to accompany him to Amsterdam in an attempt to track down his errant boyfriend. The search proved much easier than he could have hoped, as they ran into

Bubi almost immediately at the main post office. Bubi did indeed leave the country, but Christopher saw him on numerous occasions over the next twenty years, the infatuation being transformed into friendship.

Returning to Britain in the autumn, Christopher set about earning some more money by tutoring once again. One of his posts was in a small remote village in Scotland, where he had his first and only sexual experience with a woman. A little too much drink, a soft advance from her side, and it was done, without any undue worry or remorse, but it was not exciting enough to lead to a repeat performance. Recalling the incident in his recent autobiographical volume *Christopher and His Kind*, Isherwood finished his account with a breathtaking generalisation, but which is nevertheless an interesting reflection on the sort of woman he has often known and likes to have as friends: "Girls can be absolutely beautiful but never romantic. In fact their utter lack of romance is what I find most likeable about them. They're so sensible!"

By the end of November Christopher was able to return to Germany, but this third trip of the year was to be different to the others. This time he had gone to stay.

Wystan Auden had already finished his year in Germany and had taken up a tutoring job in London, so Christopher looked up the only other English contact he had in Berlin—Francis Turville-Petre. Francis had a flat in In Den Zelten, overlooking the Zoo Park. The reunion got off to a very bad start. Christopher rang the doorbell, and Francis opened the door, only to slam it in Christopher's face, screaming insults from inside. Undeterred, Christopher shouted his own name loudly, convinced that Francis must have mistaken him for somebody else. In fact, Francis had thought he was a German boy whom he had picked up on the previous evening, and who had stolen some of his belongings. The misunderstanding over, Francis invited Christopher in, and as recompense for his rudeness, asked him to stay for lunch.

Francis rented a couple of rooms from a woman whose brother, Dr. Magnus Hirschfeld, ran the Magnus Hirschfeld Sexology Institute next door. This now legendary institution was a centre for very serious study of sexual behaviour, where perversions were treated as interesting cases and everything was cloaked in the eminent respectability of German academic terminology. The build-

ing itself was imposing, being the former residence of a nine-
teenth-century prince. It was furnished with heavy period pieces,
including busts of Goethe and other heroes of the German heritage.

Magnus Hirschfeld was himself a practising homosexual and, by
the time Christopher met him, had been involved for several years
with his young secretary, the devoted Karl Giese, who referred to
him as "Papa." Hirschfeld had founded the institute in 1919, and
fought bravely against violent opposition to it from puritans and
queer-bashers. Despite having been beaten up in Munich, he had
not abandoned his struggle for fair treatment of homosexuals. He
had some support in high places, and was able to plead his cause
in the Reichstag. Indeed, for a time it had looked as if his fight to
have the anti-homosexual laws liberalised might succeed, but in
the end Germany's economic crash and political unrest meant
that plans to introduce consenting adult legislation were shelved
in favour of more pressing matters.

The institute did not treat homosexuals alone. It had a marriage guidance service, and a VD clinic, frequented by Francis
Turville-Petre.

Hirschfeld had succeeded in winning a precarious status of respectability for his brainchild, so that it was accepted as an asylum
for sex offenders, where they could stay free from the law or
outside interference, until their cases were heard in court. Hirschfeld was a supporter of Russian Soviet legislation which had de-
creed that an individual's sex life was private and therefore outside the law. Undoubtedly this was an important reason for many
homosexuals' turning to communism during the 1930s, though
they were soon to be bitterly disillusioned when the USSR turned
against that section of the community. Hirschfeld's left-wing political views added to the fuel of his detractors, but in 1929 there
were still very many communists in Berlin.

Francis Turville-Petre and Karl Giese took Christopher on a
tour of the institute's museum, which contained a remarkable
collection of scientifically labelled exhibits representing a whole
range of sexual tastes, including sado-masochism, boot fetishism
and transvestism. This eye-opening collection was to provide
Christopher with some of the necessary familiarity to write about
the masochistic Mr. Norris in *Mr. Norris Changes Trains*. Sado-

masochism, leather fetishism and similar tendencies were all well catered for in Berlin in those days, and many of the more open-minded social historians have commented on the relationship between such tendencies and some of the appeal of Nazism.

During Christopher's connection with the Hirschfeld Institute André Gide paid a visit, and was shown round the museum. All Christopher's feelings of Gallophobia—reinforced by Wystan Auden's ravings against "frogs"—were aimed at Gide, who commented politely as walking exhibits were produced and scientifically displayed, such as a boy with a pair of perfectly formed female breasts. Christopher suddenly saw Hirschfeld himself in a new and more favourable light. Hirschfeld's shambling, professorial air, which Christopher had been the first to lampoon, suddenly became noble in contrast to Gide, with his studiedly romantic cape. Christopher's reactions in this case corresponded to Hirschfeld's description of his sexual nature: infantile.

Christopher had contacted Francis in the hope of finding out about available lodgings, and he was delighted when he learnt that there was a room available in the very same flat. The available room was nowhere near as grand as Francis' chaotic apartment, but was not too expensive. It also had the supreme advantage of being "safe" for bringing back boys. Christopher's new living arrangements meant that he was able to observe Francis at close range, and marvel at his unusual character and escapades. Francis was the first of the truly exotic personalities in Christopher's Berlin experience, yet he was one of the last to be written about, appearing as Ambrose in *Down There on a Visit*.

Francis had noble looks worn down by debauchery. He was being treated for syphilis at the institute's clinic but was past the infectious stage, so that he was able to bring boys back to the flat. Often in the mornings Christopher would come across more than one strange youth, the gleanings of Francis' nights out. Despite his aura of aristocratic decay, Francis was a strongly resilient person with an ability to let all life's problems pass over him, simply by accepting them. Nevertheless, he was vitriolic in his condemnation of the mass of humanity, and railed against all those who did *not* have syphilis. He was an habitué of the different boy-bars around Berlin, and Christopher would often accompany him on these tours, though usually being careful not to drink too much.

1. Marple Hall. COURTESY OF CHRISTOPHER ISHERWOOD.

2. Frank Isherwood in 1914.
COURTESY OF CHRISTOPHER
ISHERWOOD.

3. Christopher and Nurse Avis at Marple in 1909. COURTESY OF CHRISTOPHER ISHERWOOD.

4. Kathleen, Christopher and Richard in 1912. COURTESY OF CHRISTOPHER ISHERWOOD.

5. St. Edmund's School, in 1916. Seated are Cyril and Rosamira Morgan-Brown.
Peering around her head is Christopher; seated at her feet is Wystan Auden.

6 and 7. Christopher at the Isle of Wight in 1928, the day an advance copy of *All the Conspirators* arrived.
PHOTOGRAPHED BY AND COURTESY OF EDWARD UPWARD.

8. Edward Upward in 1928. PHOTO-
GRAPHED BY CHRISTOPHER ISHERWOOD;
COURTESY OF EDWARD UPWARD.

9. Wystan Auden in the early 1930s.

10. John Lehmann in 1939. PHOTO-
GRAPHED BY HANS WILD; COURTESY OF JOHN
LEHMANN.

11. Stephen Spender in the late 1930s.
PHOTOGRAPHED BY HOWARD COSTER.

12. Magnus Hirschfield and Karl Giese in 1934. COURTESY OF CHRISTOPHER
ISHERWOOD.

13. Jean Ross ("Sally Bowles") in 1931.
PHOTOGRAPHED BY STEPHEN SPENDER;
COURTESY OF CHRISTOPHER ISHERWOOD.

14. Otto in 1931. PHOTOGRAPHED
BY STEPHEN SPENDER; COURTESY OF
CHRISTOPHER ISHERWOOD.

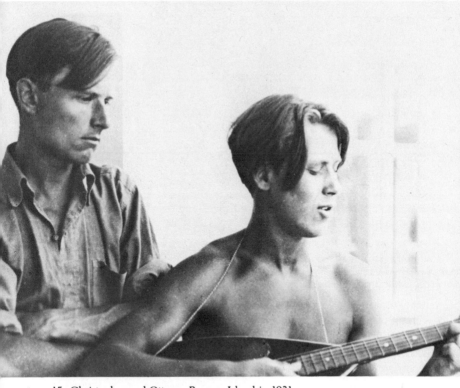

15. Christopher and Otto on Ruegen Island in 1931. PHOTOGRAPHED BY STEPHEN SPENDER; COURTESY OF CHRISTOPHER ISHERWOOD.

16. Heinz in 1933. PHOTOGRAPHED BY HUMPHREY SPENDER; COURTESY OF CHRISTOPHER ISHERWOOD.

Towards ten or eleven o'clock he would gently take his leave of Francis and go home to sleep, in order to be fresh for writing the following morning.

As has been mentioned, the first draft of *The Memorial* had been completed in London, but now came the slow and painstaking process of rewriting. Isherwood has always claimed that he likes this part of composition best. He writes straight through a work—even if he knows the first draft to be emerging poorly— then polishes very carefully over a long period of time, or often completes several new drafts. In the early days he wrote in longhand, with obsessive neatness, assiduously scratching out mistakes with a razor-blade. Towards the end of the decade he changed to a portable typewriter for the first draft. Even now, however, in writing letters, he tends to cover over mistakes carefully with Snopake rather than cross things out. He never underlines his signature, as his grandmother had told him that that was a manifestation of egotism! In Berlin he settled down into a routine of getting up quite early; then he would take his manuscript to a café in In Den Zelten, reworking the material which had lain dormant all summer. Installed at a table he would write away, drinking beer and smoking Turkish cigarettes.

Cured of his illness and fed up with the German winter, Francis Turville-Petre went south, to his beloved Mediterranean, where formerly he had done valuable archaeological work. By now Christopher could get around well enough on his own. He was not entirely cut off from his old world, however, as he made several visits to England during this period. There the domestic scene *chez* Isherwood had been clouded by Richard, who had pretended that he had got a job in order to get away from a private tutor hired to further his education. Christopher supported Richard's revolt against this situation, and added to Kathleen's discomfort by describing in clinical detail his life in Berlin. She wept a great deal because of his aggressive attitude, while he found her obstinate, stupid and pathetic. At Christopher's suggestion, John Layard (now living in London) came to see Kathleen, and submitted her to his usual form of analysis and treatment. She admitted that she had made some mistakes in bringing up her boys, and tried seriously to come to terms with their natures. While wounded by Christopher's behaviour, Kathleen did not lose her

confidence in his future, and slowly took on a new role as his un-
paid, amateur literary agent.

Christopher saw quite a lot of Stephen Spender at this time.
Stephen, like Christopher, had gone to Germany in 1929 for personal liberation, though he had chosen Hamburg not Berlin. His
host in Hamburg was a young Jew, who introduced him to interesting friends and showed him the radiant physical vitality of
German youth in a post-inflation society; the picture Stephen
later painted in his autobiography reveals much of the appeal
which the world had for Christopher:

> . . . their aims [of the young Germans] were simply to live
> from day to day, and to enjoy to the utmost everything that
> was free: sun, water, friendship, their bodies.
>
> The sun—symbol of the great wealth of nature within the
> poverty of man—was a primary social force in this Germany.
> Thousands of people went to the open-air swimming baths or
> lay down on the shores of the rivers and lakes, almost nude,
> and sometimes quite nude, and the boys who had turned the
> deepest mahogany walked amongst those people with paler
> skins, like kings among their courtiers.*

By the end of the summer Stephen had returned to England, to
do his final year at Oxford, though with characteristic energy he
spent the last few days of the long vacation printing a little volume of Wystan Auden's poems in an edition of thirty copies.

The happy home of the Mangeots had by now broken up, largely
owing to André Mangeot's peccadilloes with attractive women
musicians. Olive Mangeot sued him successfully for divorce,
though the separation was gradual. First, André moved out of
Cresswell Place, while Olive and the children continued living upstairs. André came back to live in the mews when Olive found a
house in Gunter Grove. Fowke went with his mother, while Sylvain, shortly to go up to Oxford, continued to use the mews house
as his base.

Things had also reached a nadir at 19 Pembroke Gardens, the
house into which Kathleen, Richard, Nurse Avis and the cook had
moved in the summer of 1929, following discontent with their old

* *World Within World*, p. 107.

accommodation. Christopher hotly announced that he would never live in Kathleen's house again, and in early May 1930 stormed back to Berlin.

Almost immediately, Christopher met a new boy who won his affection. "Otto"—the basis for the Otto Nowak character in *Goodbye to Berlin*—was then about sixteen and rather Slavic in appearance.

The summer of 1930 brought visits from both Wystan Auden and Edward Upward. Wystan gave Christopher a copy of his volume of poems, which he had dedicated to him. Edward, by now a schoolmaster, had become a Marxist sympathiser, though he was not yet a member of the Communist Party. Christopher was impressed by Edward's new-found austerity and political seriousness. Already surrounded by a good number of communist sympathisers at the Hirschfeld Institute, Christopher was in general accord with their leftist tendencies, although he was not politically motivated enough to align himself with them. His shallow knowledge even of the German scene at that time is indicated by the fact that in a letter home he mis-spelt Hitler's name.

Stephen Spender returned to Hamburg when he left Oxford that summer, and took a room in a boarding-house. He found several places in Hamburg which were the counterparts of *Lokale* that Christopher knew well in Berlin. In the middle of August Christopher and Otto travelled there on a two-day visit and went on a trip round the harbour with Stephen. Anxious to see more of his friend, Christopher wrote subsequently to Stephen, suggesting that he move to Berlin, which he did.

In September the Nazis increased their representation in the Reichstag from 12 to 107, with 18.3 per cent of the votes cast. The streets of Berlin that year were often the scene of bloody clashes between armed groups of the opposing political factions. In February a young SA leader, Horst Wessel, had been shot by communists, and Goebbels (already a master of propaganda) had blown up the affair into a story of Nazi martyrdom. The authorities tried feebly to ban street demonstrations, and forbade the Nazis to wear their distinctive uniforms, but their decrees were futile. Prevented from wearing brown, the National Socialists turned out in white. The SA smashed up the National Socialist headquarters in Berlin, largely over a pay dispute, and Hitler summoned Ernst Roehm (then an officer in the Bolivian Army) to leave South America and come to sort out the SA. Violence was in the air, and however much Christopher may have deplored the idea of it, he found the tense atmosphere highly stimulating.

Otto suggested to Christopher that it might be fun if he were to move in with his family in their flat in a slum tenement at 4 Simeonstrasse. Christopher readily agreed, thinking that this would mean more contact with Otto and at the same time be an interesting experience. Actually he remained with the family for only one month, but the impression he gained from his stay with them was vivid enough to provide all the background for the Nowaks in *Goodbye to Berlin.* Otto's father was a working man, a little too fond of drink, who no doubt shared his wife's pleasure at the thought of the extra income to be gained from Christopher's tenancy. Otto's mother was eager to please and effusive. However, she suffered from tuberculosis, and this caused her to move into a sanatorium in November—the immediate reason for Christopher's departure from the apartment.

When Christopher moved to other lodgings he continued to see Otto. His new accommodation was also in a poor area, at 38 Admiralstrasse, but he had a room to himself. He was delighted when the local police, with whom all foreigners were obliged to register, informed him that he was the only Englishman in the district.

A month later he was on the move again. His financial position did not require him to live in such poor places as he had occupied for the previous two months, so he went to a much more respectable district, just south of Nollendorfplatz, near the city's entertainment district. The landlady of his new lodgings at 17 Nollendorfstrasse, Fräulein Meta Thurau, reminded Christopher of a character straight out of Beatrix Potter—Mrs. Tiggywinkle, the hedgehog lady who takes in people's washing.

Fräulein Thurau became very fond of Christopher, whom she invariably called Herr Issyvoo. She is, of course, the model for Fräulein Schroeder in *Goodbye to Berlin:*

All day long she goes padding about the large dingy flat. Shapeless but alert, she waddles from room to room, in carpet slippers and a flowered dressing-gown pinned ingeniously together, so that not an inch of petticoat or bodice is to be seen, flicking with her duster, peeping, spying, poking her short pointed nose into the cupboards and luggage of her lodgers. She has dark, bright, inquisitive eyes and pretty waved brown hair, of which she is proud. She must be about fifty-five years old.

Although she was not as portly as this portrait may suggest, it fits her well. Stephen Spender, a frequent visitor to the flat after his move from Hamburg, left a less affectionate description of her:

. . . Fräulein Thurau, with pendulous jaws and hanging breasts, the watch-dog of the Herr Issyvoo world . . . in front of the table covered with a wine-coloured velvet table-cloth which had been affected by a kind of mange so that it looked like a skin of a huge cat of the same colour, I would sit amongst the tassels, the pictures of Blücher's yellowing victories, the wreckage of Fräulein Thurau's mythical grandeur, waiting an unconscionably long time for Christopher to appear. Whilst I was waiting, one or other of the characters of his as yet unwritten novels would dart out of one of the rooms opening into this one.*

Christopher's fellow lodgers provided him with an endless source of amusing tales for his friends, and the material for what most people consider to be his two best novels. Foremost among these tenants was Jean Ross, the daughter of a wealthy cotton merchant who had spent a considerable time in Egypt. About nineteen when she moved into Nollendorfstrasse, in early 1931, she was a pale, aristocratic-looking girl, with a long beautiful face. In the past she had been used to being waited on hand and foot, and never really became adjusted to a life without servants. Fräulein Thurau grumbled endlessly about the extra work Jean caused her. She was intrigued by Jean's flamboyant sex-life, but put off by her unintentionally selfish manner. Jean's moods were dramatic, and her clothes frequently outrageous. She earned her living by singing, rather badly, in a very run-down bar (nothing

* *World Within World*, p. 122.

like the swinging joint portrayed in Bob Fosse's film *Cabaret*). Her string of admirers was endless and multinational. With Christopher she established a sisterly relationship in which there was no hint of sex. She knew about his boys, whom he sometimes brought to the flat (with his landlady's implicit connivance), and listened to the ups and downs of his relationship with Otto. On at least one occasion, Jean and Christopher shared a bed without any embarrassment. However, not infrequently they had rows with each other. They were both strong but sensitive personalities, only too aware of each other's weaknesses. Jean would sometimes aim mercilessly at his Achilles' heel: his writing. *The Memorial* was still in the process of construction, and she was quite cruel in her criticism of it, though probably not deliberately so, as she was a kind, warm person. Christopher was furious once when she informed him offhandedly that perhaps some day he would write something "really great, like Noël Coward." She has reappeared on many occasions during Christopher's life, both as herself and as her fictional *alter ego*, Sally Bowles, whose tale and spin-offs have helped to keep Isherwood financially secure for much of his life.

Uncle Henry's allowance was not enough to keep Christopher in comfort in Berlin, especially after Britain went off the gold standard and the pound fell against the mark. Stephen Spender has romanticised Christopher's poverty then, with stories of dreadful meals of horseflesh and lung soup, though in fact Christopher always had enough to afford toffees, endless cups of coffee or beers in cafés, frequent evenings out on the town ("last night was positively the *last* time I'm setting foot in *there* . . ."), and for boys who demanded cash gifts or presents in kind. Both Stephen Spender and Edward Upward advanced money to Christopher at this period, but neither seems to have protested as to how it was spent. However, the main supplement to Christopher's income came from his teaching English to private pupils. From them he learnt a good deal about the state of Germany, and he was able to experiment with a few fancy theories of his own about learning a language, some of which his pupils regarded with smiling indulgence.

Among his new acquaintances was Gisa Soloweitschik, a

wealthy young Jewish girl who had been a friend of Stephen's a long time before on a skiing trip in Switzerland. Of Lithuanian origin, she studied the history of art, and had cultured, generous parents who gave Stephen and Christopher a standing invitation to lunch on Sundays at their home in Wilmersdorf. They called Christopher "Shakespeare" and Stephen "Byron." Gisa and Christopher had many arguments, Christopher still being in a stubbornly anti-intellectual mood. With her, as with other people of whom he did not completely approve, he could be cold and sometimes scathingly sarcastic. Stephen accepted Christopher's often apparently arbitrary but deeply felt attitudes towards people and ideas, and found his rebel's stand a useful bolster for his own confidence. Christopher talked to Gisa about Otto, without ever explicitly mentioning their sexual relationship. Sometimes his tribulations would bring tears of compassion to her eyes. She, in turn, spoke at length about the gathering storm-clouds for Germany's Jews. Happily, she left the country in the autumn of 1931, long before the holocaust, and married a Frenchman.

Another Jewish friend of Christopher's was Wilfrid Israel, who worked for his family's large department store. Five years Christopher's senior, Wilfrid was a British subject, born of an English mother and a German father. An elegant, distinguished young man, looking younger than his thirty years, he did not take the easy way to safety by seeking refuge in England, but stayed on in Germany right up until 1939. He escaped deportation to a concentration camp, but was killed in an aeroplane shot down by Nazi fighters on a flight from Lisbon to London. He was the basis for the character Bernard Landauer in *Goodbye to Berlin*, but it is not necessarily a faithful portrait. In view of Wilfrid's heroic activities in Germany on behalf of fellow Jews during Hitler's first years of power, Isherwood later found his depiction of Landauer's (and by implication Wilfrid's) character offensive, and felt guilty about it.

If Wilfrid Israel has gone down in history as one of the little heroes of this period, then Gerald Hamilton (Mr. Norris) will certainly be recorded as one of the great rogues. A man of unashamed villainy, he had an unbounded charm which has made him one of the most effective con men of this century. Christopher met Hamilton in the winter of 1930–31 when the latter was working as a sales representative for *The Times*. Born in Shanghai in 1890 of Irish origins, Hamilton had already travelled throughout the world and been involved in underhand dealings of many kinds. The intimate friend of both royalty and communists, he was a walking paradox. A flagrant homosexual (at one time he had a working-class communist lover), he campaigned for legalised abortion, prison reform and the abolition of capital punishment. As a Catholic convert, he had been close to the homosexual Irish patriot Roger Casement and had had ties with the Vatican. His treachery was counterbalanced by his brilliant conversation, his urbanity, wit and grace—no mean accomplishments for an overweight middle-aged gentleman who wore an ill-fitting wig. Claud Cockburn, who worked for *The Times* in Berlin before his left-wing views condemned him as "unsuitable," frequently had to tell Gerald Hamilton that *this* time he really had overstepped the mark, but on each occasion after fifteen minutes in Hamilton's company he found himself laughing. Cockburn dared not introduce new people to Hamilton, even those who had especially asked to meet this amazing man, since he knew that within a few days they would in all probability be stung for cash, lured by some eminently attractive-sounding bogus business propositions, or merely find themselves summoned in the middle of the night to stand bail. Hamilton thrived on his notoriety, particularly after the publication of *Mr. Norris Changes Trains*, and wrote volumes of autobiography, each more incredible than the last. His ultimate coup was to sit as a model for part of the memorial statue to Winston Churchill.

Hamilton was adored by Fräulein Thurau, to whom he referred as *La Divine Thurau*. He knew how to flatter and cajole, and had an expert's eye for spotting a sucker, or a "client" who had every reason not to go to the police when he realised Hamilton's duplicity. Even so, Hamilton kept barely one step ahead of the law, and occasionally found himself in prison.

At the beginning of 1931 Christopher decided that he was satisfied with the revised draft of *The Memorial*, and sent it off to Jonathan Cape. The book was divided into four parts, in a non-sequential time pattern: 1928, 1920, 1925 and 1929. In keeping with the original synopsis, it deals with a group of middle-class people trying to come to terms with the aftermath of war. Several of the characters are clearly recognisable borrowings from Christopher's family and friends.

The book opens in a Chelsea mews, where Mary Scriven (based largely on Olive Mangeot) leads an active musical and artistic life with her daughter. Also in London is a morose, artistic widow, Lily Vernon (Kathleen), obsessed with memories of her heroic husband Richard (Frank), who was killed in the war. Richard had also been an amateur water-colourist, and had lived in a large house up in Cheshire near the village of Chapel Bridge (a composite name formed of Whaley Bridge and Chapel-en-le-Frith, both in Derbyshire, the next two towns on the road from Disley to the Peak District). Courageous in her "reactionary romanticism," Lily has a son Eric—who slightly resembles Christopher himself, but is handicapped by strong glasses and a stammer. Eric helps Mary Scriven run her little concerts, having thrown up Cambridge at the time of the General Strike. But he "certainly wasn't interested in politics any more. From something he'd once said, he seemed to lump Communists and Fascists and everyone else together in one heap." And although Eric impresses some of his aristocratic and artistic acquaintances with his knowledge of working-class living conditions, even while describing tubercular children and families who live eight in a room, he is overcome by waves of sensuality:

> But why are we talking like this? Eric wanted to yell at her, becoming aware again of her half-naked body, cunningly concealed and revealed by the sex-armour, her Eton crop, her plucked eyebrows, her scent—Good God, why are you so dishonest? Quick, let's go upstairs. There must be a bed somewhere in this damned house. (p. 41.)

Eric is oppressed by his mother, with whom he no longer lives, yet he is aware of the absurdity of her effect upon him. When Lily's husband Richard had been killed, she had been told by friends that she should live for Eric. But at that time she had wondered how that could be possible, considering the boy was away at school for most of the year. The reader is given a depiction of life at the big hall (Marple), Lily's father-in-law (John Isherwood) and his wife (who resembles Emily Machell-Smith far more than Elizabeth Isherwood). Lily writes a diary, and is preparing a book of sketches of the house. Her attitude towards her environment and towards the villagers is exactly that of Kathleen's own attitude in the past. Youth must condemn Lily's cult of her dead husband, yet she is justified in mourning, as he is the Truly Strong Man, who had hidden his light under a bushel by working in a solicitor's office before sacrificing his life in a war. His opposite, the Truly Weak Man, is represented by Edward, a great friend of his, a homosexual who had performed heroic feats in war and been injured in an aeroplane accident, but whose bravado was a sham. Behind it was an insecure man chasing after worthless boys. After the war he goes to live in Berlin, where he attempts to commit suicide by shooting himself through the mouth—and fails. He has a confidante, Margaret (a younger version of Olive Mangeot), who in spite of herself falls in love with Edward and suffers accordingly.

Eric's own sexuality is ambiguous, despite his barely suppressed and aggressive desire for his female listener in the passage quoted above. Angrily he warns Edward to moderate his interest in his male cousin, yet he realises his only motive can be jealousy. One reviewer later reflected sadly that there seemed to be an unusually high proportion of homosexual characters in the book, but conceded that that sort of thing seemed to be getting more common. Reading the book with hindsight, a concise and carefully controlled portrait of some problems of homosexual life emerges, some of which must have been missed by the majority of early readers. Otherwise the book is an interesting pastel portrait of a family during those curious, early inter-war years. Valuable in itself, it is even more fascinating when seen in the context of Isherwood's own childhood and feeling towards the Test.

In March 1931 Christopher went to London to see what Jonathan Cape was doing about publishing the book. To Christopher's disbelief, Cape rejected the novel. Christopher was aware that it was much better than *All the Conspirators*, and the rebuttal hurt him. Cape, however, was working on the principle "once bitten, twice shy," and wished Christopher the best of luck in finding a new publisher. As a postscript, he added cheerfully that maybe one day he would live to regret the decision. Meanwhile, Stephen Spender suggested that Christopher get in touch with a

London literary agent, Curtis Brown, with whom he has had contact ever since.

Relations with Kathleen seemed much better on this visit and, as Christopher learned later from his mother's diaries, she was well aware how much he was suffering because of Otto. Although Christopher and the boy had fun together, and Otto possessed a healthy sexual appetite, Christopher was conscious of the fact that Otto preferred women. Otto knew the power he held over Christopher, and was not above using it. While Christopher was away in England, Otto got into trouble with the police. Stephen Spender, for ever loyal to his friends, was able to help out.

Christopher returned to Berlin on March 21 and resumed his life of English lessons, walks and talks with Stephen Spender, and frequent sorties to the cinema with Otto, who was a keen moviegoer. Stephen was amused by the violence of some of Christopher's pronouncements especially when fellow lodgers at Nollendorfstrasse, such as the bartender Bobbi, annoyed Christopher. He was beginning to show signs of strain over the fate of his manuscript and his awkward personal life.

One aspect of Christopher's character which fascinated Stephen was his ability to make friends with simple workmen or shop-assistants. During his stay in Berlin Christopher seems to have lost a good part of his class discomfort. Possibly because of the large amount of time he spent with working-class boys, he had learnt to communicate with ordinary folk without embarrassment. From that time on, his range of friends has covered men and women from every walk of life. Stephen was amazed at the way people reacted to Christopher, and recorded:

In fact, in his own neighbourhood, Christopher had trained most of the shop people to spring into automatic, swift, silent action as soon as he appeared at the shop door, as though he were a switch and they machines running on electric rails. When a certain grocer refused to act in this way, Christopher took revenge by buying his groceries at a store a few doors away, having them packed as bulkily as possible, and, thus laden, walking slowly, bowed down with his purchases, past the erring grocer's shop, hoping thus to break his spirit.*

* *World Within World*, p. 124.

Stephen and Christopher decided to go on holiday in June to the island of Ruegen, taking Otto with them. Wystan Auden came over to join them from England, where he was working as a schoolmaster in Helensburgh. His *Poems* had been published the previous autumn, and he made use of the holiday to continue writing, shutting himself in his room with the blinds drawn. Stephen had become addicted to taking snapshots, sometimes to the exasperation of Christopher. He had an automatic exposure fitting on his camera, which meant that if he ran fast enough after taking the picture, he could also appear in the photograph. From this time dates the famous picture of Stephen, Wystan and Christopher standing together, Wystan looking like an overgrown schoolboy, and Christopher grinning broadly, barely coming up to Stephen's shoulder. On the holiday, however, there was sometimes considerable strain in relations with Otto, who would take off to the local dance hall where he would chase after girls, not returning till late at night.

Stephen carried on to Salzburg, then wrote suggesting that he move in with Christopher at Fräulein Thurau's. Christopher fended off the suggestion, as he was sure it would be bad for both of them. "I think I could find you something cheaper two doors away," he wrote. "I think it is better if we don't all live right on top of each other, don't you? I believe that was partly the trouble at Ruegen. Anyhow I'm resolved not to live with Otto again for a long time." Otto, however, was still a very welcome visitor at Nollendorfstrasse, albeit in small doses.

Christopher had begun to feel oppressed and threatened by Stephen. In *Christopher and His Kind* Isherwood acknowledges that he was worried, possibly subconsciously, that Spender would invade his literary territory, for Christopher was well aware that he was living amongst a group of people who would one day form the basis for a novel. He kept copious notes, and a regular diary.

Stephen decided to go to London, and took with him a copy of the manuscript of *The Memorial*, which he showed to his friend John Lehmann. Then working at Leonard and Virginia Woolf's Hogarth Press, Lehmann was then twenty-four. He was the son of Rudolph Lehmann, one-time Liberal MP and editor of the *Daily News*, of which Stephen Spender's father had been deputy editor. An Old Etonian of the famous generation that produced Harold

Acton, A. J. Ayer, Eric Blair (George Orwell), Cyril Connolly, Rupert Hart-Davis, Anthony Powell and Henry Yorke (Henry Greene), Lehmann had graduated from Trinity College, Cambridge, before joining the Hogarth Press, who published his book of poems, *A Garden Revisited*, in 1931. He had met Stephen a few months previously through his novelist sister Rosamond Lehmann. Stephen had spoken at length to John Lehmann about his friends W. H. Auden and Christopher Isherwood, so the manuscript of *The Memorial* was planted on well-tilled ground.

Meanwhile, Christopher had made friends with a member of a family which was to cross his path on many occasions—the Manns. Klaus Mann, the eldest son of Thomas Mann, was a novelist like his father. He was constantly on the move, possessing boundless energy and a concern for the state of Germany, which soon led to his exile in Holland. He and Christopher had many interests in common, and quickly became intimate friends.

In September Christopher received heartening news. Kathleen excitedly informed him that Stephen had phoned her with the news that the Hogarth Press had accepted *The Memorial*. Christopher wrote to Edward Upward, in reply to his friend's letter of congratulations:

> Phew, that was a close one. Mater's hand was on the pen, in fact she'd already begun a pretty nasty letter inside there last week when the telephone bell rang and Stephen blurted the news of the reprieve. Richard was sent out to the grocer's for purple rockets and Nanny hurriedly rummaged out soiled Christmas festoons from the cellar.

On October 1 he returned to London to celebrate.

6

In *The Memorial*, Isherwood had fictionalised many of his childhood experiences and reminiscences, but it did not satisfy his
desire for retrospection. He therefore embarked upon an autobiography, a fairly ambitious project for an almost totally unknown
novelist. On January 13, 1932, he wrote to John Lehmann:

Dear Lehmann,

Stephen tells me that you want me to write and let you
know what I am working on and what I mean to do in the
near future. At present I'm writing an autobiographical book,
not a novel, about my education—preparatory school, public
school and University. After this is finished I shall start a
book about Berlin, which will probably be a novel written in
diary form and semi-political. Then I have another autobiographical book in mind. And possibly a travel book. So you
see, I have no lack of raw material! It is only a question of
time and energy.

Stephen also said that it was possible you might be ready
to consider a Letter from me for your series. If you would
. . . it would be called "Letter to an Enemy." The "Enemy"
is a sort of embodiment of everything I detest—and has, I
hasten to add, absolutely nothing to do with Mr. Wyndham
Lewis.

I am very glad that my novel is coming out so soon. I hope you will have the success with it that it deserves.

The Memorial was duly published the following month, almost exactly as it had been written, though the Hogarth Press had asked Christopher to expunge the clause "he can lick his arse," and requested that the time sequence be indicated. It had a most unusual and attractive brown-paper jacket designed by John Banting.

Apart from all these plans and teaching and socialising, Christopher had time to write an article for the magazine *Action,* a popular account of what was going on in Germany, and for which payment was sadly slow in arriving.

The situation in Berlin was rapidly deteriorating at the beginning of 1932. As Christopher wrote to Olive Mangeot:

Here it is rather like living in Hell. Everybody is absolutely at the last gasp, hanging on with their eyelids. We are under Martial Law, and to all intents and purposes living in a Communist regime without any of the benefits of Communism. Nobody in England can have even the remotest idea of what it is like. There are wagon-loads of police at every corner to sit on any attempt at a demonstration. You can scarcely get along the street for beggars. Hitler and the Communist openly discuss plans for Civil War and nobody can do anything.

That winter was indeed grim in Germany. Unemployment figures had passed the five million mark, and President Hindenburg had been forced to sign new emergency decrees cutting wages, prices and interest rates while increasing taxation. Membership of the Nazi Party during 1931 had risen from 389,000 to over 800,000. More and more people in authority began to accept the "advisability" of compromising with the Nazis, and giving Hitler some share of power. In February Hitler was in Berlin, wondering whether he should yet risk competing with Hindenburg.

Apart from conversations with his pupils and gossip in Fräulein Thurau's flat, Christopher was kept abreast of political developments by friends among the foreign press corps in Berlin. Violence was on the increase, which made him uneasy, yet much of his current discontent was caused by the fact that Otto had announced that he had met a very nice girl, which would mean that his relationship with Christopher would have to stop, though of *course* they would be friends for life, and could even live together as a threesome. Christopher resigned himself to the inevitable, but in fact the relationship dragged on for several more weeks.

A possible new opportunity for Christopher seemed to offer itself when Francis Turville-Petre arrived back in Germany. When Christopher heard that he would be coming, he had wild dreams of journeying with Francis to the East, but his friend had already decided to live quietly in the countryside. Francis suggested that Christopher join him, and he accepted. Their destination was to be Mohrin (Moryń), now in Poland but then part of Germany, in a flat, bleak area near the sea. Francis engaged Erwin Hansen—a friend of Karl Geise's—as cook and housekeeper. Hansen, a big, muscular man with short-cropped blond hair, worked as an odd-job man at the Hirschfeld Institute, and had previously been an army gym instructor. A committed communist, he was also an active homosexual. When asked to find someone to help him with the heavier work, he produced a boy named Heinz, then in his mid-teens.

Heinz was a very un-Teutonic-looking boy, with tight curly hair, protruding lips, a broken nose and large brown eyes. In certain lights he could look almost African, and he was highly amused when Christopher dubbed him the "Nigger Boy." Francis did not take to Heinz at all, but Christopher was quickly won over by his simple charm, and started an affair with him. Heinz proved to be a conscientious worker around the house, and was very fond of outdoor tasks such as gardening. Francis and Erwin Hansen found themselves rather bored by the experiment in living in the provinces, and returned to Berlin for weekends.

Christopher himself was in Berlin when Edward Upward passed through in April, on his way home from the Soviet Union, which had surpassed his wildest expectations. It would be some time before he and other British communists and fellow-travellers would be disillusioned by Stalin.

In the summer Christopher returned to Sellin on Ruegen Island, this time with Heinz. Both Stephen Spender and his brother

Humphrey were there, and the group got on fairly well, although there was again dissension between Christopher and Stephen. Wilfrid Israel also came to Sellin, and outlined a plan of action for the Jews when Hitler came to power. Israel believed they should go out into the streets, as a protest, and refuse to go home, even if they were fired upon. He reasoned that only by such unified sacrificial action would the conscience of the world be aroused. Nobody need be reminded of what did happen.

Christopher was working on the first draft of his Berlin novel, as he explained in a letter to Edward Upward:

> I am well started with my novel, but there's many a weary fitt [*sic*] before it's ready even for your condemnation. E. M. Forster is said to like *The Memorial* and to be writing an article boosting it.
>
> I think I have finished utterly with [Otto]. He betrayed me with a tout from S. America who promises to take him to Paris. I have found a substitute with suspicious ease. He is with me here. I suppose I ought to be undergoing some very high-class pangs. The truth is I'm bored to tears with this whole homosex business. I want my tea.

At the beginning of August Christopher went to London, where he spent the first few days with Jean Ross. She had appeared in a small part in Max Reinhardt's sumptuous production of Offenbach's *Les Contes d'Hoffmann* the previous winter, but had realised that her future was not so bright in Germany. Soon she moved into Olive Mangeot's house in Chelsea, then married Claud Cockburn.

Christopher met John Lehmann for the first time on this visit. They did not immediately warm to each other, and Christopher was rather suspicious of Lehmann with his handsome looks, formality and quizzing eyes. Although they appreciated each other, it was some time before they became intimate friends. Through John, Christopher came to know his sisters, the novelist Rosamond, the actress Beatrix, and to a much lesser extent Helen. Beatrix Lehmann went to Berlin later that year, and became very close to Christopher, as a sort of honorary sister who did not try to impose her will upon him.

Much of Christopher and John's conversation, when not on the

thorny topic of their mutual friend Stephen Spender, was about
The Memorial. Although one or two critics had liked it, it had
sold poorly. Lehmann felt rather embarrassed about the puny
amount of the first royalty statement, but Christopher good-na-
turedly informed him that it was one pound more than he had expected.

Christopher's stay in England during August and September
provided him with the opportunity of making many new friends
among the city's literary establishment, some of whom were to
have a very profound effect upon his mature life. Wystan Auden,
who was then working on the verse play *Enemies of a Bishop*
and had recently published *The Orators,* came to stay in London between jobs. He took Christopher to see two friends of his,
Gerald Heard and Christopher Wood, who lived together in a
comfortable flat in a modern block off Oxford Street. Heard was a
man of enormous erudition and intellectual curiosity. He was
blessed with an ability to discuss scientific or philosophical topics
in layman's terms, even if sometimes his arguments seemed at first
to be at a complete tangent to the topic under discussion. At the
time, he was giving a series of talks on BBC radio. The rather dry
tone of some of his books does not do justice to the man himself;
he was a brilliant talker, witty, playful and scintillating—a true exotic, if occasionally theatrical in a pleasing Irish way. He was a
dozen years older than Christopher, while Chris Wood was almost exactly Christopher's contemporary. Wood was rich and
handsome, but had none of the pretentious gregariousness of
many other young men of fortune. He was rather shy by nature,
caring nothing for his appearance, and was very modest about his
talents, in particular his musical ability. He was a good amateur
pianist, but could rarely be persuaded to play in front of people.
He also wrote short stories, flew small aeroplanes and rode a bicycle everywhere.

Inevitably, Auden and Heard tended to get together in a corner
and talk about science, so that the two Christophers found themselves keeping each other company on such occasions. Christopher
Isherwood was intrigued to discover that Chris Wood had once
visited the Hirschfeld Institute when he had been living next door.
There Wood had spotted a great beauty, whom both thought must

have been Isherwood himself. The present reality did not match up to the fleeting glimpse, and they both found this very funny.

Another two men whom Christopher met, this time through Stephen Spender, were William Plomer and his artist cohort Anthony Butts. Plomer had been born in South Africa but had lived for some time in Japan. He was a good friend of E. M. Forster and J. R. Ackerley, who referred to him as "SW" or "Sweet William." Plomer became one of Christopher's closest correspondents, and considered Christopher to be a letter-writer of exceptional brilliance. In his autobiography Plomer described the young Isherwood thus:

> "Amazing" was one of his favourite words, and his capacity to be amazed by the behaviour of the human species, so recklessly displayed everywhere, made him a most entertaining talker. . . . Christopher Isherwood, compactly built, with his commanding nose, Hitlerian lock of straight hair falling over one bright eye, and the other looking equally bright under a bristly eyebrow already inclined to beetle, an expression of amusement in a photo-finish with an expression of as he came to the conclusion of a story, and almost choking with delight at the climax, also made Taine look silly—or would have done so, if one had been thinking of him.*

William Plomer reminded Christopher of a benevolent owl, because of his big round spectacles. Plomer took Christopher to meet E. M. Forster, who for years had been Christopher's literary hero, and now became his friend. Forster was then fifty-three, but looked younger. Christopher was deeply moved by their first encounter, and on subsequent occasions sometimes found himself on the verge of tears in Forster's company. Normally contemptuous of the older generation, he was perfectly content to sit—metaphorically and literally—at Forster's feet. Forster's approval of *The Memorial* meant more to Christopher than anything else, and he was fond of saying to friends that, as far as he was concerned, his literary career was over. He did not give a damn about the Nobel Prize or other awards; he had been praised by Forster!

---

* *The Autobiography of William Plomer* (1975). The French critic and philosopher Hippolyte Taine summed up the English thus: "Le fond du caractère anglais, c'est l'absence de bonheur."

While visiting William Plomer and Anthony Butts one day, Christopher had a showdown with Stephen Spender. Spender later recalled:

> . . . Christopher showed so clearly his irritation with me that I decided I must lead a life which was far more independent of his. So the next day I called on him at his mother's house in Kensington, where he was staying. I explained that I had noticed I was getting on his nerves, and that when we returned to Berlin we should see nothing, or very little, of each other. He said he was quite unaware of any strain, and that of course we should meet, exactly as before. I went away not at all relieved, because I thought he was refusing more out of pride than friendship, to face a situation which he himself had made obvious. Moreover, he had expressed his views in the accents of ironic correctitude with which Auden, Chalmers [Upward] and he could sometimes be insulting. Next day I received a letter from him saying that if I returned to Berlin he would not do so, that my life was poison to him, that I lived on publicity, that I was intolerably indiscreet, etc.
>
> The result of this letter was that I decided not to return to Berlin.*

Certainly Christopher was upset that Stephen had told some of his friends a very great deal of the sort of life he lived in Berlin. However, the friendship did survive; they continued to write regularly, and see each other from time to time, wherever they happened to be.

Things at Kathleen's house were on unusually cordial terms. Christopher dictated the first draft of his Berlin novel to Richard, who was pleased to be of service. Kathleen and Nurse Avis were both happy at this literary activity going on under their roof. The original idea for the novel had been to have a vast canvas depicting the crumbling state of Germany and the weird people living there. Christopher had dreamed up the title long before the book was under way: *The Lost*. Actually he had thought of the title in German, *Die Verloren*, which sounded much more dramatic. He

* *World Within World*, p. 174.

wrote in his diary: "The link which binds all the chief characters together is that in some way or other each one of them is conscious of the mental, economic, and ideological bankruptcy of the world in which they live. And all this must echo and reecho the refrain: It can't go on like this. I'm the Lost, we're the Lost."

Most of the characters of Isherwood's later Berlin stories were already in *The Lost*; however, the chief character is Peter Wilkinson, a young Englishman who is picked up by Otto Nowak when taking a walk along the shores of a lake, and is seduced in a wood. The relationship with Otto is a tempestuous one, and Peter returns to England after a row. The book ends with Otto dead in the snow beneath the girders of an overhead railway.

Christopher returned to Berlin at the end of September. During the summer the political situation had followed a seemingly confused and dangerous course. Chancellor Brüning had resigned at the end of May, to be replaced by Franz von Papen, who was an improbable choice, not even being a member of the Reichstag. New Reichstag elections were called for the end of July, and the ban on the SA was removed. The communist leader Ernst Thaelmann called this action an open invitation to murder, and indeed street violence increased considerably. Von Papen effectively dismissed the Prussian state government under emergency powers a few days before the Reichstag elections. When the election results came in, they showed a massive swing to the Nazis, who doubled their support over the 1930 results, winning nearly fourteen million votes. However, although they were now the largest single party, they did not have an overall majority.

Many people became increasingly concerned about the behaviour of the SA, and wondered whether Hitler was fit to have any share of power. Papen was prepared to offer him the vice-chancellorship, but Hitler greeted the offer with contempt. Hindenburg, who was greatly alarmed by the Nazi excesses against communists and Jews, suggested that Hitler be invited to join a coalition government, but added that he should give up the idea of complete power. In September the National Socialists voted with the communists on a censure motion against Papen's government, thereby bringing it down. And though technically Papen had dissolved the Reichstag by virtue of a presidential decree as soon as he had realised what was happening, new elections were announced.

A few days before the elections, in early November, there was a transport strike in protest against further wage cuts. The communists were the main backers of the strike, but to many people's amazement the National Socialists also gave their support to the strikers, for fear of losing the goodwill of the working classes. Christopher witnessed several incidents of street violence, which he later described in *Goodbye to Berlin*. He was in quite close contact with the Communist Party, though not a member, and was then at work on a translation for a communist publication with which Gerald Hamilton was involved. Several of his friends were more deeply committed to the Left, such as Beatrix Lehmann.

In the November elections the Nazis lost nearly two million votes, though they remained the largest party in the Reichstag. The communists, however, made significant advances, taking Berlin with a majority of over a hundred thousand votes. Franz von Papen again suggested a coalition government, but Hitler refused. Papen resigned, and on November 18 Hitler was summoned to visit President Hindenburg; but negotiations failed. General Kurt von Schleicher was made chancellor on December 2, but he was doomed to enjoy his position for less than two months.

It was impossible to avoid the growing sense of political menace. Christopher took Heinz to see an aeroplane display, where little pieces of paper were dropped on the spectators' heads, reading: "This might have been a bomb, therefore Germany must arm." With typical irreverence, Christopher retorted: "This might have been a bun, therefore eat it."

Christopher received a letter from Michael Roberts, the poet who had edited a most important book of poems that year, *New Signatures*, containing work by Auden, Julian Bell, Day Lewis, Richard Eberhart, Empson, Lehmann, Plomer, Spender and A. S. J. Tessimond—a collection which perhaps more than anything else created the concept of what has now been christened the Auden Generation. Roberts was soliciting material for another volume, and Christopher considered sending part of *The Lost*. He had great reservations, however, as he admitted to William Plomer:

I rather loathe the idea. It seems so idiotic to be dressed up in a sky-blue uniform as Youth, Knock, Knock, Knocking at the door. And when Roberts writes in his letter about wishing to represent the "new spirit in literature, politics and education," I just feel frankly scared. What *is* the new spirit? How could I manage to inject some of it into a description of a sanatorium for consumptive paupers? Or have I, perhaps, got it all the time and don't know it? It's being asked to a party where one doesn't know if one's supposed to dress.*

Eventually Christopher sent Michael Roberts a piece entitled "An Evening at the Bay," which was essentially autobiographical, though presented as fiction. The story is set in Freshwater Bay, with Allen (Edward Upward) and Philip (Hector Wintle) present, as well as Christopher himself—the first time he appeared in a "fiction," and under his own name. The story makes use of entries in Christopher's little notebook of people's speech patterns and sayings. It was published in Robert's anthology *New Country* (1933) and reprinted in *Exhumations*.

Christopher spent New Year's Eve in the company of Beatrix Lehmann, fearful of what 1933 might have in store. The fact that they were so engrossed in conversation that they missed saluting the New Year at midnight was ominous according to their German friends. A few days later John Lehmann came on a visit. He had left the Hogarth Press the previous autumn and had moved to Vienna with the conscious wish to become a full-time poet. After spending the Christmas period in England, he now passed through Berlin on his way back to Austria. He stayed several weeks, and walked through the icy streets with Christopher, both of them muffled up to the eyes against the cold, while hundreds of portraits of Hitler stared at them from shop windows and street hoardings. On Sunday, January 22, accompanied by a British journalist, Christopher went to watch a Nazi demonstration of ten thousand SA men in the Buelowplatz. In order to enable the Nazis to hold the demonstration, the police had to cordon off the square, post sentries on rooftops, make a house search for weapons and stop the Underground railway. Christopher's diary record of the event is included in the final section of *Goodbye to Berlin*.

* *The Autobiography of William Plomer.*

Eight days later Hitler was summoned to the President's palace once again, and emerged Chancellor of Germany.

Christopher saw a lot of the journalist Norman Ebbutt during this period, and acted as an information intermediary, transmitting news of political prisoners which he had received from a young man.

At the end of February the Reichstag was burnt down and a general sense of despair pervaded the city. Many of Christopher's Jewish and leftist friends had already left Germany, and others were preparing to go. Gerald Hamilton had discreetly slipped away, following a police warning. Christopher's friends were of all political persuasions, but the story that they told was always the same: sudden arrests, disappearances, exile, violence, death. "The Mad Tsar," as Christopher sometimes styled himself, could not sleep calmly in his bed.

On April 1 he went to a large Jewish department store to see the effect of Nazi boycotting. Nazis were posted at the doors, informing everyone, as if they did not know, that the store was Jewish. With a start, Christopher recognised one of the guards as a boy he had known on his night prowls. Nevertheless he entered and made a token purchase.

On April 5 Christopher returned to England with most of his belongings, storing them carefully with Kathleen. He dictated his work to Richard again, and received visits from E. M. Forster, Gerald Hamilton and others, including Bubi, his first German boyfriend, who was now involved in smuggling Jewish refugees into Britain on board a Dutch freighter.

Morgan Forster showed Christopher the manuscript of his unpublished novel *Maurice*, which he had written in 1913–14 but which was not released until his death in 1970, appearing in print the following year. Forster was eminently discreet about his own homosexuality, largely for the sake of others, but he believed deeply in his own novel. Christopher was profoundly moved by the older man's humble demand for Christopher's opinion. He wriggled with embarrassment over some of the passages, especially the word "sharing" for sexual intercourse, but thought the book as a whole a noble work, superior to Forster's other writings in its passion, if inferior as a work of art. Forster nervously asked if the book had dated, to which Christopher replied, "Why shouldn't it date?" Forster was touched by Christopher's enthusiastic and emotional reaction to the book, and gently leant over and kissed him on the cheek. In his will he left the royalties of *Maurice* to Christopher, who channeled them into a travel fund for young British writers visiting the United States.

Christopher inherited a small legacy from his godmother Aggie Trevor (née Greene) at the time, and toyed with the idea of using it to go off to the other side of the world. However, he was anxious to rejoin Heinz, with whom he had fallen deeply in love, and on April 30 returned to Germany. Francis Turville-Petre had suggested Christopher join him on a small Greek island which he had rented, an invitation he now accepted. Heinz would go with him, and Erwin Hansen, who for the past few months had been bravely guarding the Hirschfeld Institute against possible rioters. Hirschfeld himself had left Germany in 1930 and settled in the South of France. He died in May 1933, and only a few days later demonstrators sacked the German premises, though fortunately the most valuable material had already been taken out of the country. Books by Hirschfeld and a bust of him were publicly burnt and destroyed in front of the Opera House. Christopher was there and cried "Shame!"—very softly.

On May 13 the little party left Germany, bound for Athens. They travelled via Prague to Vienna, where they visited John Lehmann and the League for Sexual Reform. From there they continued to Budapest, where they caught a Danube steamer to Belgrade. The last stage of the journey to Athens was by train. Francis was at the station to meet them, accompanied by some of his Greek boys, who were to cause Christopher considerable irritation over the coming weeks.

From May 21 to September 6 Christopher lived on Francis' island of St. Nicholas, situated near the shore just north of Chalcis. Christopher planned to write a very detailed diary, forming the basis for a book along the lines of Joe Ackerley's *Hindoo Holiday*, which hopefully would keep him financially secure for the next ten years—or so he wrote to Stephen Spender. Occasional breaks from the island were taken when they visited Athens for a weekend, such as for Christopher's twenty-ninth birthday in August. Sanitary conditions on the island were almost non-existent, and there was no fresh water, which meant that it had to be fetched by boat from the mainland. Christopher lived in a tent, and there was no privacy. He often lost his temper with the Greek boys because of their noisiness, total disregard for hygiene, sexual promiscuity and total indifference to the suffering of animals.

Sometimes local fishermen would tie up at the island, coming ashore to drink and carouse, and more often than not this would end in an orgy. Frequently everyone was completely inebriated. The combination of heat and rough Greek alcohol aided the sense of apathy into which Christopher had sunk. Although he continued to write his diary, he was doing little work on his books, and determined to go somewhere else. But where? Germany was too dangerous, and he had no particular wish to return to England, even if he could have obtained a residence permit for Heinz. It has appeared in print that Heinz was a Jew, but that is not true. If he *had* been a Jew, then the problem of finding a suitable place for him to live for the next five years would have been much easier. Christopher wrote of his troubles to Olive Mangeot, who promised that she would look into possibilities for a place to stay around Cateret in France. He replied, in a letter dated July 28, 1933:

> I reckon I have about twenty pounds a month certain. I can remember a time when I got through a month on that amount let alone with two mouths to feed, but that's beside the point.
>
> Actually, I fear France will be too dear. I had counted a great deal also on having Gerald's [Hamilton's] support in Paris, and now he has gone, which rather puts me off the whole business. I am toying with an alternative scheme of going by boat up the Adriatic to Trieste and from there to Vienna or somewhere in Austria. I feel much safer and more at home there, and it is no earthly use coming to England until I have found a place where Heinz and I can lay our heads. Altogether, I feel that we should be more welcome in London in the autumn and till then should not be heard and not seen. I quite realise that we are, collectively, rather a nuisance.
>
> This place continues to be Hell. I am a little better, thanks to a French tonic composed, apparently, of human blood; but

I can't be a human being again until we have got out of this heat and strident Mediterranean atmosphere, which is a series of shrieks and yells and stinks and pricks. . . .

Have just caught three fleas with a pair of tweezers. Syphilis going very strong just at present. I insist on doing my own washing-up. Francis scoffs. I may be old-fashioned, but my next holiday will be in Greenland.

Christopher and Heinz argued about what to do when they left the island. Heinz declared he was going back to Berlin unless Christopher gave him a large sum of money but, fortunately for Christopher, all the berths on the train were booked, so Heinz agreed to stay with him for a while. In this rather uneasy atmosphere they left for Marseilles by boat, arriving in the middle of September. After a couple of weeks in France they went to England. Heinz was granted a short tourist visa, and the couple went to stay at Kathleen's. Stupidly, Christopher told her that he had only just met Heinz in Paris, a falsehood which became glaringly obvious when Heinz guilelessly mentioned things that had happened to them in Germany or Greece. Kathleen was probably more hurt by this dishonesty than by the fact that Christopher was once more involved with a boy of "low" origins and moderate intelligence. Christopher's friends did their best to make Heinz feel welcome, but soon his visa expired and there was nothing for it but for him to go back to Germany.

In October Jean Ross phoned Christopher with a peculiar proposition. The telephone conversation was not recorded at the time, and there have been several versions of what was actually said, but the gist of the conversation was as follows:

Bursting with enthusiasm, Jean said that she had just met the most *marvellous* man. "He's an absolute *genius*, darling. He's making some sort of film and the woman who was writing the script couldn't go through with it, so of course I said you would be just the person, so if you could send him a copy of one of your books, so he can see how good you are. . . ."

"I've sent too many copies of my books with no result," Christopher replied gruffly, well familiar with Jean's enthusiasm for some new man.

"Well, what if I paid for half of the book, and you paid the other half?"

"Absolutely not."

"Well, if I paid for *all* of the book, and you gave me half of your first week's salary if you get the job?"

"Certainly. Done."

Christopher sent off a copy of *The Memorial*, expecting to hear no more. A few days later, however, Jean was on the phone again, and said with breathless amazement: "Darling, he thinks it's *good!*"

Thus Christopher was introduced to Berthold Viertel, Austrian poet, film director and man of letters, who was at that time employed by Gaumont-British Studios on a film called *Little Friend*, based on the novel *Kleine Freundin* by Ernst Lothar. Margaret Kennedy (author of *The Constant Nymph*) had been hired to do the screenplay, but because of other commitments could not finish it. Viertel was desperately trying to find someone to take over, and Christopher fitted the bill. The completed film bore joint credits to Kennedy and Isherwood.

Berthold Viertel was a rather eccentric man of considerable sensibility and talent. Unfortunately he involved himself in a wide range of creative fields, so that he never became pre-eminent in any of them. He was particularly proud of his poetry, but it is almost unknown outside his own country. Before coming to London he had worked in films in Austria as well as Hollywood. He was married to the distinguished Polish actress Salka Steuermann, who had worked with Max Reinhardt in Berlin, but who was by now installed in California.

Viertel had many of the characteristics of a highly educated European Jew, as well as the curious blend of practicality and wild romanticism common amongst central Europeans. He took a great liking to Christopher, and felt relieved to have someone to talk to in German from time to time, even though his English was perfectly adequate. He told Christopher that he felt no shame before him, just like two men meeting in a brothel. He had the comforting knowledge that his own family was safe and sound in California, but he watched the developments in Germany and Austria with heartfelt distress. Christopher was wildly excited by the fact that Greta Garbo, then at the height of her fame, was an intimate friend of the Viertels. He thoroughly enjoyed going into a shop with Viertel towards the end of the year, where Viertel went to buy a Christmas present for Garbo, giving her name and address to an incredulous assistant.

Viertel lapped up everything Christopher had to tell him about the German situation. They also played literary games, in which Viertel liked to refer to himself and Christopher as characters out of Dostoevsky's *Brothers Karamazov*, Christopher being cast in the role of Alyosha, and Viertel as Lucifer. In fact, their relationship was rather like that of uncle and nephew; but Christopher did not at this time feel able to talk about his own private life, since Viertel made several anti-homosexual remarks which seemed to close off any possible opening. Viertel could wax lyrical about love and heterosexuality, however.

The story of the film, which had been adapted to an English environment to suit its intended audience is intensely melodramatic. Little Felicity Hughes (played by Nova Pilbeam) is the child of affluent parents whose marriage is falling apart. Although she has everything money can buy, and is well tended by a doting governess, Felicity is disturbed by her realisation that an actor (her mother's lover) seems to be breaking up the household. Finding her mother and the actor together in Richmond Park one day, the little girl rushes out on her scooter, and is only just saved from being run over. Her father walks out in disgust at the situation, but hopes to get custody of the child. Divorce proceedings are instigated, but the child, called as a witness, breaks down in court and attempts suicide. Horrified by the extent to which their selfishness has harmed their child, husband and wife are reunited.

The plot of the film had all the makings of a real tear-jerker, but Viertel and Isherwood were determined to keep it as free of saccharine as possible. Far from being disdainful at having to write dialogue for such a film, Isherwood found it an amusing challenge, and was soon proud to discover that he could produce realistic conversations quite easily. Undoubtedly this work helped the development of his smooth-flowing style, which Cyril Connolly once called his fatal readability. And perhaps the odd thing about this film work was that it made Christopher realise that he *needed* to get involved in a truly vulgar project from time to time, and thereby be forced to extend his talent. Most of his literary friends did not share the sentiment, and thought he was either a little barmy or else doing it just for the money.

Berthold Viertel was in charge of both the direction of the film and the adaptation from the original novel, and so he worked very closely indeed with Christopher. Robert Stevenson was the associate producer, and Matheson Lang and Lydia Sherwood starred as the parents. Costumes were by Schiaparelli.

While working on the film Christopher had the nagging worry of how to arrange a reunion with Heinz. During an exchange of letters Christopher outlined a plan which would ensure both Heinz's safe passage through the British Customs and his obtaining a long-term visitor's permit. Heinz was to say that Kathleen had invited him to stay, and he would carry money sent by Christopher, but which he would claim to be his own.

Christopher went to Harwich on January 5, 1934, accompanied by Wystan Auden, to meet Heinz's boat. He waved to the boy as he came ashore, but when all the other passengers had emerged from the terminal building, there was still no sign of Heinz. Christopher and Wystan went into the Customs House to find a very dejected Heinz sitting with some stern immigration officers. On the table was the letter Christopher had sent to Heinz, outlining the way he should sell his story to the immigration people. The officials had been suspicious when they saw Heinz's passport, which recorded his profession as household servant, an idea of Christopher's, as he had not wished Heinz to shelter behind a "bourgeois" label such as "language student" or "of independent means." At first they probably thought that he was trying to enter the country not as a guest of Mrs. Isherwood, but as a prospective employee. But later, when they searched the boy's person, they found the letter, with its unmistakably intimate phraseology. Without overtly accusing Christopher of any crime, the officials smilingly made it quite clear that they understood the score, and that there was no alternative but to send the boy back to Germany on the next boat. Downhearted, Christopher returned to London with Wystan, cursing at everybody's stupidity in the affair.

Christopher spent the next two weeks revising the screenplay of *Little Friend*, and then, when it had been delivered, he left for Berlin. He packed up Heinz and their belongings and accompanied him to Amsterdam, where they found a flat. Christopher spent ten days in Amsterdam to help Heinz settle in. Then he returned to England for the shooting of the film.

Christopher's London commitment ended at the end of March, when he returned to Amsterdam. From there, he and Heinz caught a boat (the S.S. *Zeelandia*) which was going to the Canary Islands via Vigo, Lisbon and Funchal. Christopher had been looking forward to Lisbon, but it turned out to be literally a washout. It poured with rain, and he and Heinz spent hours trying to find a decent café, stumbling across a medical relief station where milk was handed out to the poor. There had been some talk of Gerald Hamilton's joining the boat, but he did not do so. The two friends spent their time on board ship playing Ping-Pong and watching films.

At Las Palmas the pair stayed at the Towers Strand Hotel, situated by the beach, living in a hut on the roof which was normally used by servants, but which was the only available accommodation. At the beginning of June they went on a trip in the hills in the interior of the island. They climbed up to El Nublo, a bleak rock which had been miraculously scaled by some young Nazis, who had planted a swastika at the top. The incident is used in Isherwood's novel *The World in the Evening*. Heinz was in his element, gleeful and singing, so that Christopher was able to enjoy the climb vicariously through Heinz's pleasure, even though he himself suffered badly from vertigo.

On June 6 they moved to the neighbouring island of Tenerife, where they lodged in a *pension*, the Pavillon Troika at Oratava, from which place Christopher wrote on July 22 to John Lehmann:

Here, amidst the flowers, our Rousseau life goes on. Heinz has just got me to cut off all his hair. He now looks like one of the boys in a Russian film. Every morning we return to our tables in the banana grove. He writes letters, making at least two copies of each. Indeed, calligraphy is dignified by him to the position of an art. One is reminded of the monks in the middle ages. This place is a sort of monastery, anyhow. It is run by a German of the Goering-Roman Emperor type and

an Englishman who dyes his hair. The Englishman loathes
women so much he has put a barbed wire entanglement
across an opening in the garden wall, to keep them out.

My novel is exactly three quarters done. I hope to finish on
the day War was declared in 1914. It is a sort of glorified
shocker; not unlike the productions of my cousin Graham
Greene. When it is done and sent off I think we shall leave
at once for another island in this group, La Palma.

The "glorified shocker" was *Mr. Norris Changes Trains*, pruned
out of the overgrown *The Lost*. The catchy title was not chosen
until just before publication in England the following year. The
American publishers (William Morrow) incorrectly informed
Isherwood that the title was incomprehensible to Americans, who
always "transfer" at stations, so Isherwood provided another title
for the U.S. edition, *The Last of Mr. Norris*, which is positively
misleading, unless one puts a question-mark at the end. The book
was actually finished on August 12.

In his introduction to Gerald Hamilton's autobiography, *Mr.
Norris and I*, Isherwood wrote: "Now and then I am asked if the
character of Mr. Norris in my novel . . . is based on my old friend
Gerald Hamilton. Sometimes I answer 'No' to this question,
sometimes 'Yes'—according to my mood and the suspected motives of the questioner. Neither answer is more than partly true"
(p. 9). The portrait is sufficiently similar, however, to be immediately recognisable to anyone who knew Hamilton, and he himself
went around publicising the fact, revelling in his fictional notoriety. Christopher and his friends very often called Gerald Hamilton Mr. Norris in their letters.

Arthur Norris in the book is a small-time con man and political
operator, temporarily in Berlin, where he plays a dangerous game
of profiteering from the stormy unrest of the early 1930s. He is
not very successful in his dealings, and is supervised by a harsh,
unpleasant male secretary. He partakes in the masochistic pleasures offered by stern young ladies in leather boots, and accepts
other people's perversions, eccentricities and dishonesty without
qualm, unless it offends *his* sense of decency. Like Hamilton,
Norris is an epicurean, a leaden butterfly tasting the nectar of
flowers across the world. He wears a wig which shows, and has rot-
ten teeth. Several critics have written that Norris is homosexual,

presumably muddling him with his real-life counterpart, or else misinterpreting his relationship with his secretary. Everything in the book points to his being heterosexual, if given to minority proclivities. Had Norris been portrayed as overtly homosexual it would have given the book a different slant. As it is, Isherwood succeeds in describing the essence of Hamilton, an outrageous but paradoxically lovable rogue.

The love of boys is represented in the novel by the Baron Kuno von Pregnitz, an *aficionado* of boys' adventure stories, firing his fantasy of youthful, wholesome Baden-Powell-cum-Hitler-Jugend camaraderie. Mr. Norris, in soliciting the baron's help, is not above dangling a handsome young friend of his before the aristocrat—the narrator William Bradshaw. The fact that Isherwood used his own middle names for the narrator hardly conceals his identity, yet Bradshaw is in many ways very different from his creator. Isherwood in Berlin was a powerful personality, even if then totally unknown, a protagonist in the dramas around him. William Bradshaw is a wet fish, sexless, gullible and terribly English. Norris twice compliments the young man on his inimitable wit, but the reader is shown none of it. This rather faceless *alter ego* was dramatically necessary if the narrator was not to divert the reader's attention away from the main characters under view. Also Isherwood, some forty years ago, was not prepared to write a homosexual-confessional novel. Had he done so, the finished product would have been very different, it would probably not have found a reputable publisher, and from a legal viewpoint it could have been dangerous. The extent of his anxiety about this can be gauged from the knowledge that he destroyed his factual diaries, from which the two Berlin novels were written, once the books were completed.

Bradshaw's feelings for Norris are characterised by grudging respect and affection. Even though he knows that Norris has financially harmed some of his own friends, William cannot condemn him. He is forgiving and protective towards Norris, and often feels sorry for him. Even when William becomes aware of the extent of Arthur's crimes, he cannot condemn him, and surmises that none of Arthur's victims were ever really angry with him. He does not moralise in the wake of Norris' temporary defeat: "Remorse is not for the elderly. When it comes to them, it is not purging or uplifting, but merely degrading and wretched, like a bladder disease. Arthur must never repent. And indeed, it didn't seem probable that he ever would."*

How Gerald Hamilton must have smiled when he read those words. One wonders how many times he thought of them over the next two or three years, as events developed in a way that will be revealed.

Mr. Norris Changes Trains was a considerable advance on Isherwood's previous two novels. Like some of Graham Greene's fiction, it is a good adventure story spiced with detailed knowledge of the inner nature of the protagonists. The background of the Nazi rise to power is succinctly and powerfully evoked, without ever directly intruding on the private drama in the foreground. The characters reveal great development in Isherwood's understanding of people, as well as an improvement in technique. His style is radically different from that of *All the Conspirators* or *The Memorial*, free of experimental pretensions, clipped and often witty. In a very few words he manages to convey an exact impression of his characters. He had made great strides forward becoming a portrait writer, a mode that would culminate in *Goodbye to Berlin*. In this method he would start with a striking but often false impression of a character, after which a fuller portrait would emerge through the action. Isherwood saw the action of his stories as a sports-track with hurdles over which the athletes (the characters) had to jump.

For many people, *Mr. Norris Changes Trains* is Isherwood's best book; but he himself later condemned it as unsatisfactory because of the narrator. He felt he had lied about himself, and had not been sufficiently conscious of the true suffering of those tragic years in German history. He wrote in 1956:

> What repels me now about *Mr. Norris* is its heartlessness. It is a heartless fairy-story about a real city in which human beings were suffering the miseries of political violence and near-starvation. The "wickedness" of Berlin's night-life was of the most pitiful kind; the kisses and embraces, as always, had price-tags attached to them, but here the prices were drastically reduced in the cut-throat competition of an over-

* *Mr. Norris Changes Trains* (1935), p. 167.

crowded market. . . . As for the "monsters" [like Arthur Norris], they were quite ordinary human beings prosaically engaged in getting their living by illegal methods. The only genuine monster was the young foreigner who passed gaily through these scenes of desolation, misinterpreting them to suit his childish fantasy. This I later began to understand.*

On August 15, 1934, Heinz and Christopher left as planned for the smaller islands of the group, and spent two weeks walking around La Palma, Hiero and Gomera. There they came across two extraordinary beggars, who wandered from island to island with ingenious visiting cards, soliciting donations. Christopher wrote a story about them, "The Turn Around the World," which appeared in *The Listener* of August 28, 1935. It was subsequently reprinted in *Best Short Stories of 1936*, edited by Edward J. O'Brien, and in *Exhumations*.

Another product of his stay in the Canary Islands was the short story "A Day in Paradise," published by *The Ploughshare* (an organ of the Teachers' Anti-War Movement) in its April–May 1935 issue. The latter is interesting, since it shows for the first time in Isherwood's writing a consciousness of social injustice (as socialists might interpret the term), though clearly tailored to suit its audience. In a rambling, concluding sentence he admits pessimistically that the exotic nature of the island visited may well obliterate images of human suffering.

In September Christopher and Heinz started on a long and complicated journey up to Copenhagen, which Christopher had selected as their next refuge. They arrived in Copenhagen on October 1 and checked into the Webers Hotel. They were tired after a journey around the coast of Denmark on a Dutch boat, during which Christopher read Plomer's novel *The Invaders* twice. The novel's grim portrait of London convinced Christopher that he should not return home for at least another six months. Copenhagen appealed to them, with its fairly easy life-style, rich cakes, good cinemas and émigré German newspapers. Heinz returned to bed almost immediately with swollen glands, but soon recovered, dragging Christopher off to sports events which bored him to distraction.

* Introduction to Gerald Hamilton, *Mr. Norris and I* (1956), p. 11.

Christopher tried in vain to persuade Leonard Woolf to publish *Mr. Norris* earlier than the spring, as he was afraid the novel would lose its topicality, but Woolf had a strong prejudice against publishing between seasons. Meanwhile, Christopher was acting as a voluntary literary agent for several of his friends, including Klaus Mann, whose *Flucht in den Norden* (Flight to the North) had been published by Querido Verlag in Holland that year.

Christopher was not friendless in Copenhagen. A young Danish acquaintance of Stephen Spender's, Paul Kryger, did as much as he could to make Christopher and Heinz feel at home. Then the two friends by chance ran into Michael Spender (Stephen's elder brother) and his German wife, Erica, in the street. Erica found them a flat in the same block as the Spenders', at 65 Classengade, and helped them buy some furniture. According to Danish regulations, however, they would have to wait three or four months before applying to stay permanently in Denmark, with no guarantee about the outcome of the final decision.

Christopher was chided by Heinz for his frequent depressions. He criticised himself for being an exile, for not rallying behind the communist forces in England, as several of his friends had done. But he knew that such action was impossible for him.

Christopher's morale over Christmas was kept high by the knowledge that Wystan Auden would be arriving shortly. He flew in on January 10, 1935, courtesy of Faber & Faber, his publishers, for whom he was writing a verse play (provisionally entitled *Where Is Francis?*) in collaboration with Christopher. The form appealed to both of them, as well as to Faber's employee T. S. Eliot, who was to publish *Murder in the Cathedral* that year. Back in Germany, in 1932, they had worked together on a verse play, *Enemies of a Bishop* (dedicated to Bubi and to a friend of Wystan's, Otto), but they were aware that it was not very good, and it has never seen the light of day. In 1934, Auden had been working on another verse play, *The Chase*, which he sent to Eliot in October, before deciding that that, too, was unsatisfactory. He sent the manuscript of *The Chase* to Christopher in November, and a correspondence ensued which resulted in a collaboration to produce a work provisionally entitled *Where Is Francis?* This was later published and staged as *The Dog Beneath the Skin*, a title suggested by Rupert Doone of the Group Theatre in London.

Years later, when Auden was asked by a journalist how he and Isherwood collaborated, he replied gravely, "with the utmost politeness." But it was not like that at all. Their communal work sessions were the occasion for much ribald banter, criticism and insult. Yet they worked extremely fast, both of them having a considerable facility with words. (A breakdown of who wrote what in the finished play can be found in Appendix Two.) Isherwood later modestly declared that he had written little of value in *The Dog Beneath the Skin.* Faber & Faber seem to have had the same impression, as they did not wish Isherwood's name to appear on the play's cover, but Auden insisted.

The play, later published and staged as *The Dog Beneath the Skin,* is very much a child of its time, urgent in its anti-fascism and aggressive in its overt suggestion that such things might also take place in England. The essential element of the plot is that of a quest. The young hero, Alan Norman (described rather aptly by Stephen Spender as "a Candide with the mental age of Peter Pan"),* takes on the challenge of finding a missing heir, Sir Francis Crewe, who has fled the constricting environment of a decent English village. Sir Francis' sister has pledged herself to Alan if he is successful. The story has obvious links with traditional British myths of chivalry. He also has thematic or stylistic reference to pantomime (especially *Dick Whittington*), Noël Coward and the life and ideals of Lord Baden-Powell. Out of the marriage of traditional material and the pet-hates of the two authors emerges a hybrid form which can be identified as a politicised Mortmere. Many elements of the old Isherwood-Upward stories, complete with vicar, scouts and absurd disguises, are present, but now with a very definite social message.

Antedating the Spanish Civil War, the play seems a clarion call to alignment against fascism; yet its political position is not so clear-cut, its ardour for the left-wing cause ambiguous. One senses an understanding of, and to some extent a pity for, some of the characters who are ideologically unsound. The Enemy is often laughed at, rather than hated. It has been suggested that the dichotomy reflects a difference in approach by Auden and Isherwood, the former being more deeply involved in making propa-

---

* "The Auden-Isherwood Collaboration," *The New Republic,* CXLI (November 23, 1959), 16.

ganda, while the latter was fascinated essentially by the satirical and comic possibilities. But this is an over-simplification. By Christmas 1934 Isherwood was quite sure of his own position *vis-à-vis* fascism, but his artistic temperament and interests would always prevent him from being a political mouthpiece.

The Dog Beneath the Skin is certainly the most successful of the three plays that Auden and Isherwood wrote together. It moves at a cracking pace, in a constant direction, and happily mixes humour with a message. It also contains some magnificent poetry by Auden, especially in the choruses between scenes.

Wystan's visit to Copenhagen was to have been the occasion for much festivity, in contrast to Christmas, which Christopher and Heinz had celebrated quietly, confronting each other across an enormous goose. As Wystan only stayed three days, however, these were spent in feverish activity on the play while Heinz did the cooking. Wystan succeeded in covering everything and himself with violet pencil marks, and had to take a bath every night to wash them off.

Mr. Norris Changes Trains was published in London in March 1935. The reviews were generally good. The *Daily Telegraph* hailed Arthur Norris as "a true original: a flabby rogue without, as one would say, a single redeeming quality, who is nevertheless one of the most delightful persons one has met in fiction for a long time, and absolutely real." The *Spectator* called the book "a feat of sustained irony." However, although the book's reception was cheering news, and promised an improvement in his finances, Christopher was very worried about the future of his life with Heinz.

Here we skate but are sad. Very soon, compulsory military service will be introduced in Germany. What is Heinz to do? If he goes back, he becomes part of the machine and won't be allowed out again for the next five years, perhaps longer. . . . In 1938, his passport will expire. He will have to get another nationality somehow, I suppose, but this is fearfully difficult and takes a great deal of time.

It had become obvious that they could not stay on in Denmark. The police had let it be known to Christopher that they considered him a "political" writer, which worried him, and he found he was liable for Danish income tax. He flirted with the idea of going to South Africa. Stephen Spender suggested America.

Christopher decided that Gerald Hamilton would be the man to help them with their problem, especially in the acquisition of a new nationality for Heinz, since his passport would expire in 1938. Hamilton was now living in Brussels, so on April 13 Christopher and Heinz moved to Belgium.

7

Christopher and Heinz stayed at 44 Avenue Longchamps during this visit to Brussels. On April 19 Christopher wrote to Stephen Spender cheerily:

> Brussels seems lively after Copenhagen. It is raffish and shabby, with dark monkeyish errand boys and great slow Flamands with faces like bits of raw meat. And there are kiosks and queer dives and the Host is carried to the dying through the streets with people kneeling as it goes by. . . . I feel delivered from all kinds of vague suffocating apprehensions.

Heinz was given a one-month visitor's visa on arrival, Germans not being too popular in many countries of Western Europe at this time. Gerald Hamilton promised to use his influence, but his influence seemed very light, or at least very slow.

Once they were installed in Brussels, Christopher went over to London on a visit, his first time home for just over a year. By this time, Wystan Auden had already decided to do a play about mountain climbing, though work on this (*The Ascent of F6*) was not begun until the following year. *The Dog Beneath the Skin* was not published until the end of May 1935. Wystan at this time was in his third and final year as a master at the Downs School in

Cornwall. While in London Christopher looked up several old friends, including Berthold Viertel, who greatly liked *Mr. Norris*.

Christopher returned to Brussels on May 12, but when Heinz tried to get his permit renewed, it was refused. There did seem some hope, however, of obtaining another from a diplomatic mission outside the country. The two friends therefore moved over the border to Holland, and approached the Belgian Consul there, who said it would be very difficult but not impossible. Meanwhile, they moved into lodgings at 24 Emmastraat, Amsterdam, where Heinz had lived early the previous year.

At this time Christopher became a regular contributor to *The Listener*, thanks to Joe Ackerley, who had been appointed literary editor in April. Although the fees offered by *The Listener* were considerably lower than, for example, the Sunday newspapers, Ackerley's professionalism, charm and literary friendships brought him first-rate contributors such as E. M. Forster, Edwin Muir and Maynard Keynes, the last mentioned being the only one with whom the delicate question of low payment arose. Christopher was only too pleased to have some extra income; his nomadic life made it impossible for him to take numerous regular pupils, as he had done in London and Berlin. Auden wrote later that *The Listener* became a major outlet for the work of their generation during the 1930s. Isherwood cannot remember if he met Ackerley before or after accepting review work but, when he did, he confirmed the general impression that Ackerley was not only a delightful personality, but also one of the most handsome men in London.

Usually Isherwood's reviews in *The Listener* were unsigned. They cover the period 1935–37, and are catholic in their range of subjects, though Christopher did ask specifically for autobiographies of non-celebrities. One of the first of his reviews was of T. S. Eliot's *Murder in the Cathedral* (June 26, 1935), while one of the last was of Auden and MacNeice's irreverent travel book *Letters from Iceland* (August 11, 1937). During the period of writing these, Christopher became more intimately involved professionally and socially with the new literary establishment. E. M. Forster, John Lehmann and others helped publicise his work, and he actively cultivated the interest and patronage of other writers, such as Hugh Walpole, for whom he had gone to great lengths to send an advance copy of *Mr. Norris Changes Trains*.

For the time being, however, Christopher was physically out of the swim of things, living in Holland. A pleasant new arrival there was Thomas Mann's daughter Erika, who had been running a very famous satirical cabaret, *Die Pfeffermuehle*, in Munich, until it was no longer safe. The rest of the family was already in exile. Thomas and his wife, Katia, had left Germany in February 1933 on a lecture tour and did not return. Mann's work was vilified and boycotted by the Nazis, who considered him very dangerous, as he was a political moderate, and a Nobel Prize winner whose support they would have found valuable, but whose enmity could be damaging. After a brief stay in the South of France, Thomas and Katia settled in Zürich. Erika was later to reopen her cabaret in Switzerland, but for the moment she came to Holland. She had heard a great deal about the country from her brother Klaus, who had worked there writing novels and editing the magazine *Die Sammlung* (founded with Heinrich Mann, André Gide and Aldous Huxley).

Erika astonished Christopher by proposing marriage. Of course, it was to be simply an arrangement of convenience. She knew it was likely that her German nationality would be taken away from her, and marriage to Christopher would give her a British passport, after which she would leave him well alone. She had already had one disastrous marriage, but that had been terminated; she was not a woman suited to the role of wife or mother. Christopher turned aside her proposal for a variety of reasons. Being married to Erika Mann (however nominally) might well complicate the already complex situation with Heinz and his permit problems. The irony that Erika could thus get a British passport while Heinz could not did not escape Christopher. While keen to be of service, he considered it to be an intrusion into his own life which he was not prepared to accept. Besides he felt he could not countenance any suggestion that he might be trying to pass as a heterosexual, even for the noblest motives. He therefore suggested to Erika that she should contact Wystan Auden, who responded immediately to her appeal. The wedding was held on June 15, at the registry office in Ledbury, Hertfordshire, after which the couple happily went their separate ways.

Although Christopher had already thought of writing a second Berlin book, he was at present working on a convoluted novel entitled *Paul Is Alone*. A detailed synopsis of this abortive work, which was in four parts and drawn from his own experience since he moved to Berlin, may be found in *Christopher and His Kind* (pp. 208–12). Like *The Lost*, it was overpacked with material. It did, however, produce the germ of substantial parts of *Prater Violet* and *Down There on a Visit*, and a small part of *The World in the Evening*.

During the first week of July John Lehmann came to Amsterdam to discuss a new literary project. For quite some time, they had dreamt of a magazine that would reflect current writing and thought throughout Europe. They had talked of it together in Berlin, but then the immediacy of the German catastrophe had overshadowed their plans. Now, on a long walk to a sports ground on the outskirts of Amsterdam, they spoke in detail of their conception of its format. John Lehmann's primary concern was that it should be international, centred on a common stance of anti-fascism and a desire to broaden communication by breaking down traditional class barriers. At the same time, artistic quality should not be sacrificed to the god of left-wing political purity. Christopher was keen on the idea that it should provide a vehicle for novella-length fiction, which was too short to be published in book form, but too long to be accepted by most magazines which printed short stories. Christopher himself proved masterful at this genre, which is far more common in German than in English literature, and of which extracts taken from his long novel *The Lost* served to provide examples.

Lehmann started discussions with several publishers when he returned to London, though for a while it was not certain whether the magazine would be a quarterly, or a twice-yearly hardbound volume similar to *The Yellow Book*. Finally the latter possibility was chosen, and the review was titled *New Writing*. Lehmann had imagined his role to be that of editor, strongly supported by an advisory committee, of which Christopher would be a prominent member. Responding to this suggestion, Christopher wrote saying that he would be honoured to sit on an advisory panel, but urging him to run the magazine autocratically and to dispense altogether with the idea of a formal committee. Consequently the idea for a committee was dropped, and John Lehmann edited the magazine alone, turning it into one of the most important periodicals of the time.

Kathleen went out to Amsterdam to visit Christopher at the beginning of August, taking the red-light district quite in her stride. Christopher had also had warning of an imminent visit from Brian Howard, whom he had as yet never met. Howard had at the time a German boyfriend named Toni, and he was living in the same house as Christopher and Heinz. Christopher had been pleased at first, thinking Toni would be good company for Heinz, but soon the boy's mannerisms and affectations got on Christopher's nerves.

Brian Howard arrived later in the month and proved to be an unusually interesting person, even though he was a snob, drank too much and was on occasions vitriolic. E. M. Forster and his charming, sedate policeman friend, Bob Buckingham, also arrived, as well as Stephen Spender. On August 27 this group plus Klaus Mann, Gerald Hamilton, Christopher and Heinz travelled down to The Hague to celebrate Christopher's official birthday. Birthday parties have always been an important part of Isherwood's life, occasions to be celebrated by a group of intimate friends, and for which generous and carefully chosen presents are given. This year the party was arranged in a restaurant by Hamilton, who suddenly found himself having to entertain the group among torture instruments in the Gevangenpoort Prison Museum, into which they had fled to shelter from a rainstorm.

Christopher shared the opinion of many that Brian Howard was one of the most fascinating and dangerous creatures of his generation. He never lived up to his promise as a poet, and made himself widely disliked by his rudeness, irresponsible behaviour, unreliability and noisiness. He was a pure hedonist, but one who contrived to make pleasure sinister. He and Christopher could never have been really close friends, but they had enough common interests to get along with each other. Howard was trying to find a place to live with Toni, as Britain had refused to allow Toni back into the country following a visit during which he had associated with drug addicts. This coincidental situation formed a sort of bond between Christopher and Brian.

Brian had the idea of going to Portugal, where life was cheap, and he would be able to buy an old house and raise animals. Toni was not in favour of it. Christopher thought that he and Heinz might be able to join them if the plan came off, but only if Gerald Hamilton and Stephen Spender would come too. Brian and Toni did indeed go to Portugal, in October, but by then Christopher and Heinz had made alternative arrangements.

Nothing materialised from the Belgian consulate in Rotterdam, as far as Heinz's permit was concerned. They therefore decided to follow up a friend's suggestion and go to Luxembourg, which did not require entry visas and were given a thirty-day Belgian permit for Heinz on the spot at the Belgian Consulate. The following day they made a bus trip through the dukedom's Petite Suisse region. The bus had to make a detour across the German frontier, but Christopher and Heinz decided to risk going for the fun of it, as the driver had assured them that passports would not be checked. They spent a quarter of an hour drinking beer and writing post-cards at a little café just on the German side of the frontier before returning safely to Luxembourg.

In Belgium, they rented a flat above Delvaux's leather goods shop in the Boulevard Adolphe Max, near the fashionable Place de Brouckère. Their landlady was a lively, amusing character who had been given the nickname Claire l'Audacieuse by one of her admirers. Had they lived there longer, no doubt, she would have followed Fräulein Thurau into fictional fame.

In October Wystan Auden came over for a weekend, bringing with him fragments he had written for his new job as a member of the GPO Film Unit. The unit, under John Grierson's inspired direction, produced some remarkable documentaries on a surprisingly low budget. Auden had been working on verse for a film called *Coal Face*, directed by Basil Wright, who brought a young composer by the name of Benjamin Britten to see him. Britten subsequently became a close friend and collaborator of Auden's.

Christopher worked hard on a piece for *New Writing*, directly inspired by his experience of living in the slum tenement flat belonging to Otto's family in Berlin in the autumn of 1930. The story was originally called "The Kulaks" but Christopher realised that the title would be misunderstood if and when it was ever published in the Soviet Union (as indeed it was), so after much

discussion with Heinz, he changed it to "The Nowaks" shortly before publication. Later, of course, it formed one of the six sections
of *Goodbye to Berlin.*

The story is fairly faithful to the real-life happenings from
which it is adapted, except that a fictional reason had to be invented for the narrator to move into the Nowaks' flat—economic
necessity. Within the structure of *Goodbye to Berlin* the time sequence is changed, so that in the book Christopher moves in with
Otto after Ruegen, whereas in fact it was before. The most
striking aspect of the story as far as the development of Isherwood's technique is concerned is the change in the role of the narrator. He is more actively a party to the story than is William
Bradshaw in *Mr. Norris Changes Trains,* and has been given the
author's own name. He observes and reports the other characters
in the story, but it is his arrival which forms the dramatic point of
departure. Some of the descriptions, notably that of Herr Nowak
recounting his war experiences, read like a first-class film script,
including stage directions. Isherwood picks out details, incidents
and habits as if he were a roving camera lens with a very sure director behind him giving the orders. He was completely aware of
this cinematographic link himself, leading to the famous passage
in *Goodbye to Berlin,* taken from "A Berlin Diary": "I am a camera with its shutter open, quite passive, recording, not thinking.
Recording the man shaving at the window opposite and the
woman in the kimono washing her hair. Some day, all this will
have to be developed, carefully printed, fixed." The passage and
the concept has been much quoted and often misunderstood. As
Isherwood explained in interview years later:

> . . . what I really meant by saying, "I am a camera," was *not*
> I am a camera all the time, and that I'm *like* a camera. It
> was: I'm in the strangest mood at this particular moment,
> not the kind of mood that I'm usually in, a mood where I
> just sit and register impressions through the window—visual
> data, as people say—in a quite blah sort of way without any
> reaction to it, like a camera. My usual mood would have been
> to rush downstairs and get into the action. The idea that I
> was a person very divorced from what was going on around
> me is quite false.*

* Interview with Robert Wennesten, *Transatlantic Review,* Nos. 42/43, p. 19.

Towards the end of October Stephen Spender arrived in Brussels with a friend whom we shall call Jimmy Younger. Stephen, too, wished to lead the life of a literary exile, and the four of them decide to go to Portugal, where at least the weather would be warmer. Just prior to their departure in early December, Christopher went back to England to arrange a few things at his mother's, and saw Morgan Forster and several other friends.

On December 10 Stephen, Jimmy, Christopher and Heinz caught a Brazilian boat at Antwerp and set sail for Lisbon. Jimmy was a young Welshman with red hair, a ready smile and a good sense of discipline, inherited from a spell in the regular army. Christopher adored his sense of fun and his vernacular. Although by no means an intellectual, he understood poetry, and revelled in political argument. Christopher also found him physically attractive.

On board ship they started a group diary, which they continued in Portugal. The ship called briefly at Oporto, then docked in Lisbon on December 17. They found a hotel (the Nunes) in Sintra, about twenty-four kilometres outside the capital. They discovered it was very easy to rent houses in the village, and chose one named the Villa Alecrim do Norte, which had five bedrooms and was owned by a tweedy Englishwoman who lived nearby. Prices in Portugal were then very cheap, so that they were able to afford both a cook and a maid.

Christopher continued working on his epic *Paul Is Alone*, while Stephen wrote *Forward from Liberalism* and the play *The Trial of a Judge*. Jimmy Younger acted as Stephen's secretary, while Heinz was kept occupied with a menagerie of animals. Right from the start, they lived in the knowledge that sooner or later the German consulate would catch up with Heinz and order his conscription.

Christopher became very popular among the ladies of the English community, accepting invitations and having them round for tea. They were pleased to have a nice young man in their midst and, like all well-bred Englishwomen, did not presume to ask themselves exactly what he was doing with Heinz. Several of them were involved in spiritualism.

The Dog Beneath the Skin opened at the Westminster Theatre in London in January 1936. Kathleen attended a preview of it, and sent details to Christopher. Auden and Rupert Doone, of the Group Theatre Company, had changed the ending and cut out one part.

At the beginning of February the inhabitants of the villa started attending the casino at Estoril, which soon became a fatal attraction, especially for Heinz. It was a particularly sinister place in the afternoon, when a smaller number of really dedicated gamblers were at the tables. The problem was, however, that the weather was so bad there was very little else to do, particularly for Heinz, whose outdoor activities were thwarted.

Meanwhile, Christopher had promised John Lehmann by post that he would write a piece for the third issue of *New Writing*. However, he was reluctant to send off a story he had just finished, which was the prototype of "Sally Bowles." He had written to Lehmann in January:

> There *is* a section of The Lost ready—about an English girl who sings in a Berlin cabaret, but I hardly think it would suit the serious tone of New Writing. It is rather like Anthony Hope's The Dolly Dialogues. It is an attempt to satirise the romance-of-prostitution racket. Good heter stuff.
>
> (dated 1/16/36)

It is mystifying why Christopher should have felt that "Sally Bowles" was any less "serious" than "The Nowaks," but it is clear that his fictionalisation of Jean Ross gave him many headaches. As early as July 1933, in Greece, he had written to Olive Mangeot that he had written the Jean part of the novel, yet nearly three years and countless revisions later, he was still not satisfied. A few weeks later, he wrote again to John Lehmann:

"I'm afraid I couldn't get the proposed story ready in time for the *next* number. It is finished after a fashion but there's something radically wrong with it at present: it must be thought over."

In the meantime, he offered Lehmann a selection from his Berlin diaries: "About five thousand words. But don't have it if you don't want. It is only mildly (heter) dirty and chiefly about my landlady, fellow lodgers, pupils, etc." Lehmann did want the extracts, but wished to settle the "Sally Bowles" problem first, so the project was temporarily shelved.

On March 14 Stephen Spender and Jimmy Younger left Portugal—not for Greece, but for Spain, from which news of republican excesses against churches and right-wing newspaper offices were filtering through. Two days later Wystan Auden arrived to start working on *The Ascent of F6* (whose original title was *The Summit*). Christopher sketched out the plot, then they wrote separate scenes (see Appendix Two). Wystan wrote indoors, protected against the spring sun, while Christopher sat outside in the garden. There is far more of Isherwood's writing in the play than there is in *The Dog Beneath the Skin.* Working intensively, they finished it within a month.

The theme of *The Ascent of F6* is motivation: the reasons behind a person's action are what make the action heroic or empty, lofty or base—it is not always easy to make the distinction between the two extremes. This theme might in part explain some of the confusion in the play, which is not as crisp as its predecessor. The complexity of the characters in *F6* may be truer to real life, but that does not necessarily make for better drama. Ostensibly, it is a play about a mountain climbing. As Isherwood explained once in an interview:

> We consciously thought of a subject, the study of a leader like Lawrence of Arabia, but translated into terms of mountain climbing—*The Ascent of F6.* We wanted to contrast mountain climbing for climbing's sake and mountain climbing used for political ends, just as Lawrence went into the desert first because he loved it, and ended up being used politically.*

The whole Isherwood concept of the Test must also be taken into account, for mountain climbing is one of the purest forms of "proving" oneself.

During Wystan's stay at Sintra they became friends with the exiled German dramatist Ernst Toller, one of whose plays was translated and adapted by Auden as *No More Peace!* Also a poet and a revolutionary, Toller was a handsome man, with great charisma, and Christopher well understood how he inspired the admiration of countless opponents of the Nazi régime. They met again a few times in the thirties, in London and in New York, and

---

* Interview with W. I. Scobie, *The Art of Fiction*, XLIX (1975).

then in 1939 Toller committed suicide in the latter city. Christopher was to record his memories of the man, and these were published years later (in 1953) in the first issue of Spender's magazine *Encounter* as "The Head of a Leader." In that piece Isherwood confesses that for a while he avoided Toller, as Toller had a shameless and efficient way of enlisting help from friends and acquaintances.

In Portugal, however, Christopher was only too glad to have the stimulation of new faces and minds. Earlier in the year he had written to Olive Mangeot asking her to collar Claud Cockburn the next time she saw him, to ask if he didn't know some interesting people in Portugal for Christopher to meet. Christopher was a great admirer of Cockburn's splendidly subversive publication *The Week*, which was one of his only sources of information during his wandering years.

Wystan left in mid-April, then Christopher set himself down to serious work on "Sally Bowles," the final draft being completed on June 21. Before sending it to John Lehmann for *New Writing*, however, he posted it to Edward Upward for his comments. He was also still at work on *Paul Is Alone*, and a resuscitated autobiographical project, provisionally entitled *Scenes from an Education*.

On June 25 the inevitable happened. Heinz received his calling-up papers. Christopher went to see a lawyer to see if Heinz could not be naturalised as a Portuguese citizen, but he was told that there was no hope.

Shortly they were joined by a friend of Christopher's from his Berlin days, William Robson-Scott. Robson-Scott had taught at the University of Berlin until he was forced to resign, largely because of his obvious anti-Nazi stance. He was a reassuring man to have around in times of trouble, English and eminently practical, with a studious face emphasised by his glasses, and short hair. He introduced some friends of his to Christopher—James and Tania Stern, who had just left Spain. They proved to be the ideal married couple for whom Christopher had been looking, and soon moved into the villa.

James Stern, a short-story writer, had had an exciting life, having followed many humble or unusual trades in various parts of the world—from being a bank clerk in Berlin to a cattle farmer in

South Africa. He grumbled incessantly, but could be wildly funny, and was, Christopher felt, a hypochondriac like himself. Tania Stern was German and beautiful, and had taught before leaving her native land, mainly Jewish and intellectual pupils. She was an expert at physical exercises, for she had her own personal system. Every day they would spend hours huddled round the radio, listening for every scrap of news about the fascist rebellion. James Stern felt the newspapers were totally unreliable, full of lies. Often he shut himself up in his room for the whole day, seeing nobody but Tania, especially if Christopher had some of his ladies around for tea. Stern loathed the social niceties, and found the overt support of the rebels among some of the English colony quite despicable. Christopher liked him for his sometimes crotchety ways, but it was with Tania that Christopher really became friends. He has always had a good way with ladies, knowing exactly how to mix flattery and clowning.

Christopher seems to have warned Kathleen during a visit she made in June that arrangements for Heinz's change of nationality were going to cost a lot of money, which she would have to produce, as Christopher did not then have capital of his own. At Christopher's urging, she entered negotiations with a lawyer found by Hamilton in Brussels, who demanded a thousand pounds for the necessary expenses, with no guarantee of a successful outcome. Kathleen called in her cousin Sir William Graham Greene of the Admiralty for advice, and obviously concurred with him that the whole deal sounded very shady indeed. However, there seemed no alternative.

Kathleen wrote to Christopher suggesting that it would be much easier for everyone if he were nearer the centre of these operations, so in mid-August he and Heinz packed up, to return to Belgium, establishing a base first at Ostend and then in Brussels again. Mexico now seemed to be the best hope for Heinz. Hamilton introduced Christopher to someone who purported to be an official of the Mexican legation in Brussels, and a large amount of money changed hands. He was told that Heinz would receive his Mexican nationalisation papers before the end of November.

Meanwhile, John Lehmann was beset by doubts about the Sally Bowles story. He liked it immensely, but wondered if it was not too long for *New Writing*. More importantly, he was concerned about an abortion episode in it. He was not sure that the printers would agree to set it, and asked if it could not be removed. Christopher replied on January 2, 1937:

> About SALLY, you know, I'm doubtful, though quite open to conviction. It seems to me that Sally, without the abortion sequence, would just be a silly little capricious bitch. Besides, what would the whole thing lead up to? And down from? The whole idea of the study is to show that even the greatest disasters leave a person like Sally essentially unchanged. . . .
>
> Surely the less pretentious Berlin Diary is really a much better bit of work? And there you have the New Humanism laid on rich and thick. I'm not at all sure that Sally wouldn't merely annoy the Left Wing, anyhow. Because it is very dilletant [*sic*] in tone.

The "Berlin Diary" was published in the third issue of *New Writing*, while *Sally Bowles* appeared as a separate book, published by the Hogarth Press in 1937. Lehmann had given up his attempt to try to persuade Christopher to change the abortion episode. Anyone who knew Jean Ross during the 1930s would have had very little trouble in recognising her as the basis for Sally Bowles, especially because of certain turns of phrase, even though the portrait was only a caricature. Several of Jean's friends were shocked by the book, and, unlike Gerald Hamilton, she avoided all possible publicity connected with it. She was a brave and kind woman, by now deeply committed to left-wing causes, and the book did not help her image much among those comrades who realised she was the model. However, Isherwood never publicly divulged the identity of Sally Bowles until after Jean's death in 1973. When some bloodhound journalists tracked her down at the time of the stage-show *Cabaret*, she politely declined their invitation to see it.

Sally Bowles is one of the most successful novellas in English literature. It has a style so smooth and seemingly simple that the reader glides through the story with consummate ease. However, when one rereads the story with a critical eye, one is struck by its economy of words for maximum effect. From the beginning, the reader is given a precise and subjective impression of Sally's physical nature which fixes her instantly in his mind:

As she dialled the number, I noticed that her finger-nails were painted emerald green, a colour unfortunately chosen, for it called attention to her hands, which were much stained by cigarette-smoking and as dirty as a little girl's. She was dark enough to be Fritz's [Wendel's] sister. Her face was long and thin, powdered dead white. She had very large brown eyes which should have been darker, to match her hair and the pencil she used for her eyebrows.

"Hilloo," she cooed, pursing her brilliant cherry lips as though she were going to kiss the mouthpiece: "Ist dass Du, mein Liebling?" (p. 2.)

The person on the other end of the line, the narrator is fascinated to learn, is the man she made love with the night before. He is but one of a stream of lovers, whose attributes, implicitly demanded by Sally, should be prowess in bed and an ability to pay off her debts. It comes as a bit of a shock to Chris, the narrator, that she is only nineteen. With gentle, unassuming questions he prises her life story out of her. Soon she moves into Chris's flat, for purely economic reasons. They become great friends, and are nearly whisked off round the world by one of her lovers. However, eventually their close relationship disintegrates.

During the winter of 1936–37 several left-wing writers from Britain went to Spain, either as reporters or as fighters for the republican government. At least for the first few months the Spanish Civil War seemed a clear case of black and white, a rallying point for all those who despised the perverted values and behaviour of fascism. Throughout the decade, poetry, drama and other writings had been full of the imagery of confrontation, of the battle between good and evil, young and old. Denied the chance of partaking in the Great War because of their age, the young writers of a slowly coalescing generation suddenly had a well-defined cause for which they could stand up and be counted. They had the necessary motivation to write literate propaganda for their beliefs, to develop what Auden called "parable-art, that art which shall teach man to unlearn hatred and learn love."*

* "Psychology and Art To-day," in Geoffrey Grigson, ed., *The Arts To-day* (1935), p. 20.

At Christmas Christopher heard from Wystan that he would be leaving for Spain in January, preferably as an ambulance driver. Jimmy Younger enlisted with the International Brigade, and came to Brussels for Christmas, but without Stephen Spender. Instead he was accompanied by Giles Romilly, a nephew of Winston Churchill. Christopher, Heinz and Gerald Hamilton did their best to give them a good time before packing them off to battle. Jimmy was very soon to be disillusioned. Stephen Spender also went off to Spain, in January 1937; he had recently joined the Communist Party and was on an assignment for the *Daily Worker*.

In early January Christopher met Wystan Auden in Paris. Wystan had left Britain in a blaze of publicity, the young poet romantically throwing himself into danger. Christopher watched wistfully from the sidelines, conscious of the fact that he too might have been carried away by the swell of enthusiasm for Spain if he was not so bound up with arrangements for Heinz.

At the beginning of February Christopher went to London to sit in on rehearsals of *The Ascent of F6*, which Rupert Doone was to direct at the Mercury Theatre. Doone and Isherwood got on well, and Christopher soon found himself absorbed into the intimate little working group that included Robert Medley and Benjamin Britten. The play opened on February 26 to a capacity audience which included Kathleen and Wystan Auden's mother. The avalanche was effectively simulated by rigging a microphone to the backstage flush toilet. Wystan returned from Spain on March 4, and went to see a performance of the play. Rupert Doone and Christopher had made a few changes in Wystan's absence, so that suddenly during the performance Wystan exclaimed in a loud whisper heard by the rest of the audience, "My dear, what have you *done* to it?"

Christopher returned to Belgium about ten days later. There was no good news about Mexico, but they now moved to France. The Sterns were living in Paris, and Tania had sensibly suggested that it would be a good idea for Heinz to learn a trade. She knew a silversmith, and fixed up for Heinz to apprentice with him.

Also in Paris were Cyril Connolly and his wife, Jean, and their friend Tony Bower. Connolly was one of Christopher's most admiring critics, and Christopher appreciated his wit and culture.

Tony Bower was an amusing, wildly generous young man, and slightly complicated things over the coming months by falling in love with Christopher.

Christopher went once more to London, on April Fool's Day. Almost immediately, he contracted a seriously infected mouth. Kathleen, hardened by her experiences with her often invalid mother, did not seem greatly worried about this, which infuriated Christopher, who felt that she ought to show more concern. In moments of delirious fury, he almost hoped he would die, just to show her. The doctor later confided that he had been puzzled and worried by the infection.

There were many visitors to the sick-bed: Wystan Auden, Edward and Hilda Upward, Tony Bower over from Paris. Wystan went over to Paris on the thirteenth, and soon phoned to London to tell Christopher that Heinz had got into trouble. He had lost his identity card in a street fight, had been identified to the police as a male prostitute and was accused of seducing a deaf and dumb chambermaid in the small hotel where he was staying. The police told him that he would have to leave when his residence permit expired on April 15. Tony Bower gallantly agreed to return to Paris and escort Heinz to Luxembourg.

Ten days later, Christopher was well enough to join his boyfriend. After a wicked Channel crossing, he stopped off in Brussels for a dinner-conference with Gerald Hamilton. Re-united with Heinz in Luxembourg, Christopher felt irrationally reassured, and ready to believe the news from the Brussels lawyer that a Mexican passport would be available very shortly. Gerald Hamilton came down to the Grand Duchy during the first week of May to confirm the report.

However, on May 12 police arrived at the hotel in Luxembourg where Christopher and Heinz were staying, and informed them Heinz was to be expelled. Christopher phoned the lawyer, who said that Heinz should go back into Germany; then a short visa for Belgium could be arranged. When Heinz crossed into Germany, he was arrested by Gestapo agents as a draft evader. A German lawyer came over to Brussels to discuss the boy's defence in the forthcoming trial. Christopher wept sometimes when he thought of his friend, but forced himself to get on with his writing. He could never know whether he had been hoodwinked or betrayed by Gerald Hamilton, but he had a terrible foreboding that he might never see Heinz again.

William Robson-Scott arrived in Brussels at a crucial moment, and as before proved a reassuring presence. Christopher was just finishing a draft of his autobiographical book, now entitled *Lions and Shadows*, like one of his first aborted novels. He dedicated it to Robson-Scott. Soon the verdict came through from Germany: six months in prison, then a year of labour service for the state, then two years in the army. Considering the way many homosexuals were treated in Nazi Germany, Heinz got off lightly.

Christopher decided to admit defeat and returned to London, where he accepted an assignment to write the screenplay for a film to be directed by Ludwig Berger, based on a story by Carl Zuckmayer. Alexander Korda was the producer. The film work cannot have made much impression on Christopher, as he remembers almost nothing about it. The film was never made, a fate shared by many of the movie projects on which he worked in subsequent years. He was never very lucky as a film writer, but at least he was always paid.

Wystan and Christopher moved to Dover together in August. The unsatisfactory climax to the Heinz affair had driven them closer together, and they maintained their unique friend-lover relationship. They rented rooms at 9 East Cliff, and wrote. Christopher finished *Lions and Shadows*, and they produced the first draft of their third and final play, *On the Frontier*. *Lions and Shadows* was autobiographical but should be read as fiction, or so Christopher wrote in its brief preface. As one or two people had requested that they have pseudonyms in the book, he decided to give everyone false names, with the exception of I. A. Richards and one or two others. However, most of the characters in the book are easily recognisable (see Appendix One). Not all of them were very pleased. André Mangeot, in a moment of expansive Gallic exaggeration, said the book had ruined his whole life. The most interesting curiosity is that Christopher felt unable to write coherently about his family, which is not mentioned at all, apart from the most fleeting, vague reference, such as to Kathleen, "my female relative." The book is often very funny, and is highly self-critical.

8

On January 19, 1938, Christopher and Wystan set off on their journey to the Far East. Several press photographers were at the station to see them on to the Dover train. Christopher sported a tartan woolly scarf and his familiar cheeky grin. Wystan was more pointedly casual, his spotted bow-tie askew, a camera slung over one shoulder, while his face had the cool, steely glare of an ace reporter.

They travelled via Paris to Marseilles, where they boarded the French liner *Aramis*, whose final destination was the Japanese port of Kobe. During the voyage out, they wrote a joint diary, part of which was destined to appear in *Harper's Bazaar* (as "Escales," October 1938). Needless to say, much was recorded in the diary which never appeared in print. Christopher was still addicted to noting down overheard conversations verbatim, and their fellow passengers provided a rich source of curious anecdote, being a mixture of colonial officials or plantation owners returning slowly from home leave, and a few idle tourists. As ever, Christopher had an ear for the absurd, the pompous and the scatological.

In the magazine article, Christopher was to write that the ship was like a hospital, and its passengers isolated from the realities of the world in boring quarantine, growing restless and peevish in their inactivity. His medical analogies hide the fact that both he and Wystan were hard at work on the play *On the Frontier*. Wystan was also to write several poems, some of which were later published as part of their oriental travel book, *Journey to a War*.

The ship made stops in Egypt, Djibouti, Ceylon and Vietnam, allowing the travellers brief forays into town and countryside which were welcome respites from deck and cabin life. In Egypt they acquired some pornographic postcards, but began to have second thoughts about the advisability of arriving in conservative Hong Kong with obscene material in their luggage, so nervously lobbed the cards out of their porthole. Unfortunately, the wind was blowing in the wrong direction, and they were dismayed to see one of the pictures flurrying into the deck below. Christopher tore downstairs to try and retrieve it, but found half a dozen sailors sitting round a table eating supper. The sailors did not seem to have spotted the card, which lay face down on the floor, but Christopher decided it was too risky to pick it up, so planned to get it back later. Of course, by then it was gone.

On February 16 they arrived in Hong Kong, finding it disappointingly grey, the harbour shrouded in a chilly, drizzling fog. They stayed with the vice-chancellor of Hong Kong University, and were fêted by the local expatriate dignitaries, from the governor downwards. Wystan, currently (as Christopher described it in a letter to John Lehmann) "in a Proust fit" enjoyed the lavish hospitality and outdated gentility greatly, but for Christopher the visit was marred by a severe bout of the local stomach upset known as the Hong Kong Dog. Nonetheless, he was able to write cheerily to Lehmann:

> If I am killed in China, I'd like my name on the [*New Writing*] notepaper just the same, with a cute little black cross against it! Our plans are taking shape. Next Saturday, we cross for one night to Macao, the Portuguese colony which provides stolid Hong Kong with its nightlife; there are even special late boats, leaving there at three in the morning! On Sunday afternoon, we return here, pack and leave early on Monday for Canton by river-boat. There are no Jap troops round Canton, but the Jap planes bomb the railway every afternoon, and drop bombs all round the city. On the whole, people say, they've behaved well, in so far as they've stuck to

military objectives and avoided actually slaughtering civilians.
The chief danger is that they're very bad shots.

(dated 2/24/38)

Few Chinese would have agreed with Christopher that the Japanese had "behaved well." This was a bloody, brutal war—a fragrant example of colonial expansionism without any concern for the Chinese civilian population. But Christopher relied entirely on the comments and judgements of his new acquaintances, and there was no shortage of people in the expatriate community in Hong Kong who admired Japanese "discipline." Auden and Isherwood had set out on their Chinese journey woefully unprepared. Not only did they not know the language (therefore being dependent on sometimes dubiously objective interpreters), but they were ignorant of Chinese history, and had minimal information about the actual state of Sino-Japanese hostilities. However, in their very ignorance, they sometimes proved to be interesting observers.

From the outset, Christopher noted everything that was comic or absurd, so that at times his travel account sounds like a jolly romp. Even if he and Wystan found much to laugh about, however, they were both made increasingly aware over the coming months of the horrible realities of war. Their superficial flippancy hid a far deeper appraisal of the senseless butchery around.

Their initiation was gradual. They travelled without incident by river-boat from Hong Kong to Canton, giggling at the sight of a British officer in white ducks who was practising golf shots on the deck of a Royal Navy steamer, or pointing excitedly at a Japanese gunboat. Approaching Canton itself, they could distinguish the different European "factories," trading-houses with the nation's flag, swastika or other emblem painted clearly on the roof to show Japanese bombers they were neutral territory. In keeping with the red-carpet treatment that they were to receive during much of their tour, they were met at the quayside by a car from the British consulate-general. They stayed in a missionary compound just outside the city, and Christopher blanched over tea and sultana cake in the neat drawing-room of his hosts' house, as they carried on a polite conversation, apparently oblivious to the air-raid that had suddenly started around them.

The following morning, Christopher and Wystan trotted off with their notebooks and pencils for the first of a series of interviews with authoritative Chinese and Europeans, many of whom were extremely distinguished or knowledgeable, even if the young travellers were not always quite sure to whom they were talking. Their first quarry was Tseng Yang-fu, who was at that time both mayor of Canton and a member of the central committee of the Kuomintang (KMT). A graduate of Pittsburgh University, and a former political vice-minister of railways, he was the ideal person to tell them about the all-important problems of communications, in their own language. As they drove to the interview in a chauffeured limousine, a Union Jack fluttering from the bonnet, they wondered what on earth they were going to ask the mayor. Suddenly they had to come to terms with the fact that officialdom would see them as competent war correspondents, even if they themselves found the concept distinctly ridiculous. Christopher's report of Tseng Yang-fu's folksy interpretation of the knot of the Sino-Japanese situation is a pretty deplorable indication of journalistic shallowness, couched in the spelling of a music-hall Oriental:

> We not wan' to fight Japan. Japan wan' to fight *us!* Japan velly foolish. First she wan' to be number *tree* power. Then number *two.* Then number *one.* Japan industrial country, you see. Suppose we go Japan, dlop bomb—woo-er, boom! Velly bad for Japanese, I think? Japanese come to China. China aglicultural country. Japanese dlop bomb—woo-er, boom! Only break up earth, make easier for Chinese plough land! Much people is killed of course. Velly cruel. But we have lots more, yes? Ha, ha, ha, ha!*

Fortunately, the perspicacity of Christopher's note-taking improved over the coming weeks.

The next day, they were entertained by the governor of Kwangtung province, and met other leading political figures, but they were anxious to get up-country, nearer the action. They kitted themselves out for the journey ahead, buying collapsible camp-beds and mosquito nets, and had visiting cards printed with

* *Journey to a War.*

their names rendered phonetically into Chinese characters as Au Dung and Yi Hsiao-wu. Any attempt at appearing to be intrepid adventurers, however, was ruined by Auden's refusal to admit any discomfort. As he was suffering from corns, he travelled through hell and high water in carpet slippers.

The journey by train to Hankow was long and potentially dangerous, though their major problem turned out to be boredom. Thanks to the influence of the governor, they had been given the best possible accommodation, in a two-berth cabin in the first-class coach, but the passing countryside and people were not enough to entertain them for the two days and three nights of the journey. They whiled away the time by reading aloud from Anthony Troloppe's *Framley Parsonage* and Sir Walter Scott's *Guy Mannering*, or screeched themselves into hysterics by singing operatic arias in falsetto, to the consternation of other passengers. As in their preparatory school-days, they became entangled in violent religious arguments, causing Auden to prophetically exclaim: "One of these days, my dear, you're going to have *such* a conversion!"

The Chinese Nationalist Government, under Chiang Kai-shek, was then based in Hankow, which had become the centre of furious diplomatic and military activity. At the time, the Kuomintang and the Communist Party were just about on speaking terms, in the hope of forming some sort of common front against Japanese aggression. Chou En-lai himself was in town, as well as a herd of pressmen, ambassadors, missionaries, spies and military of numerous nationalities. Christopher and Wystan camped down in a big empty room of the British consul's residence.

Their list of helpful contacts reads like an extract from the *International Who's Who*. They visited the left-wing American ecclesiastic Bishop Roots, whose house had been nicknamed the Moscow-Heaven Axis, since Agnes Smedley, long-time friend of the Chinese Communist Party, had moved in. The Dutch documentary film-maker Joris Ivens (who had earlier co-operated with Ernest Hemingway on the film *Spanish Earth*) was able to give them considerable information about the Eighth Route Army and Mao Tse-tung. Someone suggested that it would be possible for them to fly in one of the dangerous little planes that went over the Japanese lines from time to time, but fortunately for Christopher's nerves, nothing materialised.

Christopher's biggest shock in Hankow, however, came from news that had nothing to do with China. He and Wystan paid a call on one of Generalissimo Chiang Kai-shek's German military advisers, General Baron Alexander von Falkenhausen, whose ADC greeted them cheerily with the tidings that the Bundeswehr had just marched into Austria. Their minds were reeling from the enormity of the news, worry for their friends and the possible consequences of the *Anschluss,* yet they had to go through the motions of putting intelligent questions about the Far East situation to the gaunt general in pince-nez. Little did they realise that only two months later, Hitler would recall a protesting von Falkenhausen to Germany, where he was approached by Adam von Trott zu Solz to assassinate the Führer.

Mme Chiang Kai-shek had the English visitors round for tea the following day, and Christopher fell under the spell of her exquisite, almost terrifying charm. She dazzled him with her ability to switch roles in mid-conversation, at one moment the super-cultivated woman with a broad knowledge of Western and Oriental literature and art, at the next, a technical expert, discussing aeroplane engines or machine guns. He had heard that she could be ruthless and cold-blooded, but witnessed only her graciousness. She looked tired and rather ill, but gave the two men a lecture on her New Life Movement, which she hoped would restore dignity and prosperity to an ailing China. On their way out, Christopher and Wystan ran into the Generalissimo himself, and persuaded him to pose for a photograph with his wife, in which he stiffened visibly like a schoolboy on parade.

In terms that would have had his London left-wing friends at his throat, Christopher concluded that whatever the Chiangs' faults, and even though they were by necessity cut off from the lives of the working people of China, it was "impossible not to feel that the leadership of the Chiangs is vital for China, as long as this war continues. And Madame herself, for all her artificiality, is certainly a great heroic figure."*

Sadly, Christopher was never able to make a direct comparison with Mao Tse-tung. Through friends of Agnes Smedley's, he was

* Ibid.

offered the chance of visiting the Eighth Route Army, but turned it down, on the grounds that too many journalists had been to see them. Wystan did, however, briefly meet Chou En-lai.

Leaving the city, Christopher and Wystan headed for Cheng-chow, moving nearer the front line. Indeed, the front line was moving nearer them. The terrain was depressing. Auden stared at the miserable mud plain around Minchuan and christened it "The Bad Earth." Daily, they met doctors and missionaries, getting wildly conflicting reports. A pro-Franco Spanish bishop informed them that the Japanese would be a jolly good thing for China, as they would sort out some of the mess of the incompetent Chinese, but others clearly did not agree. At Suchow, they found missionaries bricking up the walls of their compound in preparation for the expected Japanese occupation.

They acquired the necessary passes to go to the front, and on March 27, set off for the battle in a rickshaw, later transferring to horseback. They saw no real action, though there was the odd exploding shell and a few Japanese planes flew overhead. A Chinese guide pointed out a position saying, "Over there are the lines to which we shall retreat," to which Auden remonstrated severely, "But you *mustn't* retreat!" Their remarks were no longer facetious. They had seen the maimed and the dying in field hospitals, and smelt the odour of gas-gangrene. Their sympathies were consolidating behind the Chinese in the brunt of overwhelming Japanese force, but they were rapidly becoming sickened with the whole institution of war.

In mid-April, they returned to Hankow, to find the capital transformed by spring. Japanese air-raids had become more frequent, but socialising continued unabated. Through the British ambassador, Sir Archibald Clark-Kerr (a great admirer of *Sally Bowles*, and an extremely unstuffy diplomat), they met the traveller and journalist extraordinary Peter Fleming, who was then working in China as the *Times* correspondent. Christopher found him a subtly comic figure, with his sleek good looks and pukka sahib air. Yet he was conscious of the fact that Fleming was a professional in a game in which he and Auden were rank amateurs, and they found Fleming's company instructive as well as amusing.

Fleming accompanied them in May on the first leg of a journey to Shanghai, by a complicated route avoiding Japanese-occupied territory. They marvelled at Fleming's ability to say and do exactly the right thing, thus ensuring co-operation from the Chinese. To keep up their spirits, they recited passages from an imaginary book entitled *With Fleming to the Front*.

In the summer of 1938, the Japanese still respected the neutrality of the Foreign Settlements in Shanghai, in which lived many of the diplomatic corps, the traders and the missionaries. A large number of Chinese had fled into the safety of these colonial havens when the Japanese occupied the city. The westernised part of Shanghai offered everything that the traveller could wish for, from strictly Chinese entertainments to the latest American movies. Prostitution was rife, and the city was renowned throughout the Far East for its boy whores. Although staying with the British ambassador (currently in Shanghai), and often occupied in photographing and documenting the abysmal poverty and working conditions in the city, Christopher and Wystan nonetheless found the opportunity to spend many afternoons in the bathhouses that were staffed by attractive and willing youths.

The period in China was the longest that Wystan and Christopher ever spent together. Christopher's despotism and sulks often irritated Wystan, and Christopher could be infuriated by his friend's dogmatism, yet in general their relationship was amicable, more friends than lovers, yet very special friends.

Now that their stay in China was drawing to a close, they had to make a decision about where to go. They had deliberately not made any specific plans. They decided to return to Europe via New York, thus making a complete tour of the world since their departure from England, but got a nasty shock when the American consulate in Shanghai refused their applications for entry visas. Fortunately, they were able to make use of their friendship with the British ambassador to obtain a reversal of this decision; a persistent refusal from the American consular official, which would have meant that the friends would travel back entirely through Canada, would probably have changed the whole direction of Christopher's life.

They crossed the Pacific on the *Empress of Asia* of the Canadian Pacific Line, which called at three Japanese ports en route, a prospect they were not relishing, as they were both by now sworn enemies of imperial Japan. One stop-over was long enough for them to travel to Tokyo and stay overnight. They ran into a delirious mob that was seeing off a band of soldiers, which so shook Wystan that he dropped and broke his only pair of glasses.

However, the ten-day sea voyage from Yokohama to Vancouver enabled them to rest from their physical and mental exertions in Asia. They travelled by train across North America, making no significant stops before New York. There they were met at Penn Central by the writer and fashion magazine literary editor George Davis. They had known Davis in London, and were delighted when he immediately handed over wads of dollar bills that he had earned for them by selling travel articles that they had sent.

For nine days, Davis gave them a wild guided tour of New York: the streets, bars and restaurants of Manhattan; Coney Island on the Fourth of July; the chic literary parties, where everyone was dying to meet them and hear of their experiences. They revelled in their instant popularity, and Christopher's senses were hit harder by the city than by any other since Berlin. Christopher's instant love-affair with America was clinched by a blind date that he initially treated as a joke, but which developed into something much bigger.

George Davis happily assumed the role of pimp in the extravagance of his hospitality. He offered to find Christopher a boy of his own specifications; half disbelievingly, Christopher asked for an intelligent eighteen-year-old, blond "and with sexy legs." Such a boy was produced almost immediately, but as he was to progress into a life far removed from that of a call-boy, we shall accept his pseudonym of Vernon. Christopher was immediately attracted to him, not only because he was physically what he wanted, but also because he seemed to represent the youth and health of America which Christopher was ready to embrace. The final days of this first visit to New York were spent largely in Vernon's company.

Wystan and Christopher arrived back in London on July 17. Tempers had run short on the voyage across the Atlantic, and at one point Wystan had got quite maudlin, weeping in self-pity that it was always Christopher that had the best sexual adventures. Christopher even refused to have Wystan stay the night at Kathleen's house, their first day in, though not so much from any falling out as from a wish to be quite alone to enjoy the adulation due to a returning traveller back from a distant war.

Immediately, Christopher looked up old friends; indeed, he went to see his "honorary sister" Beatrix Lehmann perform the very evening of his return. At the end of July, he went to stay with John Lehmann in the Isle of Wight. His friends were avid for his news, and his adventures no doubt made him even more attractive than usual to casual homosexual acquaintances in London. He joined up with Jimmy Younger, Stephen Spender's former friend, going with him for a short holiday to Ostende in August.

Constantly on the move, he was soon in Dover with a group that included E. M. Forster, Joe Ackerley, William Plomer and T. C. (Cuthbert) Worsley, the last-mentioned having served in Spain in an ambulance unit. Although these friends could discuss the tragedies of Spain and China, their current preoccupations were naturally nearer home, as storm clouds were gathering over Europe, and war seemed inevitable. Back in London, Christopher started a journal of the crisis, from which he later quoted in the novel *Down There on a Visit*.

John Lehmann was able to give Christopher up-to-date information about Germany, as he had recently been on a brief visit to Berlin. He had even seen Heinz there, finding that the boy was managing to cope fairly well, resigned to the way things were going. Christopher thought much of him, but he was also thinking a great deal of Vernon. He had only recently returned from many months of Wystan's company and a brief affair with Jimmy Younger, and was taking advantage of the opportunities for casual encounters offered by London. His private life was thus as complex as the growing world situation, and neither did much to help him make plans for his immediate future.

Sometimes he felt fearfully depressed by the twisting turns of events. His political position had never been as rock solid as that of many of his friends, such as Edward Upward, Jean Ross and Olive Mangeot, but his intimate connections with Germany and his recent experiences of war had made his stance even more uncertain. Nonetheless, under John Lehmann's steady influence, Christopher did write to the British Foreign Office, offering his services in propaganda work in the event of war. He and Lehmann could always share a flat together in wartime London. Suddenly a reprieve appeared in the form of Chamberlain's Munich agreement. Christopher was wildly excited, but at the back of his mind, he wondered whether events had only been postponed.

Wystan, just back from a holiday in Belgium, was clearer about his intentions. He had also been deeply impressed by America, and wished to return for a lengthy period. Christopher agreed in principle to accompany him, but first they should finish their China travel book—a galling prospect, for although the events were chronologically not very distant, they had been pushed into the background by their vivid impressions of America and the awful European crisis.

Meanwhile, London literary life continued unabated, and Christopher found himself invited to an increasing number of fashionable and impressive tables. On one memorable occasion in November, he was summoned to the home of the great London hostess Lady Sybil Colefax. Virginia Woolf met him on the doorstep, and although it was not their first encounter, she noted in her diary that night:

He is a slip of a wild boy: with quicksilver eyes: nipped; jockeylike. That young man, said W. Maugham, "holds the future of the English novel in his hands."

This was not the first time Christopher had met Somerset Maugham either, but he was certainly unaware just how much the older novelist admired him. In fact, he was quite sure Maugham must consider him a very wet fish, as, slightly tipsy, Christopher tried to tell a funny story, which fizzled badly, causing him to flee the house in embarrassment.

Christopher had contact with other members of the so-called Bloomsbury Group at this period. In fact, the economist Maynard Keynes sponsored Auden and Isherwood's play *On the Frontier* in its first production at the Arts Theatre in Cambridge, opening on November 14. Keynes's wife, the former ballerina Lydia Lopokova, played the leading female role. Otherwise the team was very much that of the Group Theatre, with Rupert Doone directing, Robert Medley doing the designs and Benjamin Britten the music. The play was received kindly by the audience, but Christopher was aware that it was by no means as good as the previous ones.

Wystan and he finished *Journey to a War* in Belgium, where they had gone to spend Christmas and New Year. Wystan produced one of his scurrilous private poems (as yet unpublished) to mark the occasion of New Year 1939, full of slanderous but amusing references to their mutual friends. Celebrations were slightly dampened, however, by the fact that Christopher caught a dose of the clap. The treatment in those days was a painful affair, but Christopher viewed the business as one of the unavoidable realities of existence. Far from keeping quiet about it, he told many of his friends about his malady, even writing to E. M. Forster for amused sympathy.

Their outstanding literary commitments now out of the way, Wystan and Christopher finalised their decision to return to the United States, and booked a passage on the French ship *Champlain*, due to sail for New York on January 19, the first anniversary of their departure for China. They returned to London for a few days of hectic farewells, the warmest to a romantic youth with whom Christopher had become quickly involved even at this eleventh hour, in keeping with his sometimes reckless emotional as well as physical promiscuity. Christopher felt moved and guilty as the young man travelled with him in a taxi to the station in London, yet only hours later, Wystan and Christopher were grinning together like schoolboys on board the *Champlain*, excited by the prospect of new travels and adventures. As ever, Christopher's ego showed a remarkable instinct for survival.

PART THREE
America

9

As Auden and Isherwood's reasons for going to live in America were soon to come under considerable close and unkind scrutiny in Great Britain, it is important to know why Christopher went. Yet there is no simple answer. Like many hundreds of thousands of immigrants before and since, he saw the United States as the land of the future, a place where he could find new horizons. He had a particularly romantic image of the Far West, and both he and Wystan had been profoundly impressed by their short visit a few months previously. New York had seemed vital. Christopher had grown tired of wandering in Europe, even if such an existence were now possible, which seemed unlikely in view of the deteriorating political situation. Although he had many dear friends in London, he had no real wish to settle in England again. This was partly because he wished to be free of demanding family ties (Kathleen was already over seventy), but also because he enjoyed being a foreigner. As a foreigner, one is different, and although Christopher never adopted the more outrageously eccentric or obnoxious behaviour of some of his contemporaries, such as Brian Howard, who wished to flaunt their peculiarity, nonetheless he did savour being different. In America, he could enjoy the ultimate luxury of being a foreigner *and* living in a country where everyone spoke his language, could commission work from him and buy his books. He had a better chance of obtaining film work there than anywhere else in the world except London. Also, several men whom he greatly admired had gone before him, most notably Aldous Huxley and Gerald Heard. Finally, America meant Vernon. Whatever peccadillos great and small Christopher had enjoyed since his last brief visit to America, as soon as the ship pulled out of Southampton harbour and headed for the open sea, his vivid imagination was dreaming up fantasies of a vigorous, Whitmanesque life with the blond with the sexy legs.

As the *Champlain* pulled into New York Harbor on January 26, Christopher was immediately aware of a change in the city, now in its winter clothes. Even the ship itself, covered in snow and ice from a blizzard, seemed eerie. Premonitions that maybe New York would not live up to his wonderful memories were temporarily swept aside by the sight of familiar faces. Erika and Klaus Mann were on the quarantine launch to greet the new arrivals, while on shore, Vernon was waiting.

For a while, Christopher and Wystan lived at the George Washington Hotel, and rejoined the social whirl they had left behind, the previous summer. But soon it seemed to have lost much of its appeal. No longer were they the centre of attraction, visitors from a distant war. They were just two Englishmen among a never-ending stream of new arrivals from Europe. Nonetheless, they did have many fascinating new friends, such as the poet and balletomane Lincoln Kirstein, who later gave Christopher many important introductions to people throughout North and South America. They remained close friends for many years, then suddenly the relationship was broken off, and Isherwood became a taboo subject for Kirstein.

After a few weeks in the city, Christopher and Wystan moved into a flat at 237 East Eighty-first Street, and became better acquainted with poorer areas of town, a development which partly calmed Christopher's social conscience. They rewrote the ending of *The Ascent of F6*, which was performed in an intimate production by the Drove Players in April. The avalanche at the end of the play was simulated by a door being slammed off-stage, an effect which particularly appealed to Christopher.

One of Christopher's first literary engagements in America was an invitation to a Pen Club dinner, to which he went unaware

17. Salka Viertel as
a young woman.

18. Gottfried Reinhardt and Christopher viewing set for *Rage in Heaven* in 1940.
COURTESY OF GOTTFRIED REINHARDT.

19. Dodie (Smith) and Alec Beesley in the 1940s.

20. Swami Prabhavananda and Christopher in 1942. PHOTOGRAPHED BY AND COURTESY OF MARGARET KISKADDEN.

21. Denny Fouts ("Paul"). COURTESY OF CHRISTOPHER ISHERWOOD.

22. Bill Caskey and Christopher in 1949. PHOTOGRAPHED BY WILLIAM CASKEY;
COURTESY OF CHRISTOPHER ISHERWOOD.

23. Christopher in 1946. PHOTOGRAPHED BY WILLIAM CASKEY; COURTESY OF CHRISTOPHER ISHERWOOD.

24. Christopher, Kathleen and Richard outside Wyberslegh Hall in 1947.
COURTESY OF CHRISTOPHER ISHERWOOD.

25. Christopher and Don Bachardy in 1953. COURTESY OF CHRISTOPHER ISHERWOOD.

26. Drawing of Christopher in 1976 by Don Bachardy.

that not only was he expected to speak, but that he was also billed as the first speaker. Off the cuff, he made a speech about cross-cultural misunderstandings, based on an old *Reader's Digest* joke about a foreigner who arrives in New York for the first time and sees a woman fall out of a high office-block window and into a dustbin. The foreigner exclaims: "America must be very wasteful. That woman was good for another ten years at least." Christopher sat down, feeling rather pleased with himself, then noticed that a senior member of the American literary establishment was glaring at him. "Charming," the other writer said, cuttingly. Only later did Christopher discover that the Pen Club meeting was a deadly serious anti-fascist affair, a fact that had been communicated to all the other speakers but not to him.

On April 6 Wystan and Christopher were invited to give a lecture at the Keynote Club on West Fifty-second Street. The subject was to be "Modern Trends in English Poetry and Prose." Louis MacNeice, who had recently arrived in New York, also took part. MacNeice and Auden both read poems, while Isherwood gave a more general talk, drawing on some of his experiences in China. In the front row of the audience were some youths, including the young poet Harold Norse (then twenty-two) and his friend Chester Kallman. According to Norse, Kallman had suggested that they go to the lecture and wink at Auden, who was their literary hero. Auden read first,

> . . . babbling in his own Oxonian diction and teetering over the edge of the platform with long shoe-laces untied. We all thought he was going to fall; and the place was overheated. Somebody offered to open a window, and Auden screamed "Oh, I would LOVE that!," and we all broke up. He went on reading on the very edge of the platform and didn't see us at all. He was near-sighted. But Christopher did. We were winking and grinning and Isherwood was grinning back while Auden and MacNeice read. After the reading we went up and said we were from the Brooklyn College *Observer*, and could we interview them. Auden kind of trumpeted, "Oh, ah, see Mr. Isherwood." Christopher was very warm and sympathetic and wrote their address on a calling card and gave it to

me saying he *hoped* I'd come and see them. I was all ready, but Chester took the card. . . .*

Kallman duly called at the apartment two days later, but Auden, who must have had some inkling of what was going on, obviously expected someone else, for he exclaimed on seeing Kallman at the door, "But it's the wrong blond!" Notwithstanding, the two became immediately close, and a few days later Wystan presented the young man with a copy of Blake which he had inscribed:

> When it comes, will it come without warning
> Just as I'm picking my nose . . .

Chester Kallman stayed with Auden off and on for the rest of his life, though in later years they spent quite long periods apart. Chester and Christopher never really got on, and Auden sometimes claimed outrageously that this was because of Christopher's inherent anti-Semitism. What is more likely is that Chester was jealous of the previous relationship Christopher had had with Wystan, and possibly saw him as a threat. Auden was unfailingly generous to Kallman, whose character was far from being golden, particularly towards the end. Wystan's feeling for Chester was no doubt totally genuine, but it is rather typical of him that the first move should have come from Chester. Unlike Christopher, Wystan was not an avid hunter for sex, his mind usually being far too preoccupied with the poem on which he was currently working. However, when a convenient sexual opportunity presented itself, he rarely turned it down. The subordination of his private life to his muse was no doubt one of the reasons why Wystan had been able to go along for so long with the stop-go physical relationship with Christopher.

America saw the end of the Auden-Isherwood literary collaboration, their swan-song being yet another ending to *The Ascent of F6*, which was revived in London in June at the Old Vic, with Alec Guinness in the role of Michael Ransom. Another American production was scheduled for August at the Bucks County Playhouse, Pennsylvania, but it never came off. They never wrote another play together, nor did they fulfil an obligation to John Leh-

---

* Harold Norse in an unpublished interview with W. I. Scobie.

mann to write a travel book about America, to be entitled *Address Not Known*. They had written a scenario for a film called *The Life of an American*, but nobody ever made it. The scenario begins with a reference to the famous camera passage in *Goodbye to Berlin*, and reads:

> An interesting and cheap four-reeler could be made in which the part of the central character was taken by the camera. The hero sees life through the lens of the camera, so that the audience identifies itself with him. To make this possible, the story must be as ordinary as possible.*

Isherwood still had a lot to learn about selling a product to American film moguls.

Goodbye to Berlin was published by the Hogarth Press in 1939. It included the four stories "Sally Bowles," "The Nowaks," "The Landauers" and "On Ruegen Island," plus two extracts from "A Berlin Diary." All of these had appeared in John Lehmann's *New Writing* or *Penguin New Writing*, with the exception of "On Ruegen Island." The basic inspiration for that story was Christopher's visit to Ruegen in the summer of 1931 with Otto and Stephen Spender. However, in the story the boy Otto has an affair with a Peter Wilkinson, observed in all its torrid finality by the narrator. Thus Christopher writes from the standpoint of Stephen, who observes the unsatisfactory arrangement collapsing as a consequence of the pressure of Otto's attraction to girls, and exaggerates Peter's (i.e., his own) obsession and misery. However, Peter is not a faithful self-portrait of Christopher. According to *Christopher and His Kind*, some of Peter's mannerisms were modelled on William Robson-Scott. The book itself works beautifully. The six sections balance each other well, forming a composite picture of a mood, portraits symptomatic of their time and place. To Christopher's disappointment, however, its initial reception in America was very cool.

The last small thing that Auden and Isherwood wrote together was an article for *Vogue* magazine (dated August 15, 1939), headlined "Young British Writers—On the Way Up; Ten Authors Discussed by Two of Their Brilliant Contemporaries." The open-

---

* Quoted in Edward Mendelson, "The Auden-Isherwood Collaboration," Christopher Isherwood Issue of *Twentieth Century Literature*, October 1976.

ing blurb made a prize blunder by referring to their newly published "novel about Spain, *Journey to a War*," but the article itself
is worthy of study. The first two paragraphs are almost an apology
for Isherwood's own fictional method of the period:

> Times of crisis, like our own, are unfavourable to the art of
> the novelist.
>
> The realistic novelist, trying to write about Europe today,
> is like a portrait-painter whose model refuses to sit still. He
> may hope to catch certain impressions, jot down a few sugges-
> tive notes—but the big, maturely considered masterpiece
> must wait for better times. Most of what passes for fiction is,
> of necessity, only a kind of high-grade news reporting. The
> writer is far too close to his violently moving, dangerous sub-
> ject.

The ten writers chosen for the Auden-Isherwood accolade were:
George Orwell, Ralph Bates, Arthur Calder-Marshall, Graham
Greene, Stephen Spender, Rex Warner, Edward Upward, Henry
Green, William Plomer and James Stern. Cecil Day Lewis and
Louis MacNeice did not qualify because they were poets; Stephen
Spender scraped through because he had published some prose.

By the late spring Christopher had decided to leave New York
for California. He found the eastern metropolis overpowering, and
wrote to John Lehmann on May 2.

> Oh God, what a city! The nervous breakdown expressed in
> terms of architecture. The skyscrapers are all Father-fixations.
> The police cars are fitted with air-raid sirens, specially de-
> signed to promote paranoia. The elevated railway is the circu-
> lar madness. The height of the buildings produces visions
> similar to those experienced by Ransom in F6. . . .
>
> I myself am in the most Goddamawful mess. I have discov-
> ered, what I didn't realise before, or what I wasn't till now,
> that I am a pacifist. And now I have to find out what that
> means, and what duties it implies. That's one reason why I
> am going out to Hollywood, to talk to Gerald Heard and
> Huxley. Maybe I'll flatly disagree with them, but I have to
> hear their case, stated as expertly as possible. And I have to
> get ready to cope with the war situation, if or when it comes.

At this stage Christopher's newly found pacifism was not based on any religious convictions. His thinking about the probability of war with Germany had inevitably confronted him with the possibility of pointing a gun at, or dropping a bomb on, Heinz. This he could never do. But, he reasoned, if he could not drop a bomb on Heinz, then he could not drop a bomb at all. Was not every German somebody's Heinz? The physical horrors of war as witnessed in China had also left their mark on his consciousness. This decision to become a pacifist, arrived at during the calm of the Atlantic crossing, necessitated a complete reappraisal of his entire political and moral standpoint.

> . . . as I now began to realise, my whole political position, left-wing anti-fascist, had been based on the acceptance of armed force. All the slogans I had been repeating and living by were essentially militaristic. Very well: throw them out. But what remained? I told myself that I should have to put my emotions back from a political on to a personal basis. I would be an individual again, with my own values, my own kind of integrity. This sounded challenging and exciting. But it raised a disconcerting question: what were the values to be?*

Christopher was convinced that Huxley and Heard might have an answer. Joking about his journey to visit these wise men, Christopher reminded friends that a fortune-teller had told him that the letter "H" would be important for his future. The real name of Vernon also began with that letter.

Gerald Heard, Christopher Wood, Aldous Huxley and his Belgian wife, Maria, had all settled in the Los Angeles area in 1937. Rumours had filtered back to Christopher and his friends in London that Heard was studying yoga, and they laughed at the thought of him dressed up in turbans and levitating over the desert. Even if Christopher was not ready to admit the possibility of his taking up a religion, he was in harmony with Heard's pacifist beliefs, and was convinced of the man's intellectual integrity. He corresponded with Heard, who whetted his appetite by writing that every pacifist should acquire medical knowledge, so that a

---

* Isherwood, *An Approach to Vedanta* (pamphlet, 1963).

team of psychologically sound, well-equipped healers could be formed from them. The idea of becoming a healer appealed to Christopher, and he was hungry for more details. He also wished to meet the Huxleys, Berthold Viertel's wife (and the film world in general), and become acquainted with the farthest edge of the western world. Early in May Christopher and Vernon set off across the country by Greyhound bus, passing through Washington, New Orleans, Houston, El Paso and Albuquerque.

They settled at 7136 Sycamore Trail in Hollywood. Christopher Wood lent Christopher some money to tide them over for a while until Christopher could get some work writing for the movies. There seemed some possibility of his landing a job at MGM on a Bernard Hyman production of Eve Curie's best-selling biography of her mother, *Madame Curie*, to be directed by George Cukor and starring Greta Garbo. Huxley had been approached by Anita Loos to write the script in 1938 (his first Hollywood movie work). His treatment was then passed along to many other writers, including Scott Fitzgerald and Salka Viertel, but the project was dropped before it reached Christopher's hands. As Tom Dardis has surmised in *Some Time in the Sun*, perhaps the thought of Greta Garbo in a lab coat, sweating over bunsen burners, was too much of a gamble to take. A version of the film was finally made under Sydney Franklin in 1943, with Greer Garson as Marie Curie.

Christopher described his new life in a letter, dated July 7, 1939, to John Lehmann:

Here I am living very quietly, seeing hardly anyone, and hoping vaguely that when Berthold arrives he will get me a movie job. Life with [Vernon] reminds me very much of life with Heinz—except that he is even more serious, hates going out in the evenings, reads Suetonius, Wells and Freud, and goes to Art School. If I were happier inside myself, I would be very happy. But I never cease worrying about Europe. My "change of heart" about War, and the use of force generally, has only strengthened and been confirmed. I am sure this is how I will feel for the rest of my life. I'm afraid this will mean that I shall lose a lot of friends but, I hope, none of the real ones. I am often very homesick for London, and the

Hogarth Press office, Stephen's jokes about his psycho-analysis, walks with Morgan [Forster] near Abinger Hammer. Peggy's [Beatrix Lehmann's] imitations, rows with my Mother. When I think of my friends, I remember them all laughing. The Past appears entirely in terms of jokes. The driving-forces, which separate people, are so dull, really. Just their needs and greeds; sex and money and ambition. Oh dear, why do we have bodies? By the time they've been satisfied, there is only half an hour a day left over for Talk. And talk is all that finally matters.

Christopher's disenchantment was not only a revolt against the demands of the flesh, and disgust caused by the divisive nature of politics. He had turned against his dominant ego, was sickened by his own ambition, by Christopher Isherwood the public manifestation. Was ever ground so fertile in which to sow the seeds of Eastern religion?

Christopher's first meetings with Aldous Huxley were positive but reserved. He thought Huxley nice but bookish and inclined to be pontifical. He never lost his initial impression that Huxley and he were very different sorts of people, but that did not stop them soon becoming friends. Huxley's was essentially a great intellect, while Christopher relied more on intuition. Christopher took very easily to Maria Huxley, small and chirruping at the side of her tall, often solemn, husband. Without being a calculating hostess, Maria created some memorable parties, almost by happy accident. She became Christopher's first honorary sister in America.

Gerald Heard was more influential in Christopher's version to the Hindu philosophy to which he and Huxley had been attracted: Vedanta. Vedanta is the philosophy preached by the Vedas, the most ancient of Hindu scriptures, and teaches man to recognise his real divine nature. The aim of a man's life is gradually to manifest that divinity, which resides within him, though it is perhaps hidden. It is thus totally opposed to the dualism of some Christian sects. Vedantists believe that Truth is universal, so they are tolerant of other religions, saying that all beliefs can be valid routes to the knowledge of God if engaged in sincerely with a pure heart.

In India there was a renaissance of Vedanta in the nineteenth century, thanks to the work and teachings of the mystic Ramakrishna (1836–86). Immediately after his death, several of Ramakrishna's disciples bound themselves together in a group, led by two men, Vivekananda and Brahmananda, in order to carry on the spirit and teaching of Sri Ramakrishna. Ultimately, in 1897, this group became an order, which had its headquarters at Belur Math, near Calcutta. Swami Vivekananda visited the United States in 1893, as an unofficial delegate to the World's Fair Parliament of Religions in Chicago. His speeches made a strong impression on American audiences, and he toured several cities giving lectures. Six years later he came back to America and supervised the opening of various Vedanta centres, arranging for swamis from the newly founded Ramakrishna Order to come over from India and direct them. During this second tour of America he became acquainted with three sisters in Pasadena, California. One of these was a widow, Carrie Mead Wyckoff (later known as Sister Lalita), who kept in touch with disciples of the Ramakrishna Order after Vivekananda returned to India, where he died in 1902.

In 1928 Sister Lalita met Swami Prabhavananda, then assistant to the head of the Vedanta Center in San Francisco. The following year she invited him to Los Angeles, and put her own house in Ivor Avenue, Hollywood, and also her income, at the society's disposal. Thus the Vedanta Society of Southern California was formed, first on a very modest basis, but around 1936 the congregation grew considerably. Enough money was raised to build a small, onion-domed temple in the garden, which was dedicated in the summer of 1938. Both Huxley and Heard were very involved in the group, largely because of the personal example of Swami Prabhavananda. Gerald Heard spoke often of the swami to Christopher, but he himself had many talks with Christopher before taking him to see Prabhavananda.

Heard told Christopher that every individual has two selves: the apparent, outer self and the invisible, inner self. Everyone is familiar with the outer self, but the inner self is secret, unchanging and immortal. It has no individuality, and because it is infinite, has access to the infinite, just as sea-water has access to the sea because it *is* the sea. One's quest, therefore, should be to gain an understanding of the inner self, for which end meditation is an accepted means. Heard recommended that Christopher start gradually, having little sits of ten or fifteen minutes at a time, letting his mind fall into calm, then reminding himself of what he was searching for and why. Heard himself regularly meditated six hours a day, his whole life governed by what he referred to as "this thing." Heard's terminology was highly individual, and his manner frequently very funny. This was quite in keeping with the practice of the Ramakrishna Order, for often laughter was a means to Truth.

By the end of July Christopher felt and understood enough to ask for an interview with Swami Prabhavananda, with the aim of learning meditation. Prabhavananda was remarkable for the fact that he steadfastly refused to *appear* remarkable, making no effort whatsoever to make an instant impression upon people. His manner exuded humility, and at all times he insisted that he was directed not so much by his own ideas but by the example of the late Brahmananda, whose disciple he had been. Brahmananda had died way back in 1922, but Prabhavananda managed to convey the impression that his guru still directed the activities of the society.

Christopher found the swami to be small and unobtrusive, impressive by his very mild authority, devoid of grandeur, ostentation or severity. He seemed to represent a higher attainment than the normal run of life, while at the same time displaying a blatant human weakness by chain-smoking, a fact that unsettled many visitors. Christopher, however, found him easier to accept because of this, as he was not trying to present a false face of perfection.

Such was the joyous spontaneity of Swami Prabhavananda's smile and manner that Christopher sometimes found himself with tears welling in his eyes. But the first meeting was awkward for Christopher, who had to thrash out his prejudices against religion, the word God (say "The Self," said Prabhavananda), the quasi-mystical ritual and meditation techniques. The swami listened to his objections and reservations one by one, then quietly outlined a programme of action and non-action. He recommended that Christopher first open himself up to feel the all pervading Existence around him. Next, he should consciously emanate good will to all those around him, both those visibly near and those far off.

He should think of his body as a temple, containing the inner self; the reality of infinite knowledge and infinite peace.

Christopher was worried by apparent contradictions, which he discussed with Prabhavananda at a very early stage. How could work in the flashy, movie world be compatible with Vedanta practice? More importantly, how could the religion be reconciled with an active homosexual life?

The first point was easily answered: one had only to live like a lotus on a dirty pond, living in the world, but being manifestly pure. The second point was more complex. The swami had no objection to homosexuality *per se*; the object of sexual desire was irrelevant. What was important was the degree to which sexual and other animal desires ruled one's life. The swami and other devoted disciples practised sexual abstinence, in the belief that sexual activity distracted from the energy and totality of the spiritual quest.

Over the next few years, Christopher had to evolve his own standards in relation to this matter. Often Christopher and Gerald Heard discussed this "intentional living," the need for and the degree of self-discipline, abstinence, release from the power of possessions, the avoidance of pretension, particularly at a later stage, when one might be tempted to feel smug in one's spiritual superiority.

Christopher was right when he supposed that his new attitude to life might bring ridicule from some quarters, or even broken friendships. But his decision to follow Vedantist teaching brought far more antagonistic reaction from his acquaintances than did his pacifism. Several of his friends even now cannot quite understand what prompted him to take it up, and with them the topic is never mentioned. At times, this lack of sympathetic understanding could be wounding. The most distressing opposition came from Wystan Auden, himself increasingly devoted to the pomp and circumstance of High Anglicanism. He bluntly referred to Vedanta as mumbo-jumbo, and remained mercilessly critical of it. This did not help the friendship, but in any case they were fated to drift apart for many reasons, not least of which was that of climatic preferences. Christopher loved sunny California, which Wystan visited but hated, preferring New York. They did not correspond much, and saw each other very rarely during the next few years.

Others felt that the main objection to Vedanta was its "irrelevance" to the time, a thesis propounded by J. B. Priestley among others, pinpointed in this extract from *Letter to a Returning Serviceman* (1945):

> As you know, Robert, there are some brilliant literary acquaintances of ours who have pleasantly exiled themselves to Southern California (the choice is significant), where they announce themselves as a kind of new Yogi men, meditating hard to enlarge or change human consciousness. I for one have no quarrel with them, and am prepared to consider all reports of progress they mail to us from Hollywood, but I believe they are on the wrong track, that the change of consciousness has already happened, and that the evidence for that change is best found in the heat and muck of social conflict from which they have fled.

The anti-pacifism attacks were also not slow in arriving. During 1939, as the inevitability of a European war impressed itself upon all those of sound mind, Britons in America were faced with the straight choice of returning home and being prepared to fight, or of remaining in America and being accused of cowardice. Benjamin Britten, who had gone to America with his friend Peter Pears in 1939, suffered considerable emotional strain over this problem before returning to England in 1941. John Lehmann was not alone in his exasperation against Auden and Isherwood when war broke out: he felt that they should be in England sharing the experience and writing about it, and he was far from overjoyed to receive the following Auden poem, "September 1st, 1939":

> There is no such thing as the State
> And no-one exists alone;
> Hunger allows no choice
> To the citizen or the police;
> We must love one another or die.*

In November 1939 one of the first volleys was fired in what later became an anti-Auden-Isherwood campaign in both press

* Quoted in John Lehmann, *I Am My Brother* (1960).

and Parliament. Christopher had written a chatty, rather indiscreet letter to Gerald Hamilton about some of the German refugees he knew in California. William Hickey (Tom Driberg) of the *Daily Express* saw the letter, and printed parts of it in his column of November 27:

> The studios here are very cagey about producing anything abut the war, so I am working on a Chinese story [for Goldwyn], and spend nearly all my time with Viertel (the director of "Little Friend") and his family. [Aldous] Huxley lives in the same street; I see him daily. Also Gerald Heard. I have got very absorbed in Yoga, but it is too difficult to write about, so I won't. I have no intention of coming back to England. . . .
>
> The refugees here are very militant, and already squabbling over the future German Government. God help Germany if some of them ever get into power. Others are interested, apparently, in reconquering the Romanisches Café, and will gladly sacrifice the entire British Army to make Berlin safe for night-life. So much silly hate. So many pontifical opinions. So much I-told-you-soing.

Not only did this unfortunate letter put fuel in the fire of the "anti-coward" forces, but it also puzzled and hurt many of Christopher's German friends in California when inevitably it filtered back. He had learnt the lesson the hard way, that anything a writer or public figure writes or says can be flung back at him from unexpected quarters.

Throughout the 1930s refugees flooded out of Germany and Austria in the wake of the Nazi rise to power. A high percentage of these were Jews, but many were merely political opponents of Hitler's régime. Between 1933 and 1941 nearly two hundred thousand immigrants arrived in the United States from Austria and Germany. America was the ultimate goal for many of the refugees, though others went to Mexico and South America, and about seven thousand found themselves stranded in Cuba. Many had had to leave all their possessions behind. It is worth remembering, though, that there was a much smaller but significant flow in the opposite direction, as overseas Germans returned to the Fatherland in the belief that the Third Reich would see the realisation of a tremendous new Germany.

Europe's loss was America's gain, in so far as many of those who chose to leave Germany and central Europe were men of talent: writers, artists, film-makers, scientists and professionals. Hollywood naturally attracted much of the fresh talent, and a colony of émigré *literati* grew up in Christopher's new home town of Santa Monica. Salka Viertel became a focal point for these exiles. Without seeking social brilliance in the way that Lady Colefax or Lady Ottoline Morrell had done, she ran what was to all intents and purposes a *salon*. Thomas and Heinrich Mann were among the regulars, as were Arnold Schoenberg, Otto Klemperer, Bruno Walter and Max Reinhardt. Frequent visitors included Greta Garbo and Aldous Huxley.

Frau Viertel was born Salka Steuermann, the daughter of an artistic-legal Jewish family from Galicia, now in the Soviet Union but then a part of Poland. She had a successful acting career in Vienna and Berlin (including a stint with Max Reinhardt) before going to America with her husband Berthold. Her pianist brother Edward was one of the greatest interpreters of the music of Schoenberg, Berg and von Webern. In California Salka Viertel became a close friend of Greta Garbo, and wrote scripts for her, including the original treatment for *Queen Christina* (1933), directed by Rouben Mamoulian for MGM, and *Anna Karenina* (with Clemence Dane). She was a member of the Hollywood Anti-Nazi League, founded by Prince Hubert von und zu Loewenstein, Otto Katz (alias Breda) and others. Hollywood took its politics seriously under the influence of a committed nucleus. Berthold and Salka Viertel hosted a successful evening for André Malraux when he came to speak about Spain, and fifteen Hollywood stars gave fifteen thousand dollars each for medical aid when Ernest Hemingway and Joris Ivens toured with the film *Spanish Earth*. Salka Viertel worked with James Hilton on the screenplay of a film with the title *The Cargo of Innocence*, based on a true incident of the sea-rescue of shipwrecked Spanish orphans and nuns. However, before it could be made, America had abandoned Spain to her fate, and the subject was no longer considered interesting. Salka became an American citizen in February 1939.

By the time Christopher frequented the Viertels' Mabery Road home, Salka and Berthold had long since taken to living separate private lives, though Berthold stayed in Santa Monica on visits. Salka had her sons Hans, Peter and Tommy with her, and Gottfried Reinhardt formed part of the household. Gottfried, the younger son of Max Reinhardt (whose Salzburg château, Leopoldskron, had been expropriated by Goering), also worked for MGM, and it was he who gave Christopher his first major U.S. film assignment. Salka had taken Christopher under her wing, having received high praise about him from Berthold, who had written from London: "Isherwood [is] one of the finest and most original writers. He observes very sharply, behind his mask of boyish charm. He lived in Berlin and speaks German. I find his *Berlin Diary* a stylistic masterpiece, the humour is quite devilish. You will like him."*

The film for which Gottfried was to be producer was *Rage in Heaven*, based on a novel by James Hilton. Reinhardt thought Isherwood would be ideal to work on the script, as he was familiar with the mores and speech-patterns of the sort of wealthy London upper-middle-class characters in the story. And although he had trouble convincing the boys in the front office at MGM, who had never heard of Christopher, a contract was obtained. Christopher was basically in charge of dialogue, while the story-line was written by Robert Thoeren. The young Ingrid Bergman was chosen to play the leading female role, costarring with Robert Montgomery and supported by George Sanders. W. S. Van Dyke II directed the film. When Robert Montgomery read the Isherwood-Thoeren script, he felt he could contribute little or nothing to the role, and was extremely unhappy when MGM refused to release him from his contractual obligation. For a while, it seemed that the film might never be made. When shooting began in late 1940, Montgomery thought Van Dyke a studio workhorse, not giving enough time for adequate rehearsals. Reinhardt, on the other hand, had the impression that Montgomery was not co-operating, and MGM made an unofficial complaint to the Screen Actors' Guild

* Quoted in Salka Viertel, *The Kindness of Strangers* (1969).

that he was not giving a performance. Reinhardt thought the rushes looked so awful that it seemed as if drastic action might have to be taken, until Christopher suggested adding a prologue to the film in which a doctor explained that Philip Monrell had been in a lunatic asylum and was suffering from a condition whose symptoms corresponded exactly to the way Montgomery acted. Montgomery was unaware of the changes, but had the last laugh, as his interpretation was well received in many trade and popular papers.

However, *Rage in Heaven* was not really a roaring success. Rumours circulated around Hollywood that Montgomery was being "punished" by being cast in this medium-budget picture. Van Dyke shot it completely in eight weeks, though that for him was a quite leisurely pace.

Meanwhile, the Auden-Isherwood controversy had exploded with full force in Britain. In June 1940 Major Sir Jocelyn Lucas (Conservative, Portsmouth South) asked the Parliamentary Secretary to the Minister of Labour "whether British citizens of military age, such as Mr. W. H. Auden and Mr. Christopher Isherwood, who have gone to the United States and expressed their determination not to return to this country until the war is over, will be summoned back for registration and calling up in view of the fact that they are seeking refuge abroad."* The Government did not follow up this demand, which was based on a fundamental misunderstanding of Wystan's and Christopher's position. Needless to say, the press had a field day, and the matter was not quickly laid to rest. The two writers were caricatured for posterity by Evelyn Waugh in *Put Out More Flags* as the poets Parsnip and Pimpernell. Waugh never met Isherwood, but he was not an enemy of his, usually being complimentary about his books.

In early July 1940 Christopher received news of his Uncle Henry's death, which of course meant that he would inherit the estate. However, he had no wish to become entangled once more with the past and believed that the money and houses would mean more to his brother and mother than they could do to him. He therefore signed everything over to Kathleen and Richard, in-

* *Sunday Dispatch* (June 9, 1940).

cluding an annual income of several thousand pounds. The day
the news of Henry's death arrived, Christopher wrote in his diary:

> I was fond of him and he of me. He always thought of me as
> being after his money—as indeed I was. But this seemed to
> him perfectly natural and proper. He had the eighteenth cen-
> tury conception of the relation between uncle and heir.
>
> I often used to wonder just when this would happen—and
> I always half-knew that when it did, when Marple and all the
> money became mine, it would be too late. It is too late now—
> not merely because of the War but because the absurd boy-
> hood dream of riches is over forever. It is too late to invite
> my friends to a banquet, to burn the Flemish tapestry and
> the Elizabethan beds, to turn the house into a brothel. I no
> longer want to be revenged on the Past.

In the sunshine of California, the ghosts of his oppressive heritage had been lain. To take on the responsibilities of the estate
would have tied him to a past which he wished to forget, even if
he no longer felt the need to be revenged upon it. To have run
the estate during wartime from American exile would have been
nigh impossible, and by signing his inheritance away, he was acknowledging to Richard the debt that he owed him for looking
after Kathleen—and the debt to Kathleen for looking after Richard. Christopher anyway had a horror of the idea of possessions,
particularly real estate, which was to last well into the 1950s.

Evidently Christopher did not realise to what extent Marple
Hall had deteriorated structurally. Richard had spent weekends
there from time to time with the caretaker, but it was already
largely uninhabitable and needed massive repair work. Richard
meanwhile was doing his national service as a farmworker on a
farm attached to Wyberslegh, then later he transferred to another
farm adjoining Marple Hall Park. As owner, Richard could now
let Kathleen come back to live at her beloved Wyberslegh, but
not until alternative accommodation could be found for the elderly lady tenant then occupying the house. As it happened, a few
months later Wyberslegh was hit by some small German incendi-
ary bombs, but soon after the house was ready for Kathleen's reoc-
cupation. Richard and Nurse Avis of course lived with her there.

Christopher was naturally in a quandary about what he should do about the war. He toyed at one point with the idea of joining a Quaker ambulance unit, but he did not know enough about motor maintenance to qualify. And although he enjoyed the life-style and intrigues of the film world, his conscience would not let him rest. While he churned out dialogue for a film about Chopin, friends in London were suffering the Blitz. Letters from Europe kept him posted of developments there, and first-hand accounts came from new arrivals such as Tony Bower, who established himself as a correspondent for a film magazine. He appears in the role of Ronnie, one of those on the periphery of the drinking, bitchy Hollywood scene in the Paul episode of *Down There on a Visit*.

In the late fall of 1940, Swami Prabhavananda decided to initiate Christopher, who had by this time been attending the Vedanta Society for about fifteen months. Asking Swami Prabhavananda to be his guru was one of the most important decisions, if not *the* most important, of Christopher's entire life. The ceremony was held on the birthday of Ramakrishna's Holy Mother:

> The initiation took place before breakfast, right after the first of the day's three meditation periods. Before going into the temple, I was provided by one of the women of the family with a small tray on which were arranged the flowers I was to offer: two red roses, a white rose and a large daisy. The Swami was waiting for me inside the shrine; its curtains had been drawn for privacy. First, he told me to offer the flowers: to the photographs of Ramakrishna and Holy Mother, to the icon of Christ, and to himself—because the guru must always receive at least a token of an initiation-gift. Next he taught me my mantra, making me repeat it several times until I was quite sure of it. Next he gave me a rosary and showed me how to use it.*

Even if the decision to commit himself to Vedanta was taken at a time of great personal questioning, it remained valid, and Christopher maintained a close, devotional friendship with Prabhavananda until the latter's death in 1976.

Christopher continued to work for MGM for the first few months of 1941, until his contract expired in May. He contributed

* *An Approach to Vedanta.*

to Victor Saville's A *Woman's Face*, starring Joan Crawford, and bits and pieces for *Crossroads*, a remake of a French film about amnesia. One day, at the end of March, one of the trade gossip-columnists dropped by at Christopher's office at the studios and asked if he might use the phone. As Christopher carried on with his work, he heard the reporter shout down the phone: "No—*no*, you dope—the name's Woolf—W-O-O-L-F—sure, I'm sure—sure, I've heard of her, you ignorant bastard—she was a great writer—British." Thus Christopher learnt of Virginia Woolf's suicide. Klaus Mann asked Christopher to write a memorial piece about her for a new magazine he had founded, *Destiny*; the piece appeared in May. Christopher recalled the occasions when he had sat at Virginia Woolf's feet, riveted by the talk. So much so, in fact, that on one occasion in London a few years previously, he had been to the Woolfs for tea, then stayed on for supper at Virginia's suggestion. He sat in rapt attention to the literary gossip until about ten o'clock, when suddenly he remembered that he ought to have been in a hotel in Croydon with a young man—a recent conquest, with whom he was due to leave for Paris for a romantic weekend, but whose very existence he had forgotten in his admiration for Virginia Woolf.

During the spring and summer of 1941, refugees continued to arrive, to swell the Santa Monica émigré community. Augusta Steuermann (Salka Viertel's mother) turned up, sprightly but emaciated after a harrowing wait in Moscow, and a long journey across the Trans-Siberian and the Pacific. Bertolt Brecht and his wife, Helli, arrived with their children in July. Brecht did a minimal amount of work for the film studios, but hated the life, writing: "Every morning to earn my bread I go to the market where they buy lies."* Although Brecht understood English, he did not attempt to express himself in that language. He would talk late into the night with friends about the war, while Helli served tea and home-made cakes in their simple but spacious wooden bungalow on Twenty-sixth Street. Christopher knew Brecht, but there was a degree of mutual antagonism. Brecht took him to task over his translation of the lyrics of *Dreigroschenroman*, and generally gave the impression of being a very uncomfortable person, wary

---

* Quoted in Salka Viertel, *The Kindness of Strangers*.

and tough, with an almost peasant cunning. Christopher was horrified by Brecht's political position, with its implicit acceptance of the authority of the state.

Doyen of the German writers was Thomas Mann, though some people would say that his brother Heinrich was the greater writer. Thomas Mann sometimes referred to Christopher as "the starry-eyed one," and was amused by him. When they first met, in California, there was a family reunion, including Erika and Klaus. A journalist happened to be present, and Thomas Mann introduced all of his family in turn. "And who is that?" asked the reporter, pointing to Christopher. "Family pimp," Thomas Mann replied.

One English friend who had a more sympathetic view of Vedanta than many was Somerset Maugham, who was in Los Angeles that summer awaiting his grandchildren, who were due to arrive from England. Maugham told Christopher that he intended to write a novel about India and Hindu mysticism that autumn— the book that appeared as *The Razor's Edge*. It has sometimes been said that Christopher was the model for the main character of the book, but he denies it.

In July, Christopher joined about twenty-five others at La Verne, for a month-long seminar run by Gerald Heard. The programme was divided up between meditation, discussion, physical labour and relaxation, several of the participants being Vedantists or Quakers. Just before he left Santa Monica, Christopher wrote to John Lehmann:

> I think it should be interesting. God forbid that I should make any more rash promises, but, *supposing* I were to write a short plain account of the doings and findings there, would you feel inclined to print it? I feel so terribly sorry about all the times I've let you down that I rack my brains to find any conceivable way of appeasing you.
>
> Later plans are still very vague. I may go East to see Wystan, but this depends on whether or not he has been conscripted: he had been ordered to report for duty on July 1, and I haven't heard from him since. Most probably they'll reject him because he's too old. Tony Bower, as Cuthbert (Worsley) will have told you, is already in the army.
>
> This fall, I hope to get some fulltime job working with the

Friends, either on relief or refugees, and thence possibly to
China next Spring—but all that depends entirely on circumstances outside my control.

(dated 7/3/41)

The full-time employment with the Quakers did indeed materialise. It was natural that Christopher should find the Society
of Friends the most sympathetic of the Christian sects. They
preached pacifism and tolerance, were usually free of religious dogmatism or bigotry and believed in the Inner Light, or that of God
in every man—a concept similar to some aspects of Vedanta. At
La Verne, Christopher had long talks with a Quaker named
Harold Chance, who wrote to Friends in Philadelphia about
Christopher's wish to work in some Friendly concern:

> Up until recently he has been employed by one of the Holly-
> wood Movie Companies as a script writer and, I understand,
> at a salary of between $500 and $600 a week. A few months
> ago he decided he was wasting his life at that kind of job,
> quit the work with enough savings to last him a year or so
> and since that has been rather closely associated with Gerald
> Heard and his group here in Southern California. He has
> worked some with Raymond Booth and Raymond has some
> thought that he might be able to use him in the refugee part
> of the work in the west, particularly if he had a little more ex-
> perience in some of our Refugee Hostels. . . .
>
> I have found Christopher a most interesting person. He ap-
> parently has a rather brilliant mind, at least he expresses him-
> self very well, though he is very much English in that expres-
> sion. . . . I might add that I do not think that he is
> ambitious in his desires as to the type of service, in fact, I
> think for a year or so he is quite eager to do some very hum-
> ble chore if necessary. . . .

(dated 8/9/41)

Raymond Booth sent a strong letter of support asking Friends
to look favourably on Christopher's application. Consequently, in
October, Christopher went to Haverford, Pennsylvania, just outside Philadelphia, to help out at the Co-operative College Workshop there. He had gone straight to the heartland of American
Quakerism.

10

Haverford provided a great contrast to life in both California and New York. The community was both affluent and tranquil, located in attractive wooded country. For generations, the area had been dominated by the Quakers, who had originally arrived with clear visions of a New World peaceable kingdom in William Penn's state, but who had gradually adapted to many of the ways of society at large as they welcomed others into their territory. Perhaps because of the integrity of their handling of affairs, many became successful businessmen, so that not all the doyens of Haverford Quaker circles lived out the principle of simplicity that had always been a traditional cornerstone of Friends' belief and practice. Nonetheless, there were many men and women there of considerable sincerity and goodness, and the town's Quaker-endowed college educated many upright young men and contributed to the world of scholarship, particularly in religious affairs.

Haverford Friends Meeting had more than its fair share of "weighty" (i.e., influential) Friends. Most notable among these was Rufus M. Jones, a very eminent Quaker theologian and historian, then nearing his eightieth birthday. Friends Meetings for Worship (at least in the type of Quakerism found in Europe and the eastern seaboard of the United States) take the form of silent gatherings. Silence may be broken by any Friend who feels moved to speak, and was so, often week after week, by Rufus Jones, who frequently ministered at great length. Christopher quickly became familiar with the elderly but vigorous figure, with his white moustache and round, steel-rimmed spectacles. On some Sunday mornings, however, Christopher would travel to the Meeting at Radnor, a few miles away, where ministry tended to be very brief, although many people spoke. One Quaker, curious to learn Christopher's reactions to the community, asked him how he compared the two meetings. Christopher replied in Hollywood jargon that Haverford was a "long serial" while Radnor was "short subjects," a remark that became an "in" joke among local Friends. Although rarely frivolous, Haverford Friends were quite able to laugh at the world and at themselves. Nonetheless, Christopher sometimes caused eyebrows to be raised, particularly because of some of the remarks made by a lively young man with whom Christopher shacked up for a while (having left Vernon in California). Christopher was appalled yet admiring one day when the said young man, coming out of meeting one Sunday morning, looked up at a picture of Elizabeth Fry in the hallway and said very loudly, "I never liked that picture of you, Chris!"

The Co-operative College Workshop, where Christopher worked, had been established to help incoming refugees from Europe adapt to American life. Christopher helped with teaching English to Germans and Austrians, but much of the Quaker program was concerned with informing the new arrivals about American customs and institutions. A very high percentage of the immigrants were intellectuals, and went on to teach in colleges or take on other responsible positions. The workshop wardens reported back to Friends' committees that they found Christopher keen and always ready to pitch in with the washing-up, but applied to him exactly the same adjective that Thomas Mann had used: starry-eyed.

While working with the Quakers, Christopher became a very good friend of a young lecturer in Spanish at Haverford College, René Blanc-Roos. Apart from his academic activities, Blanc-Roos coached the college wrestling team, and had an occasionally pugnacious attitude which greatly appealed to Christopher as a contrast to all the worthy gentleness around. Blanc-Roos was a warm but severe admirer of Christopher's work, and insisted that he keep himself on form by writing something, anything, so as not to lose the habit. The result was a story, "Take It or Leave It," published in the *New Yorker* in October 1942. With the advantage of hindsight, one can see its lack of spontaneity. Its construction is completely artificial, quite unlike anything else Isherwood wrote. The writer appeals to the reader to write the story for him, giving the outline, and asking for the details to be fitted in. Even the characters are unnamed ("I can't waste time inventing names for them"). The idea has a certain cleverness, but it is one of the stories that this writer likes least of Isherwood's work. Nevertheless, he was very grateful to Blanc-Roos for making him write something, and later dedicated *Prater Violet* to him. During Christopher's time at Haverford, he would conduct furious arguments with Blanc-Roos about literature and sex, reading aloud from Rimbaud and drinking together. Some years later, when Blanc-Roos went through a period of great depression, following the early death of his wife, Christopher (who hates writing letters) wrote daily to him, and found the experience a rewarding one.

While Christopher was living at Haverford America joined the war, following the Japanese attack on Pearl Harbor. Christopher had already taken out his first citizenship papers, so making himself eligible for military service. However, the draft board in Pennsylvania was quite used to conscientious objectors, and immediately classified him as such. From the beginning, he said that he would be prepared to serve in a medical corps if given an assurance that he would never have to carry arms. This they said they could not guarantee, but later they changed their minds and he agreed to enlist, thinking he would probably end up in a forestry camp. However, he never joined up, as the age limit was lowered and he was declassified.

Christopher stayed with the Friends in Pennsylvania until July 1942, when the hostel closed, having outlived its usefulness. He did not live up to the Quakers' early hopes that he would go on to work for them in the West, however, as he was offered alternative occupation with the Vedantists. In later years, Christopher wondered whether he should not have stayed with the Vedanta Society in 1941–42, rather than go to Haverford, but came to the conclusion that the break had been profitable. Not only did it give him a fresh experience (drawn upon in the novel *The World in*

the Evening), but it also allowed him to reflect from a distance
upon his involvement with the Vedanta philosophy. The certain
points of similarity between the two religions confirmed his con-
viction in the latter, though he probably would have become a
Quaker had he not met Prabhavananda. Nonetheless, his attitude
to the Society of Friends was ambivalent; he greatly admired
them, but thought many too puritanical.

The work that the swami proposed to Christopher on his return to California in the summer of '42 was a translation of the
great Sanskrit classic, the *Bhagavad-Gita*.

The *Bhagavad-Gita* was originally part of the great Sanskrit
epic *Mahabharata*, the longest poem in the world, with over one
hundred thousand couplets (about thirty times as long as *Paradise
Lost*). Roughly 80 per cent of the *Mahabharata* is comprised of
stories, centred on forces of good and evil, to a large extent po-
larised as the Padavas and the Kuravas. The *Mahabharata* talks a
great deal about war, which is not symbolic, whereas the dialogue
between Krishna and Arjuna in the *Bhagavad-Gita*, set against the
background of war, almost certainly is. This point was of crucial
importance for Christopher, the newly self-discovered pacifist. He
even wrote a sizeable article about it for the Vedanta Society's
magazine, *Vedanta and the West*, for which he did a considerable
amount of work.

Working with the swami on the translation of the *Bhagavad-
Gita* was both a valuable literary experience and an ideal way of
learning in depth about Vedanta. Christopher of course knew no
Sanskrit, nor did he seriously ever try to learn any. Prabhavananda
looked after the purely linguistic side of the translation, after
which they worked together on finding the nearest English render-
ing of the exact meaning.

Sometimes, a friend of Aldous Huxley's, Margaret (Peggy) Kiskadden, would sit in on these translation sessions. Once she
suggested that she heard "two voices" in the text, which caused
quite a heated discussion. Huxley was called in to arbitrate.

Christopher saw a very great deal of Peggy Kiskadden over the
next ten years. Originally, she had lunch with him every Tuesday
at the Swamitage, as she called it, then she moved in for the period Monday to Friday, leaving her children by her first marriage
in the care of one of the nuns from the Ramakrishna Order. She

had met Christopher through Chris Wood and Gerald Heard, and she remained very close to Chris Wood right up to his death. Gradually, she took on the role of another honorary elder sister to Christopher. She followed closely the hot and cold relationship with Vernon, and Vernon's successors, and would be read letters from England, sympathising with bad news and sometimes proffering advice, which was not always well received.

Initially, Christopher combined work on the translation with a resumption of his past Hollywood life. He took on an assignment at Paramount with Lesser Samuels, whom he had known from his Gaumont-British days, this time working on a Somerset Maugham story, *The Hour Before Dawn.* Christopher's contribution was mainly to a tribunal scene, as Paramount wanted someone who was familiar with the experiences of conscientious objectors. This sudden call from Paramount put a stop for a while to a new novel on which Christopher was working, tentatively called *Prater Violets* (in the published version, the final "s" was dropped). The book was to be a study of Berthold Viertel and his relationship with Christopher during their time together on *Little Friend.* In fact, the period spent at Paramount proved to be a godsend for the book, as Lesser Samuels was able to provide all the relevant technical jargon which Christopher had partly forgotten.

However, early in 1943 Christopher accepted an invitation to go and live in the Vedanta Center in Hollywood, leaving the home in Alto Cedro Drive in Beverly Hills, where he had stayed on his return from the Quakers. Vernon had gone off travelling independently, though later he turned up in California again and lived in another Vedantist community. Finally, he married, and had a son whom he named after Christopher.

Christopher's stay at the Vedanta Center provided him with the opportunity to try out different aspects of self-discipline, such as sexual abstinence, vegetarianism and long periods of meditation. He had practised partial vegetarianism while working with the Friends, but never really made up his mind about the morals of it. In fact, only a few of the devotees at Ivar Avenue were vegetarians, and the swami with all his cigarettes was a walking example of the possibility of sanctity without total asceticism, though Prabhavananda did suddenly one day give up smoking for good.

Even at the Vedanta Center, though, Christopher did not totally abandon film work. He was soon busy on a film script with Aldous Huxley. This was an original screenplay about a faith healer, which they entitled *Jacob's Hands*. As Huxley wrote to Frieda Lawrence on April 10: "I hope we shall be able to sell it, as it will solve a lot of economic problems and will make it unnecessary to go into temporary slavery at one of the studios."

However, none of the studios would touch the script, which puzzled Huxley and Isherwood until they learnt from a friend that the reason was fear of objection from the medical profession. Huxley wrote off to the MCA at length telling them why doctors should have no grounds for complaint, but to no avail. The film was never made, though an adapted radio drama was produced. Hollywood seemed omnipotent in frustrating the Huxley-Isherwood partnership, which had got off to an ominous non-start as early as August 1940, when Huxley had wanted Isherwood to work with him on a film version of *Lady Chatterley's Lover*, which had also petered out because Christopher was under contract to MGM.

Christopher's main writing at this time (indeed, since his arrival in the United States) was his diaries, but he did find the courage to work on *Prater Violet*. He wrote to Gerald Hamilton on June 12, 1944:

> The greatest problem at present is the time element. Owing to my habit of writing about things which happened ten years ago, I find myself in a totally different epoch; and somehow I have to *allow* for the war, without mentioning it. I'm afraid this may make the thing seem very old-fashioned. But there is virtue in that, too; if one can somehow present it as a period piece.

Prater Violet, which was finished at the end of 1944, is probably the most successful of Isherwood's "dynamic portraits," finding exactly the right balance between the character in the limelight and the narrator. The book has a good sting in the end, where the narrator reveals that he has a sex-life, something which has been hidden all the way through. The story is almost a straight account of events at Gaumont-British (Imperial Bulldog), though simplified and exaggerated. Not all the characters were real people, or at least not at that time and place. Lawrence Dwight in the novella, for example, is largely based on René Blanc-Roos. To increase the dramatic intensity of the story the director's wife is still in Austria, therefore directly threatened by Hitler's rise to power. In real life Salka Viertel had been safely in America at the time of *Little Friend*. The portrait of Berthold is endearing without being at all flattering. There are also amusing glimpses of home life with Richard and Kathleen Isherwood, and an ironic look at the Christopher of the mid-thirties.

Although Christopher admits to promiscuity at the end of the book, he is nonetheless ambiguous about the sex of his partners. As yet he felt it quite impossible to identify overtly with a homosexual in a story without drawing the reader's attention away from the main narrative. In the book, the director is allowed to talk poetically about his idea of heterosexual relationships:

"Women are absolutely necessary to a man . . . he needs them like bread. I do not mean for coitus . . . one needs their aura, their ambience, their perfume."

Berthold Viertel, who okayed the manuscript before it was sent off to Christopher's publishers at the end of 1944, quite liked the book, though he wrote rather wistfully that he was ending his life as a "tragic Punch." Graciously he added that he was pleased that all the time he and Christopher had spent working on *Little Friend* had not been in vain.

The longer Christopher remained at the Vedanta Society and worked with the swami, the more he became aware that for him religion was primarily a relationship

> leading at long last to direct union with the Atman [the reality which is within us, as opposed to the reality in its universal aspect, or Brahman]; a relationship for time being with some individual who can give you a dim glimpse of the Atman within him, simply by being what he is. Such an individual doesn't have to be perfect. But he must have no pretenses; he must be, at all times, neither more nor less than himself. If there is clarity in his character, then you can look into him, as it were, and, very occasionally, get a glimpse of the something else, the element which is not-he, not his personality, not his individual nature. And then you can begin to

have faith in his faith. You can feel that he is holding you, like a rock-climber on a rope, just as he himself is being held by the rope that goes on up above him. That is what the disciple demands of the guru. It is a tremendous demand.*

Many of Christopher's friends never really understood the sincerity of his belief in Vedanta. John Lehmann and others in London received his news with increasing dismay, though Morgan Forster faithfully maintained that Christopher must know what he was doing, and defended him in absentia against his numerous critics. Nonetheless, Christopher began to realise that a monk's life was not for him. The tolerance shown by the swami, and the Vedanta Society as a whole, meant that Christopher could be accepted in the community even with his carnal past and present, yet he had to flee the center from time to time, to get a breath of the sensual air outside.

Typical of this need was his friendship at this time with an extraordinary young man by the name of Denham (Denny) Fouts whom he had first met in London in 1938 and who subsequently appeared barely disguised in several novels and short stories, including Gore Vidal's *Pages from an Abandoned Journal*, Speed Lamkin's *The Easter Egg Hunt* and Isherwood's own *Down There on a Visit*, in which their relationship is described in great detail in the Paul episode, though with the usual fictional embellishments, particularly at the end. According to Truman Capote, who wrote at length about Denny Fouts in his *Esquire* articles in 1976, Denny grew up in Florida, and worked as a teenager in his father's bakery. When he was sixteen, he was swept off one day by a passing cosmetics tycoon, and thus began his career as the Best Kept Boy in the World. He left his original benefactor in Capri, following a trail of aristocratic and wealthy connections of both sexes (including, according to Capote, an heir apparent to a European throne), that took him round the glory spots of the world. Shortly before the war he met Peter Watson, British heir to an oleomargarine millionaire, who had put up money to finance Cyril Connolly's literary review *Horizon*. During the German bombing of London in 1940 Watson insisted that Denny re-

---

* *An Approach to Vedanta.*

turn to the safety of the United States, accompanied by Jean Connolly (Ruthie in *Down There on a Visit*).

Denny was far more complex than most gold-diggers. Although he was an expert at manipulating people, and had a brilliant sarcastic wit which he could flash on and off when necessary, he still retained a quality of innocence, which was one of his most attractive traits. He believed implicitly in other people's honesty, and never locked his doors, with the result that he was often robbed. His major weakness was a reliance on hard drugs. He was quite often ill, not only because of his addictions, but also because of hernia trouble.

Denny worked as a cook in a forestry camp, as did the former singer Michael Barrie (later Gerald Heard's secretary). Christopher became very close to Denny, and they studied Heard's teachings together. Later, Denny was expelled from the forestry camp for being homosexual, as he announced candidly to Alec and Dodie Beesley, English acquaintances of his to whom he turned when this disconcerting experience occurred. They financed him for a while, their London agents being reimbursed by Peter Watson. Christopher soon became a good friend of the Beesleys, going to their home for Sunday lunch for several years.

Denny found an evening job in a bookstore in Hollywood after he was asked to leave the forestry camp. In the day-time, he worked as a janitor, using his duty hours to study algebra, German and Shakespeare, in order to gain a high school diploma, which he had never had time to acquire during his world travels. Every Saturday during the summer of 1943, he and Christopher would go to the beach to swim. Denny's studies bore fruit, for soon he was able to go to college. He lived in a small flat near the beach at Santa Monica, the main room dominated by a giant Picasso which Peter Watson had presented to him, and which he had shipped over to California from the Museum of Modern Art. Christopher wrote to Gerald Hamilton on April 13, 1944:

I admire the colouring [of the Picasso], but maintain that it has a very sinister quality, as I slept under it on Denny's sofa, having terrible nightmares about Nazi Germany, in which the British Embassy was full of paintings. The First Secretary, a rather Bertie Wooster young man, explained to me cheerfully: "You see, we keep them for contrast." There was also a frightening blind old lady who had shot off a man's hands, and was fumbling about and fretting because she had lost her ammunition.

Another important new friendship dating from Christopher's time in the monastery was that with the young playwright Tennessee Williams, who, like most of his peers, had come to Hollywood in the hope of earning some money in the movies. He turned up one day at Ivar Avenue with a letter of introduction from Lincoln Kirstein. He knocked on the front door of the Vedanta Center, and asked for Christopher, who came out shortly and told him that it was meditation time, inviting him to come in and meditate with them. Williams agreed to do so, but found he was unable to share the mood of the meeting, and thought it a very unfortunate way to meet a man whose writing he admired so much.

However, Christopher phoned Williams soon afterwards, and they became great friends, having common interests not only in literature and movies, but also in boys. Often they would go to the pier at Santa Monica for fish dinners, during the blackout. As Williams later recalled in his *Memoirs*: "There was almost a sentimental attachment between us but it didn't come to romance: instead, it turned into a great friendship, one of the continuing friendships of my life, and one of the most important ones." Tennessee's admiration for Christopher's work continued to grow, and on at least two occasions he told friends that he thought Isherwood to be the greatest living novelist in English—a complimentary minority opinion.

Christopher considered Tennessee a true exotic, with his southern drawl and wild talk. He savoured the playwright's scurrilous stories, and adopted the stance of a concerned older brother in a way that became quite a familiar pattern in many of his relationships with younger men. When Tennessee bought a second-hand motor scooter, Christopher protested anxiously, remembering only too clearly his own humiliating and dangerous Cambridge experiences on two wheels. Tennessee developed a great liking for Santa Monica, so rented a two-roomed apartment there, in the southern, poorer part of town, behind the muscle beach.

Christopher succumbed to the temptation of working with Warner Brothers for most of 1945. He got rather a kick out of being able to march through the forbidding door of the studio that separated the nerve centre of the movie world from the outer offices full of hopeful writers and would-be starlets, but the work itself was not intellectually satisfying. This never demoralised him in the way it did many other "serious" writers, but he was able to moan to his friends, writing to Olive Mangeot that he was working on "a bad script of a bad story"—Somerset Maugham's *Up at the Villa*. Gottfried Reinhardt's brother was in charge. However, the film was never made. After the *Villa* script, he did some work on *The Woman in White* with John Collier, based on Wilkie Collins' novel, but almost nothing of his contribution was retained in the screened version.

During 1945, Christopher had succeeded in living what was in effect a double existence, moving in both the Vedantist and movie worlds, but things had developed in such a way that he now felt it right to physically move out of the Vedanta Center, while retaining close links with it.

11

The problem of balance between the spiritual and the carnal is one that has beset Man for thousands of years. It is an element, too, that must be considered for an understanding of Isherwood's character and thought. Traditionally, the two natural longings of Man have been seen as opposing forces; complete devotion to one demands the rejection of the other.

In the late thirties Christopher had discovered that an active sexual existence without spirituality was an empty and rather distasteful experience. His wartime connection with Vedanta, and specifically with those fine disciples of it who moved in the Hollywood community, confirmed that total commitment to a religious, meditative life barred a demanding sexual life. Such abstinence, from his own viewpoint, was equally unsuitable. Eastern religions in general admit contradictions more readily than does the Western heritage of Judaeo-Christianity. Several of these religions accept the coexistence of opposites within a single entity, of which the Taoist symbol of yin and yang is the clearest manifestation. Was the old theory of separation of body and mind in fact justifiable? Had not Swami Prabhavananda, indeed, accepted Christopher as a favoured disciple, even though he knew of Christopher's attachment to the world of the flesh? The essential realisation for Christopher was that sex and spirit, both God-given, rightly reside in the same body in healthy coexistence. However, it would still take him several years to find the right balance.

A parallel dichotomy which had to be resolved was that between the Old World and the New. Christopher had no wish to live the life of an expatriate, clinging to a British passport, playing cricket and—to push the cliché-image—nibbling cucumber sandwiches. He had applied for American citizenship, let American vowels infiltrate his speech, yet as a first-generation immigrant on the doorstep of middle age, he knew he could never be totally accepted as an American. Somehow he had to adjust to the American idiom, in both his life and his work, without losing the qualities of his intensely English vision of the world. His assimilation into the mainstream of American life was hindered by several things. Hollywood and its dormitory satellites were paradoxically the most American and the least American of places. They produced celluloid images of the American dream, but they were not representative in the way that Chicago or Cedar Rapids were. In Santa Monica he was surrounded by other recent immigrants, predominantly Jews, who had come not so much because they wanted to but because they had had to leave their homelands, and America seemed the next best thing. Many of them intended to return to Europe when conditions were more normal. In Germany Christopher had deliberately sought out the majority, to live among the indigenous workers. He found their real-life private dramas were the more interesting for their anonymity. In America, however, Christopher cultivated minorities, having realised that he was more at home with them. Away from Europe the social hangups evaporated, and of course he was older.

Many people found the war years sexually stimulating, in the sense that brief encounters were more frequent. There was an urgency about then too which appealed to some tastes, as did the blackout. Servicemen on leave would hang around the corners of Sunset Boulevard and other Hollywood streets, ready for a party that could easily become an orgy. The beaches north of Santa Monica became regular meeting-places and the scenes of nocturnal orgies. Christopher became quite a habitué of "The Pits," as one stretch of beach north of Santa Monica was called. He loved the thrill, the hint of danger and even the anonymity of this al fresco promiscuity. Such activities went on for a few years after the war, when the area became increasingly settled by people who objected to the libertine reputation of the place, causing a big police clean-up.

During the latter half of 1945 Denny Fouts's apartment near the beach at the bottom of Santa Monica Canyon became vacant, as he returned to liberated Europe. Christopher moved in, sharing this apartment at 137 Entrada Drive with a young Irish-American, William Caskey, seventeen years Christopher's junior.

Christopher had been fascinated by Bill Caskey the first time he saw him washing dishes at Cafe J, one of the popular hangouts near the beach. He had gone into the kitchen to help, in order to make the young man's acquaintance. Bill's family were Kentucky horse people, and for a while he had worked in photo-finish at a race-course. He was an attractive, dark-haired man with a disarmingly quick wit and an aggressive ability. His violent temper intrigued Christopher. Bill had seen much since he left Kentucky, and had acquired several rich or influential friends before choosing to go it alone in Santa Monica. He was a fine photographer, and over the next few years took hundreds of excellent portraits of Christopher and his friends.

As this was the first time that Christopher had lived with anybody of intelligence and ability en ménage, and on a more or less equal footing, he decided it was necessary to draw up a set of rules that would guarantee the enterprise's success. Caskey was rather dubious about the whole idea, but agreed to give it a try. Many of the rules were concerned with individual freedom and respect, and included one which stated that neither of them should bring back sex-partners to the flat while the other was in town. Caskey stuck to the rules for quite a while, until he realised that Christopher was incapable of doing so, so then he abandoned them too.

Christopher was rather ill for part of the winter of 1945–46, and had to be operated on for an infection of the prostate gland. He hoped to visit England during the summer of 1946, but that trip was put off for several months. Meanwhile, Christopher and Bill moved out of Denny's flat into an apartment over Salka Viertel's garage, at 165 Mabery Road. She later gave an impression of Christopher in her book *The Kindness of Strangers*:

> He still looked like an adolescent; one could detect the fine lines around his blue, wide-open eyes, only because they were lighter than his sunburnt face.

In the morning, on his way for a swim, he would stop by for a cup of coffee and a chat. . . . The chat would transform itself into an absorbing discussion, which on my side tended to be rather emotional. At this time I was "unbalanced" to say the least, but Christopher had unlimited patience and understanding. Then one of us would say something atrocious and hilarious, and suddenly we laughed and the world became bearable again.

The immediate post-war years were the most glittering as far as Salka's *salon* was concerned, however "unbalanced" she may have felt herself to have been. One visitor of increasing regularity was Charles Chaplin, who became the victim of much irrational hatred. During the war he had made a famous speech urging help for America's Allies, the Soviet Union. In the hysterical anti-communism that was whipped up at the time of Winston Churchill's Iron Curtain speech and the following years of hunting Reds under beds, Chaplin became a prime target. His "Soviet" pronouncements were thrown in his face, and he found himself on trial in a blown-up paternity case that took on considerable political overtones. Eventually he was found not guilty; but the criticisms continued, especially when he married the eighteen-year-old daughter of the playwright Eugene O'Neill, Oona, shortly after the trial.

Christopher saw quite a lot of the Chaplins, but they struck him as a rather stuffy couple. This stuffiness may well have been evident on the occasion of one of Bill Caskey's most spectacular outbursts. Bill was remembered by everyone for his occasional flashes of temper, though for most of the time he was quiet and pensive; if he had not been so, he and Christopher would never have been able to live together so long, as he would have prevented Christopher from writing.

However, on the occasion in question, Bill and Christopher had been invited to the Chaplins' for dinner, and Bill was looking for a place to sit down. He was called over by Nathalie Moffat, daughter-in-law of Iris Tree, and a former *protégée* of Jean-Paul Sartre. She had acquired quite a reputation as a wit and a free-liver (her most famous quip being her description of Simone de Beauvoir as "an alarm clock inside a fridge"). Expansively, she called to Bill: "Oh, Billy, do come and sit here. I just *love* pansies." Bristling, Caskey shot back: "Nathalie, my dear, your slang is out of date. The correct word is 'cock-suckers.'" The gathering was scandalised. The Chaplins stopped inviting Bill and Christopher, but this may have been because someone told them that Christopher had peed on their sofa one night when paralytically drunk.

A frequent, almost daily, caller at Mabery Road was Greta Garbo, who fended off visitors and admirers so effectively that she sometimes found herself in need of company. Often she would call round at Salka Viertel's and cheerily ask if she could not go for a walk with her. If Salka was not at home, then Garbo would go round the back and dig out Christopher or Bill. Meeting Garbo had been one of Christopher's greatest dreams when he came to the States, but her unannounced visits were sometimes very inconvenient. On one occcasion, when Christopher and Bill heard her outside the door, they hid under the table until she went away.

Then generally accepted to be the epitome of beauty, Garbo did everything she could to make herself as unattractive as possible in public, presumably to escape recognition, though sometimes the very bizarreness of her drab clothing drew attention to her. Although Garbo hated to be contradicted or dictated to, Salka Viertel would sometimes be quite stern with her, and on one occasion, when she was organising a birthday outing for Christopher, at which Garbo would be present, absolutely insisted that Garbo wear a dress instead of her usual baggy slacks. To everybody's amazement, she did.

Hovering around California in the latter half of 1946—more often than not as a moth around Garbo's flame—was the British photographer Cecil Beaton. He had spent the war years in many remote corners of the world as an official photographer, from western China to the deserts of the Middle East. Were it not for the poignancy of unrequited passion, Beaton's insistent courting of Garbo (whom he had known in pre-war days) in Beverly Hills, New York and elsewhere, had about it a Waugh-like comedy. As they had several friends in common, Cecil Beaton looked up

Christopher in California, but later seemed to put a damper on the possibility of a greater friendship. Bill Caskey wondered whether Beaton had merely wished to use Christopher and himself as yet another link in the chain that would bind him to Garbo. Beaton was of course by no mans the only person frustrated by Garbo, either emotionally or professionally. Tennessee Williams was extremely anxious that the great actress should play Blanche DuBois in the film version of *A Streetcar Named Desire* in 1947, but she turned him down.

On January 21, 1947, Christopher left, on his own, for England. Having a rather superstitious streak in his complex character, he deliberately chose the date to coincide with the sailing date of the *Aramis* to the Far East nine years before. He flew from New York to Gander, where the passengers disembarked for light refreshments and the plane refuelled for the transatlantic crossing. Christopher stayed awake through the dark and icy night, watched the sunrise and the descent to Shannon in Ireland. His mind full of memories of his childhood period in the troubled province, he noted the flag of the now independent nation and the Gaelic announcements that came over the loudspeaker. Bad weather delayed departure until the afternoon, but then he was soon coming in to land at Bovington, setting foot in England for the first time for eight years and since a major war. Wartime cheerfulness was clearly still in force. A lady at the immigration and health control shrugged when she heard Christopher had no vaccination certificates, and said: "Oh well, never mind—you've got a jolly good sunburn!"

On arrival in London Christopher went straight to John Lehmann's flat. There he reunited with many of his old friends. John Lehmann saw a big difference in him:

> Perhaps he didn't realise that his accent and some of his mannerisms had changed as much as we noticed at once. These changes did not, however, show themselves continuously: I had the impression, talking to him during the three months of his visit, that he was, in spirit, being pulled to and fro across the Atlantic all the time.*

* Lehmann, *The Ample Proposition* (1966).

Christopher stayed at John's for two days. He was struck by two things in London: the shabbiness and the goodwill. He was startled also by a new acceptance of officialdom and regulations, and a readiness to queue. Next, he went up to Wyberslegh to stay with his mother and Richard. That winter was extremely severe and there were coal shortages. Tired from the demands of a war that was over, the population moaned piteously at the weather. Nanny was now very frail, and Kathleen looked after her, rather than the other way round. Accustomed as he was to the material comforts of American life, Christopher was alarmed by the lack of basic household aids. When he said that there should be a refrigerator, Kathleen replied that the food kept cool enough in the larder, which was in the cellar where the coal supply was also kept. He offered to buy his mother a vacuum-cleaner, but she indignantly refused. He stared in dismay at pans caked in grease, and tried to be of service without seeming too fussy. Richard tried to cheer him up with endless cups of tea.

After eight years of separation, Christopher had wondered how he would react to his family and the house. Despite the noticeable physical deterioration around, they were essentially no different from when he had known them before; it was he who had radically altered. He now saw himself as a foreigner, in a real as well as metaphorical sense. He was even more acutely aware of the traits that infuriated and bored him, yet he had learnt a certain tolerance and patience that had been notably lacking in his youth. Plaintively he wrote to William Plomer, in a letter dated January 27, 1947:

> . . . my dear Nanny has suddenly turned into an aged crone who laughs toothlessly at mysterious private jokes. My Mother, at 78, is quite unchanged, and a miracle of energy. She does all the cooking; and presently we are going to trudge through a snowdrift to collect Nanny's old-age pension. It is cold beyond belief. . . .
>
> I hope to emerge from this retirement around March 1st, for a *mad* fortnight in London, and am already counting the days and muttering "February hath 28 alone."

In March he visited Edward Upward, and then went to Cheltenham to see Olive Mangeot and Jean Ross, and her young daughter Sally. He tried to go to Stratford to see Beatrix Lehmann, but was prevented by floods. On returning to Wyberslegh, he wrote to Edward Upward on March 22: "After reading a lot of reviews of Prater Violet, I have decided to be an *emotional* writer. You must tell me how. It seems, according to most critics, that I'm incapable of LOVE." Two days later he continued:

> I've faithfully promised to write "The School of Tragedy" this year, and I still don't in the least know what it's about. I would like to produce something rather like a Huxley novel, with serious discussions; but, unlike Huxley, with convincing characters. Also there's going to be a LOVE scene, if it kills me. As usual, the really attractive relationship—the battle of two elderly Quaker spinsters for an elderly Austrian Jewish refugee—can't be described, because it actually happened. It's heartbreaking. *Why* must people be so touchy? I would have loved it—the bitchery, the perms, the diets, the cyanide glances—and the wedding—with half the Quakers drunk on Californian port which I'd smuggled into a bedroom—George Moore would have swooned with pleasure.

Christopher left Southampton by boat for America on April 16, after a farewell party at John Lehmann's at which he met several artists, including Keith Vaughan, whose work he liked immediately, taking several samples back with him to the States. In New York Christopher occupied an apartment at 207 East Fifty-second Street, rented from James Stern. He wrote on April 28, to John Lehmann:

> Just to let you know that I arrived on Friday, after a bugger of a voyage, with strong head-gales. I avoided being sick by doggedly overeating and dosing myself with whisky. We were all vaccinated, which made me a bit sick after landing but I'm fine now. Jimmy's apartment is a dream (I even have a room all to myself to work in) and Caskey is sweeter than ever, and I am very very happy. . . .
>
> In a few days I hope to start driving the plough over the terrain for my new novel. I have terrible stage-fright about this, but the only thing is to make a start. At all costs, I'm resolved, this time, not to be funny. I don't care how dreary

and boring it is, as long as it isn't the kind of book anybody could possibly read for pleasure on a train. People like being amused more than anything, I've decided.

Getting started on the book proved phenomenally difficult. On July 8 Christopher wrote to Edward Upward:

My novel won't start. I really don't know why. Partly it's New York, which is noisy and jittery and hot. Partly it's a kind of stage-fright. I just gasp and stammer whenever I try to speak the opening lines. . . .

This is a messy, unsatisfactory period in my life. I flap about and feel fussed and get nothing done. But in October we sail for Colombia, Ecuador and W. J. Turner-land. I have a friend in Argentina who is one of Peron's deadliest enemies, so we'll probably finish in prison.

Christopher's main problem with the new novel (destined to become *The World in the Evening*) was the creation of the main character. On July 30 he wrote again to Upward:

I am determined to write in the third person and abolish "Christopher Isherwood," but this other character has to be such a lot of things which I am, and also am not. He has to be: my age, an orphan, rather rich, born in America of a wealthy Quaker Philadelphia family but educated in England and having spent much of his life in Europe. In youth he was a bit of a Cote d'Azur playboy, was married and divorced: he has a bad conscience about the kind of life he led and has reverted to Quakerism, largely because of the social service involved. He doesn't really get on with the Quakers, however, because they are such awful puritans, and he can't just write off art and sex and pleasure as being wicked in themselves. At the same time he is "religious"—i.e. he believes in the validity of mystical experience, to a degree which makes him a bit impatient with the super-intellectual liberal materialism of the Central European refugees.

Christopher continued discussions by post with Upward over the next few months. Meanwhile, Stephen Spender arrived from England, and he, Wystan Auden and Christopher posed together

on Fire Island for a photograph recapturing the posture of one
taken on Ruegen Island fifteen years before.

Worries over the novel were shelved during preparations for his
forthcoming visit to South America, based on which Christopher
was to write a travel book for Random House and Methuen. He
was peeved that Ecuador had a revolution just before he left New
York, as he had been hoping for a Mortmereish air-raid on Quito
while he was there, in which nobody would be hurt and planes
would drop fireworks and flags. On September 19 Christopher
wrote a quick note to Edward: "Just leaving. Usual jitters and
misery. Why do I do these things? My dog and I are tired of roving. . . ."

Bill Caskey was horrified just before their departure when
Christopher put several thousand dollars into an ordinary check-
ing account. Caskey argued that at least the money ought to be
put in an interest-earning deposit account, if not invested, but
Christopher scoffed at the idea. The incident fitted into a whole
syndrome of Christopher's not wanting to have possessions or
liabilities, which also meant that in the forties Christopher refused to buy a house, even when sudden large sums of money
from film work would have enabled him to.

Christopher kept a detailed travel diary during the six months
of wandering in South America with Bill Caskey. The finished
book about the trip (*The Condor and the Cows*) was to prove an
ideal opportunity for Christopher to ruminate over his attitudes
about life, especially on religion and politics. Often on the journey, he asked himself what on earth he was doing in South
America on what appeared to him to be a very artificial assignment. In fact, the book that emerged is one of his best, though it
is almost never read these days.

They sailed from New York to Curaçao, in the Dutch Antilles,
where Christopher installed himself with a beer on the balcony of
a hotel in Wilhelmstad. There, rather typically, instead of dissecting the nature and habits of the local population, he dreamed up
a new persona for himself as an expatriate in Curaçao, living off
the stimulation of the never-ending parade of transient visitors:

I should have everything I want. I should make friends. I
should meet extraordinary characters. There would always be

new faces, new people passing through. I'd entertain them all. I'd become a famous figure. In Europe and the States, travellers would say to each other: "So, you're putting into Wilhelmstad? Oh, there's a man there you mustn't miss on any account. Known all over the Caribbean. They call him Curaçao Chris. . . ."*

The idea is of course preposterous. He would have gone crazy in Curaçao within a week, and indeed there were many occasions on the South American journey when boredom set in cruelly. Christopher never had the unflagging enthusiasm of the real traveller or travel writer, nor did he enjoy the almost masochistic discomforts so relished by the explorative in less developed parts of the world. Where he could travel first-class, he did. Where he couldn't, he moaned. He was usually more than ready to accept hospitality when it brought the comforts of Europe or North America.

From Curaçao, the ship called at a couple of Venezuelan ports before docking at Carthagena, Colombia, where they disembarked. Most of their journey through Colombia was by river-steamer, distinctly reminiscent of Mark Twain. For nine days, they slept, ate, played deck games and kept a look out for alligators. The boat was sadly lacking in fellow-passengers of real interest or genuine eccentricity.

A train which climbed a narrow single track up steep mountains for more than eight thousand feet brought Bill and Christopher to Bogotá. They arrived in the capital at night, having been warned by fellow passengers that it was a den of thieves and cut-throats. They installed themselves in the Hotel Astor, the rendez-vous for bejewelled, bridge-playing ladies of good families. The town itself struck them as being most undistinguished, though Christopher was surprised by the large number of bookshops and the wide selection therein, confirming Bogatá's reputation as a place of immense culture, where even the shoeshine boys were reputed to quote Proust. As an admission of defeat, so far as coming to terms with the city was concerned, however, Christopher and Bill went to see a Bob Hope movie on their third evening there.

* *The Condor and the Cows.*

In the hope of exploring other channels they called at the U. S. Embassy (Christopher had become an American citizen in 1946) and at the British Cultural Institute. It was a shrewd move, as they were thus introduced to some of Colombia's intelligentsia, including the essayist Edgardo Salazar Santacoloma (with whom they discussed Shakespeare), the poet Leon de Greiff and the novelist Eduardo Zalamea Borda. Christopher particularly liked Zalamea, who took him to see the offices of the Liberal newspaper *El Espectador*, for which he worked. Significantly, when the editor asked Christopher what were his political beliefs, he replied that he was a Liberal—and not entirely out of politeness. Christopher was by now totally unimpressed by extremism of any sort, particularly as both Left and Right had failed miserably in his personal litmus test—their attitude to homosexuality. The Communists, after 1934, referred to gays as "fascist perverts," while the Nazis had branded them "sexual bolsheviks" and sent them to concentration camps. Christopher naturally drifted towards wishy-washy liberals who didn't really mind what people did with their private lives, and who were against the petty tyrannies of totalitarianism.

Throughout all these early cultural exchanges Bill Caskey sat "looking like an unplugged lamp," until he took to going off on his own with his camera, leaving Christopher to his literary pleasantries.

They went to a bullfight, which Christopher found very exciting and not in the least disgusting, but he hoped that he would never have to see another, as he felt it was hypocritical to watch a spectacle in which he would be terrified to participate. It is hard to imagine the Christopher of ten years previously reacting so favourably to a bullfight, surely a stylised Test for the Truly Weak Man? Certainly, he had often been critical of the exploits of one of the great bullfight enthusiasts, Ernest Hemingway. (Hemingway had once greatly amused a mutual friend by saying that Auden and Isherwood could not *possibly* be homosexuals, as he *knew* how homosexuals wrote!)

While in Colombia, both Christopher and Bill suffered from fearful digestive problems, but at their next stop, Popayán, they had several solicitous helpers including the country's leading literary critic Sanín Cano. On November 6 they left for Pasto, a thirteen-hour bus ride across difficult terrain, round many hairpin bends and blind precipitous corners, the road flanked by little black crosses marking where less fortunate travellers had gone over the edge. A mail-car then took them to the Colombia–Ecuador frontier, from whence a series of awkward connections took them to Quito:

> That is the irony of travel. You spend your boyhood dreaming of the magic, impossibly distant day when you will cross the equator, when your eyes will behold Quito. And then, in the slow prosaic process of life, that day undramatically dawns—and finds you sleepy, hungry and dull. The equator is just another valley; you aren't sure which and you don't care. Quito is just another railroad-station, with fuss about baggage and taxis and tips. And the only comforting reality, amidst all this picturesque noisy strangeness, is to find a clean pension run by Czechish refugees and sit down in a cosy Central European parlour to a lunch of well-cooked Wiener Schnitzel.*

While in Quito they met several members of Los Contemporàneos, a group devoted to the creation of a modern, indigenous Ecuadorian art, who came together every Saturday in the studio of the painter and sculptor Guayasamín. Perhaps stimulated by his rounds of cultural visits, Christopher translated a poem by Humberto Navarro—"Ballad of Absence"—into English. On December 1 he gave a talk to the British Cultural Institute about the Hollywood film industry.

Three days later, they left the Ecuadorian capital by train to Guayaquil, where they found a Polish pension called At Home. Christopher received what he thought was a violent kick in the seat of his chair, but it was only an earthquake.

After a tedious and awkward journey largely by truck, they got to the Peruvian border, arriving in Lima on December 14. There, they found some welcome mail was waiting, including the manuscript of a novel called *The City and the Pillar*, by the young writer Gore Vidal. The diaries of their mutual friend Anaïs Nin showed that Vidal had expressed a wish to meet Isherwood the year before, as he felt their writings were so "similar." Vidal said

* Ibid.

that he wished *he* had written *Prater Violet*. His own novel, however, was far franker about homosexuality than any of Isherwood's work up to that time. Christopher liked it a lot, especially because the young homosexual lovers in Vidal's novel were shown to be clean-cut, athletic all-American boys—a real innovation in the then comparatively small canon of serious homosexual fiction.

Christopher and Bill stayed out of town, in the seaside suburb of Miraflores. Their social rounds began with a lunch given by the American ambassador and former governor of Tennessee, Prentice Cooper, who revealed himself to be an ardent naturalist, whose home menagerie included a pet jaguar. Christopher avoided playing with that particular beast, but braved a few cautious pats of the ambassador's vicuna.

Christmas was spent among American expatriates, though festivities were dulled by the consciousness of the poverty of much of the local population, and the sight of bread-lines outside shops in the poorer neighbourhoods.

The prospect of travelling sixty hours in local buses to reach Arequipa proved too daunting, so they took a plane on January 9, 1948. At Arequipa, they stayed in the comfortable establishment run by the legendary Tia Bates, then well into her eighties, who had entertained the Duke of Windsor and Noël Coward, and reputedly received hundreds of letters from admirers, friends and grateful guests across the world. Christopher noted that she seemed to reserve her greatest favours for young U. S. Army men and airline pilots.

Later in the week the two travellers went up to the twelve-thousand-foot-high plateau around Lake Titicaca, where the scenery struck Christopher as being like the Tibet of his imagination (the only one of his dream-places that he has never been able to visit). Indian culture was far more evident here than it had been in other parts of their tour. A detour to Cuzco brought them some new insights into the Spanish colonial heritage, but also landed them amongst hordes of tourists. Nevertheless, they were able to enjoy the wonders of the Inca remains around Machu Picchu.

A confrontation with a Protestant, who enraged the Catholic Bill Caskey with lurid stories of the venality of Catholic priests, led Christopher to write down his own feelings about the ever-present Church in South America:

> Even if you discount fifty per cent of all criticism, it can't be denied that the Church in South America is a disgrace to Catholicism, and that the conditions in some parishes are bad enough to satisfy the producer of a Russian anti-religious movie. But I loathe the prudery of the average Protestant, who judges nothing but external behaviour, refusing to see that the Catholics, even at their worst, have much to teach him about the value of sacraments and the psychology of prayer. And how dare a comfortably married minister sneer at the backslidings of would-be celibates? He simply doesn't have their temptations. As for the militant atheists of the Left Wing, their smug stupidity appals me. It is all very well to brand certain cults and legends as superstitions, and to attack the political crimes of the historic sects, but have they never stopped to ask themselves what religion is *for?* How in the world do they imagine they can make their free democratic community function when they have removed the whole spiritual basis of consent?*

The passage shows very clearly how Christopher's experiences with the Quakers, Gerald Heard and the Vedanta Society had changed his attitude to organised religion in particular and spirituality in general. Less than ten years previously it would have been unthinkable for Isherwood to have written such a statement.

Bill and Christopher crossed Lake Titicaca into Bolivia, where, in early February, Christopher began to show symptoms of altitude sickness, so he was unable to accompany Bill on a trip to photograph the Oruro Carnival and Diablada Festival. Christopher used his time to make non-fatiguing social calls on some of the large European refugee colony. Georg von Terramare, the Austrian dramatist, told him that there were so many Austrian refugees in La Paz that he had been able to find a cast and an audience for a play he had written in Viennese dialect.

A long and dusty train journey took Bill and Christopher into Argentina. Berthold ("Bubi"), Christopher's friend from Berlin, met them at the station in Buenos Aires. He had had many ad-

* Ibid.

ventures since he had last seen Christopher in England during his refugee-smuggling days on the Dutch tramp-steamer. He had worked as a stoker on a German boat along the west coast of Africa, before being arrested by the Gestapo, then had come to settle in South America. Now he was part-owner of a small factory. But he was still the same energetic, amusing soul, anxious to please. Christopher was touched to see that Berthold had copies of his novels on his shelves in the comfortable living-room of his suburban house, a token of friendship, as he still did not know enough English to read them. He acted as the visitors' guide to Buenos Aires, which seemed to Christopher to be the most truly international city in the world, with its British banks and companies, German restaurants and Parisian boulevards.

Victoria Ocampo, a friend of Wystan Auden's, also lived in Buenos Aires, and edited a literary magazine called *Sur*. Christopher found her an unashamed aristocrat—fearless, generous, commanding, demanding, not caring a damn about fashion, a woman of impulse, with the necessary temperament and money to give free reign to her desires. Christopher, Bill and Berthold went to stay with her at the seaside resort of Mar del Plata, all three of them losing heavily at the local casino. Since Victoria Ocampo was a strict teetotaller who refused to serve liquor to her guests, the three men had brought a secret provision of whisky with them, and would gather before dinner in the room of another house-guest for a tipple. They were caught out on the first evening when their hostess walked into the room. Instead of being annoyed, however, she sat down and calmly asked them to explain the reasons for their addiction.

Most of March was spent in the capital on a social whirl, which meant that Christopher wrote only a few lines in his diary each day. Berthold proved to be an almost embarrassingly generous host. Christopher also went twice to visit the Ramakrishna Mission at Bella Vista, the only one in South America, and paid a call on Jorge Luis Borges, who dazzled him with his knowledge of classical and modern English literature.

Originally, Christopher's idea had been to return to New York from Argentina, but a change in plans enabled him and Caskey to go to Europe. They caught a French boat from Buenos Aires on March 27. The ship put in for a few hours at Montevideo, and

again at Rio de Janeiro, where they visited a friend. The sea journey then took them across the Atlantic to Dacca, Senegal. They
travelled second-class, sharing a cabin with an old European who
infuriated Caskey because he had a chamber-pot which he used in
the cabin at night. Caskey found the procedure so disgusting that
one day he threw the offending vessel out of the porthole.

En route to Le Havre, the friends found themselves hounded
by a young Jewish intellectual, who was fascinated to learn that
the Englishman knew leading members of the London literary
scene. Each time he approached them, he would ask a question
such as "And do you know E. M. Forster?" Their patience and
good manners finally broke when he asked them one day: "And
do you know Christopher Isherwood?"

They spent a few days in Paris, where one evening Caskey went
along to Pigalle and was slipped a mickey finn. He woke up the
next day in a cage in a police station, robbed of money and
traveller's cheques, which put Christopher into quite a state. His
mystical calm could break down quite easily under pressure.

Sitting in the Deux Magots at St.-Germain-des-Prés one day,
they were approached by a young man who introduced himself as
Gore Vidal. Christopher thought him wildly attractive, and the
three of them went sight-seeing together; Vidal irritated Caskey at
Versailles by running down a register of historical figures deciding
which were gay. Isherwood shares many people's opinion that
Vidal is at his best in his essays, and believed Vidal to be
America's one true aristocrat. Isherwood has kept in touch with
Vidal ever since, dedicating *A Single Man* to him. Vidal returned
the compliment with *Myra Breckinridge*.

Bill Caskey persuaded Christopher that they ought to go to see
Denny Fouts, who was living in Peter Watson's flat in the Rue du
Bac. By this time, Denny was using quite dangerous quantities of
heroine, cocaine and opium ("If it's good enough for Cocteau,
honey, it's good enough for me"). It was a rather depressing encounter. Later Fouts went on a cure, but died in Rome of a heart
attack.

One day Christopher and Bill ran into Wystan Auden and
Chester Kallman, who were just off to Ischia. Caskey announced
that, as he was a Catholic, he ought at least to see Rome, which
Christopher had also never visited, but instead they went to Eng-

land. There they saw many of Christopher's old friends and went to stay for a while at Wyberslegh, where Kathleen alarmed Caskey with her habit of lifting up her dress to warm herself by the fire. Wallpaper which had curled off the wall from damp had, rather unskilfully, been stuck back on again. Nanny's health had deteriorated even further, and later that year she died.

They returned to London in the second half of June, which gave them about a month before sailing to New York, and during this time Christopher received an offer from MGM to work on a new film, *The Great Sinner*, to be based on Dostoevsky's novel *The Gambler*. He returned to California to work on the script, which had already passed through Ladislas Fodor's hands.

Fodor had had the idea that Dostoevsky himself should be in the film as a character who becomes a gambler. It was not easy for Christopher to make some of Fodor's work gel with his own, but he was pleased that at least some of Dostoevsky was left in the finished movie. During the shooting he found himself standing in for the actor Frank Morgan, who was meant to speak with the voice of Christ when Dostoevsky robs a poorbox in a church. Christopher was given a microphone and an enormously long cable, and told to speak the lines in the concrete entrance hall of the studios, to make the voice reverberate. Just as the red cue-light went on for him to speak, a door opened and in walked a carpenter. Christopher looked at the man right in the eye and declaimed in the loudest possible voice: "And they parted my garments among them, and they cast dice for my robe!" He had never seen anyone so startled in his life.

On November 6, 1948, Christopher wrote to John Lehmann from his new home at 333 East Rustic Road (the "haunted" house at the bottom of Santa Monica Canyon):

My life, since I reached California, has been divided into two phases. The first, before Caskey joined me, was work at the studio, on the Dostoevsky picture, which is now being shot. (Called "The Great Sinner"—did you know he actually meditated writing a book of that name, the old ham!?) It is not Dostoevsky, but it's somewhat magnificent, owing to $3,000,000 worth of sets, costumes and high-powered talent.

Anyhow, I disclaim all responsibility—unless, of course, you like it! This first phase also included a lot of whisky drinking and a good deal of running around town, in the process of which I lost nearly ten pounds and a great deal of sleep. Then Caskey arrived and found this house, which we hope to stay in for a couple of years. It is very nice, and really quite rustic, under some sycamores, near the ocean, beside a creek. I feel like Vanzetti's description of Sacco "a worker from his boyhood, with a good job and pay, a bank account, a good and lovely wife, and a neat little home at the verge of a wood, near a brook. . . ." Madly respectable!

Caskey paints, carpenters, sews and cooks untiringly, and so far we have had only *one* wild party! I am churning out a travel-book, which is going to be my longest and worst work, I fear. I just can't do straight journalism, and the truth is that South America *bored* me, and I am ashamed that it bored me, and I hate it for making me feel ashamed. However, I am determined to go through with it and then get on to the novel, which at least will be an *honorable* failure.

The Condor and the Cows turned out to be far from his worst book. The title was chosen to represent the two geographical extremes of South America: the Condor of the Andes and the Cows of the Pampas. Christopher was well aware of the fact that there was no reason for his having gone to South America, except that he was commissioned to write the book, but travel writing is such an accepted and popular diet for the general public that that did not matter. The book gave him an ideal chance to ramble on about all sorts of ideas and theories about life in general, as well as about South America in particular, which he could never have slotted comfortably into his sort of fiction.

He now looks back on the book with affection. Published in 1949, it is not well known in the States, but sold quite well in England. The English edition (dedicated to Kathleen) had ninety-four photographs by Caskey, whereas the American edition (dedicated to Bill's mother) only had thirty-six.

Undoubtedly one of the reasons why work on the novel was going so slowly during this period was the fact that Christopher was drinking rather heavily and living a fairly degenerate existence, which sapped his creative energy. However, he did manage to write his diary some of the time, on better days, standing upright for an hour or so to work on it, often chewing his knuckle as he thought.

To clear his head in the morning, he would do the washing-up from the night before. He had a room where his most precious books and papers were kept, and he would lock it if people were coming round for a party. He was known to fly into a rage if anyone touched his typewriter. In contrast to the calm of his later years, Christopher at this time would often get excited, and he and Caskey had some quite spectacular rows in public and private, which secretly both of them rather enjoyed.

Neither of them had been qualified to vote in the election which swept Truman back into the White House, but they followed politics closely, particularly during what William Manchester has so aptly dubbed the Age of Suspicion. Indeed, the house in which they were now living had formerly been inhabited by the wife of one of the Hollywood Ten. While Christopher had been in South America and Europe, the communist witch-hunt had been pursuing its gruesome course. A good many of Christopher's friends became directly or indirectly involved. Congressmen Thomas, Rankin and Stripling fought the "Reds" in the guise of the U. S. Congressional Committee Regarding the Communists' Infiltration of the Motion Picture Industry. Jack Warner and L. B. Mayer had to defend their reasons for making films such as *Mission to Moscow* and *Song of Russia*. More than five hundred prominent Americans signed a petition protesting against the hearings, and a Committee for the First Amendment was formed by those forces in Hollywood who saw the affair for the ignominy it was. Thomas Mann was cheered when he addressed a meeting thus:

> I have the honour to expose myself as a hostile witness. I testify that I am very much interested in the moving-picture industry and that since my arrival in the United States nine years ago, I have seen a great many Hollywood films. If communist propaganda had been smuggled into them it must have been most thoroughly buried. I, for one, never noticed anything of the sort. . . . As an American citizen of German

birth I finally testify that I am painfully familiar with certain political trends. Spiritual intolerance, political inquisitions, and declining legal security, and all this in the name of an alleged "state of emergency." . . . That is how it started in Germany.*

Unfortunately, not everybody had the common sense and courage of Thomas Mann, nor the moral integrity of Lillian Hellman, who wrote a letter that was a landmark of the McCarthy era, refusing to testify about any of her friends or their beliefs. Nineteen people were originally summoned to Washington to explain themselves. Eight of them were dropped from the list of the Un-American Activities Committee. Bertolt Brecht, who figured in the remaining eleven, went through the interrogation, then immediately left on a plane for Switzerland, later moving to East Berlin. Helli Brecht sold the house in Santa Monica, then followed with the children. The remaining "suspects" became the Hollywood Ten. Salka Viertel, who had arranged an amicable divorce for Berthold while Christopher was in South America, also found herself under accusation of being a communist. She was refused an exit visa when she tried to see Berthold in 1953, but a skilled lawyer managed to obtain a permit for her in the end.

At this time Christopher learned that Edward Upward had broken with the Communist Party. He wrote on February 9, 1949:

> I can't help feeling glad about the ending of your political activities. Just as I imagine you were glad when I stopped living with the Vedanta people. But I don't want to underline this, or I shall say something stupid, not knowing the circumstances. I know the break must have been painful for both of you, but it is sure to make your writing easier. And your writing is your real job, your real debt to any kind of social order. We need you more now than ever. The very fact that you've saved up your powers all these years is an advantage.

Edward Upward charted the course of his relationship with the Party in his unjustly neglected trilogy of novels, *The Spiral Ascent*, in which Christopher appears in the role of the poet Richard. Christopher remained one of the greatest believers in Up-

---

* Quoted in Salka Viertel, *The Kindness of Strangers*, p. 236.

ward's talent, and repeatedly showered Upward's work with praise. After much discussion and soul-searching, Upward had finally agreed to have *The Railway Accident* printed, and Christopher wrote a foreword for it, which he posted that May.

Christopher still kept in touch with the Vedanta Center, and in 1949 worked on a translation of Patanjali's yoga aphorisms, finally published in 1953 as *How to Know God*. The possibility of a visit to India was mooted, but nothing came of it. Bill Caskey viewed the whole Vedanta business very cynically, and usually referred to the Hollywood Center as "Heaven."

In May Stephen Spender was expected on one of his many visits to America in the post-war years. Having just seen his portrait in Spender's frank article about some of his friends, printed in the *Partisan Review*, Christopher wrote on May 19 to Edward: "You are lucky not to be included in the memoirs he printed in the Partisan Review. I shall be embarrassed ever to show my face in New York again. It is like being featured in the Kinsey Report."

One of Christopher's closest friendships during this period, and indeed for the rest of the composer's peripatetic life, was with Igor Stravinsky, who lived in Santa Monica with his wife, Vera. Christopher considered Stravinsky to be one of the three remarkable men he had met in his life (the other two being E. M. Forster and Swami Prabhavananda). In the winter of 1948–49, Igor Stravinsky was working on *The Rake's Progress*, but also travelled enormously both inside and outside the States, conducting, composing and leading a glittering social life. He was fond of Christopher, and amused by him, and thought Bill Caskey a riot. Often they would get together with Aldous and Maria Huxley, who had little difficulty in persuading the group to go to eat at their favourite hangout, the Farmers' Market in Los Angeles, where there was a wide variety of health foods, exotic fruits and nuts—as well as the sunflower seeds that Aldous was then eating in great quantities, in the belief that they would help his troubled eyes. Sometimes these visits to the Farmers' Market would set Christopher off on his vegetarian fads again, though they never lasted very long. The place was the haunt of all kinds of European intellectual émigrés, movie stars and weirdos which the party loved to observe, though they themselves were often the centre of attention, the wiry, intense Stravinsky and gangling Aldous Huxley both being extremely famous in their lifetime, and instantly recognisable.

Talking of the composer in an interview with the British journalist W. I. Scobie, Isherwood recalled:

> I always think of Stravinsky in a very physical way. He was physically adorable; he was cuddly—he was so little, and you wanted to protect him. He was very demonstrative, a person who—I suppose it was his Russian-ness—was full of kisses and embraces. He had great warmth. He could be fearfully hostile and snub people and attack his critics and so forth, but personally, he was a person of immense joy and warmth. The first time I came to his house he said to me: "Would you like to hear my Mass before we get drunk?"

And drink they did, on many occasions. Stravinsky was fond of one particular fatal brew called Marc de Borgogne, which usually made Christopher (who has a very low level of alcohol endurance) tiddly in a very short space of time. Once Christopher actually passed out on the floor, then came round to see:

> . . . at an immense altitude above me Aldous Huxley, who was very tall, standing up and talking French to Stravinsky who never seemed to get overcome however much he drank. And Aldous, who I think was very fond of me, was looking at me rather curiously as much as to say "Aren't you going a little far?"*

It is interesting to interpolate how Christopher struck Stravinsky's shadow companion and devoted biographer, Robert Craft. Writing in his diary on August 10, 1949, after one of those Farmers' Market lunches, Craft recorded about Christopher:

> His manner is casual, vagabondish, lovelorn. One does not readily imagine him in a fit of anger or behaving precipitately or enduring extended states of great commotion. At moments he might be thinking of things beyond and remote, from which the conversation brusquely summons him back to earth. But he's a listener and an observer—he has the observer's habit of staring—rather than a propounder and expa-

---

* W. I. Scobie in *The Art of Fiction* (1975).

tiator, and his trancelike eyes will see more deeply through, and record more essential matter about, us than this verbosity of mine is doing about him.*

It took Christopher a long time to appreciate Stravinsky's music, and indeed the composer accused him of falling asleep to it, but then Christopher was never notably musical. This did not stop him having good friends within the tight-knit world of musicians, of whom Stravinsky was the closest. He knew Virgil Thomson in New York and, of course, Benjamin Britten, among others.

Christopher was seeing Aldous Huxley professionally as well as socially at this time, as they had started working on another of their ill-fated joint movie projects. This one was to be set in South America, with a sort of Hungarian Mr. Norris in it—an idea which encouraged Christopher to speculate whether he should not resuscitate an old idea of writing a sequel to *Mr. Norris Changes Trains*, set in South America. For the first time in Christopher's American period since his earliest Californian days, money had become a serious problem. Bill Caskey supplemented the household income by working as a gardener, then his father died, and he came into some money, though he had to tend the family business in Kentucky for several months in the first part of 1950.

Financial worries made it impossible for Christopher to visit either India or England during 1950, as he wished to do. Swami Prabhavananda went to the subcontinent in the late spring, and, since Gerald Heard went to New York at the same time, Christopher found himself coping with the weekly Sunday morning lectures at the Vedanta Center during the summer. Not wishing to take on the role of minister, he gave readings (including Upward's university poem about Buddha), with very little comment.

At the beginning of December 1949, Christopher and Bill rented a new house, at 31152 Monterey Street, Coast Royal, South Laguna, about sixty miles down the coast from Santa Monica. Christopher explained the move in a letter to Edward Upward, dated December 5:

This is by means of an attempt at a New Period—goodbye Hollywood, allons to serious writing, retirement, art, and no

---

* Robert Craft: Stravinsky: *Chronicle of a Friendship, 1948–1971* (1972).

more parties and telephone calls. Actually, I don't know what we are going to use for money; and I'll probably come scampering back if I get the least sniff of a job. . . .

My novel is alive again and I'm determined to finish it, even as an interesting failure. I am feeling my way toward an Anglo-American style, and this is itself very hard. It *ought* theoretically to be wonderful and funny to be a detached mongrel, talking a bastard jargon, but I fear this will only come with much more practice.

As one means of easing monetary worries, Christopher reluctantly accepted the offer of a job reviewing books for the American magazine *Tomorrow*. He did not like reviewing, and always refused to review anything he had not enjoyed reading, on the grounds that it was a waste of the readers' time to describe poor books when there were so many good ones clamouring for recognition, and also because he did not like to hurt other writers. In January 1951 Christopher wrote a résumé of his activities in a letter of January 24 to Edward Upward:

My novel is really extraordinary. I mean, I simply haven't the slightest idea what is going to happen in it, or if it is the least good. It is becoming much more like a Freudian analysis, and I'm far more interested to see what I shall discover about myself than to see how it will develop as an artwork. However, the practical result is the same: I have to go on writing it, and I will. Certainly, all this obstruction shows that there's *something* I'm very very unwilling to admit.

Other tasks: reviewing Stephen's autobiography [*World Within World*] (which I think is exceedingly interesting, though there is something in it to enrage everybody, myself and yourself included), editing a new anthology of essays from the Vedanta magazine, getting on with the Patanjali translation, collaborating on a dramatisation of my Sally Bowles (with a very intelligent N.Y. Jew and . . . Speed Lamkin, who is one of our most promising writers—he wants to be the Rastignac of Los Angeles and is writing a novel about the old movie stars), reading manuscripts by young writers who get scholarships at a sort of literary stud-farm called the Huntington Hartford Foundation, in which I'm a member of the advisory board. . . . All this just in case you should think I'm lounging on the beach.

The Huntington Hartford Foundation, started in 1949 by a multi-millionaire who had built it on 135 acres in Rustic Canyon, was intended to assist artists, writers and musicians with three months' free room and board, plus studio, in which they could find absolute quiet and complete freedom from financial worries while they developed their talents. By June 1951 there were 160 people there. Among Christopher's colleagues was Robert Penn Warren, as well as Speed Lamkin, a young man from Louisiana, whose novel *The Easter Egg Hunt* was dedicated to Christopher. (Christopher himself appears briefly but recognisably in it as Sebastian Saunders, along with Denny Fouts—Danny Hunts.) There were several little houses on the Rustic Canyon property, though Christopher had the use of a studio apartment over the stables. He alternated between there and his South Laguna home. Sometimes, he alarmed Bill by swerving back to the Foundation at night in his little old Ford in a state of semi-inebriation, but Bill was not in a position to protest, as he himself had been hauled up in front of the magistrates for driving under the influence.

A major event of 1951 was the dramatisation of *Sally Bowles*, which came about largely thanks to Alec and Dodie Beesley. Several of Christopher's friends were worried about his financial situation, so the Beesleys came up with the idea that a dramatisation of *Sally Bowles* would be one way that he could earn some royalties, and that John Van Druten was the best person to do it. Aware that the proposal would have to be stage managed if it was to succeed, the Beesleys waited for an opportunity at Van Druten's ranch on the other side of Palm Springs. The plan was that Alec Beesley should pop his head up out of the swimming-pool and say very casually, "Say, do you think it would be possible to make a play out of Chris's *Sally Bowles?*" To make the situation seem natural, the general conversation would be steered towards the problem of dramatising novels. John Van Druten would rise to the bait, as indeed he did, producing *I Am a Camera* in a few weeks.

Neither the Beesleys nor Christopher were wildly enthusiastic about the play in script, but it was a quite different matter on stage. It opened in Hartford, Connecticut, on November 8, 1951, with Julie Harris in the lead. It was she who made the play. Isherwood later recalled:

> I first set eyes on Julie at the studio of a New York photographer, where she and I were to enact meeting, for publicity purposes. Julie entered in costume as Sally Bowles. Since we had not been formally introduced I decided to treat her as Sally. Hugging my lost companion, I exclaimed reproachfully that she had stayed the same age while I had grown twenty years older. My scene of improvised whimsy was played to conceal a certain dismay, a disconcerting sense of strangeness. This was not simply an actress dressed up as one of my characters. Here was something other, an independent presence which Julie, under John's direction, had mediumistically produced. Oh yes, it was *like* Sally Bowles, but it wasn't my creation. It wasn't Julie's. It wasn't John's. It had a life of its own. But it was determined to survive if it by any means could. It would use any of us to do so.*

The play transferred to the Empire Theater in New York at the end of the month, and was attended by many celebrities on its first night. Christopher and John Van Druten walked back and forth across the back of the auditorium to catch the feel of the audience. During the interval Christopher went into the lobby, where Stravinsky rushed up to him, embraced him and murmured, "Inferior to the novel!" Marlene Dietrich then approached Stravinsky with a wild "Cher Maître," but Stravinsky did not introduce them. So Christopher stood around awkwardly, feeling very foolish.

At the end of the show, Christopher walked back to the house where he was staying near the docks, absorbed in an account of the amours of a friend of his, so that he completely forgot about the play until the notices appeared in the morning's papers. Some critics, like Brooks Atkinson of the New York *Times*, had reservations about it, but it soon became obvious that it was a hit. John Van Druten did his own directing, William Prince took on the

---

* "Saturday Review" column, *The Times*, August 15, 1975.

role of Christopher Isherwood and Olga Fabian gave a cameo performance as the landlady. A British production, starring Dorothy Tutin, was also successful. As the Beesleys had hoped, Christopher did well out of it financially, though there was some bitterness caused when John Van Druten (then a relatively wealthy man) insisted on a 60-40 split of royalties, rather than the more usual 50-50.

Although *I Am a Camera* brought Christopher's name into the American press during 1951, he was talked of in the British newspapers because of an entirely different matter. The *cause célèbre* of 1951 in London was the disappearance of the two diplomats Burgess (recently returned from a tour of duty in Washington) and Maclean (head of the Foreign Office's American department). Guy Burgess and Donald Maclean, it seemed, had been warned by Kim Philby that the Foreign Office had caught on to their connection with Moscow secret service agents. On May 25 therefore they disappeared. Newspaper headlines screamed "Where Are They?" and some people even suggested that they were hiding in Ischia with their good friend W. H. Auden. Stephen Spender was engagingly indiscreet with certain newspaper reporters about Burgess's friendship with his group of writer acquaintances, with the result that Christopher soon found himself being visited by two clean-cut FBI agents. He soon made it obvious that he knew nothing of the Burgess and Maclean affair, but they stayed for a long time, as if fascinated by the opportunity to talk to a genuine limey writer. Burgess did indeed reach Moscow, where the Russians fixed him up with a very charming friend.

At the end of the year, *I Am a Camera* successfully launched, Christopher left for England on the *Queen Elizabeth*.

12

On his two previous visits to Europe Christopher had studiously avoided going to Germany, unsure of how he would feel about visiting Berlin *après le déluge*. In 1952, however, he plucked up enough courage to accept an assignment from *The Observer* to write a piece about Berlin. This was published on March 23, and he wrote:

> I dreaded meeting the people I had known. I dreaded seeing familiar places in ruins. I had quite made up my mind to go, but my unconscious still protested; so I developed symptoms of a duodenal ulcer and nearly broke my leg on a staircase. Throughout the flight from London, I expected to crash, and was almost disappointed when he landed safe at Tempelhofer Feld in a mild snowstorm: "a psychosomatic snowstorm, obviously," one of my friends commented later.

He had not warned Fräulein Thurau, his old landlady, that he would be coming. When he arrived at her door she let out a Wagnerian scream of joy that must have been heard throughout the block. She knew about her *alter ego* as Fräulein Schroeder, but did not seem disturbed about it, though she told him she was annoyed because he had written that she "waddled." She did not do so, being much thinner than her fictional incarnation. She said that "Otto" had been round recently, looking very well dressed, but still a spiv, and had wanted to buy her carpets. Heinz was living happily with a wife and a son, named after Christopher. Heinz had written to Christopher soon after the end of the war, to let him know that he was still alive; but Christopher had not been able to bring himself to tell Heinz about his visits to Europe in 1947 and 1948.

Back in the Western Atlantic at the end of spring, Christopher went on a trip to Bermuda with a young Irish-Minnesotan, who miraculously stopped him drinking for a while. Christopher then caught a train from New York to San Francisco, where he joined up with Bill Caskey, who had taken the opportunity of the Korean War to join the Navy. Christopher went on a mountain trip with Caskey, then returned to Los Angeles to find the Huntington Hartford Foundation in uproar over its director. Christopher became slightly involved in this dispute, getting his fingers burnt, and retired to the relative tranquillity of the Vedanta Society. There he finished his Patanjali translation and part of his latest novel, *The World in the Evening*.

Among Christopher's friends in Los Angeles was a very remarkable psychologist, Evelyn Hooker. Dr. Hooker was involved in a comprehensive study of homosexuality, then a very frowned-upon subject in conservative California. She worked from the assumption that homosexuals were not necessarily sick people, but that they were a phenomenon, forming a group which was an ideal subject for social-psychological research. She interviewed hundreds of homosexual men of all kinds, and became a very familiar and loved figure in the gay bars of Hollywood at a time when they were very much outposts of a threatened minority. Christopher's relationship with her was based on a professional interest and a growing friendship.

Christopher explained to her that he had been having problems in finding somewhere to live, and she half jokingly suggested that he could always move into the summer-house at the bottom of her garden. To her amazement and amusement, he followed up the suggestion with alacrity, and commissioned a very close friend of his, the architect and writer Jim Charlton, to refurbish it. Thus he moved into 400 South Saltair Avenue, Los Angeles.

Although he was now living alone, Christopher still saw Bill

Caskey (just returned from the Orient) from time to time, and in November they went on a trip south. Christopher wrote to William Plomer from Hermosillo, Mexico, in a letter dated November 21, 1952:

> We have been making a little trip through Arizona and down the western coast to Mexico to a place called Guaymas, where they catch big Hemingway-fish with spikes on the end. It was full of Hemingway characters who had lost control of their dialogue. One of the nicest things about South Western America is that it has Mexico next door. How I wish you could indulge in another far-fling and come here!

Bill Caskey travelled widely as a sailor, before settling down to a life as a photographer and artist, specialising in nightmarish *objets trouvès*. He finally installed himself in Athens, Greece, during the late 1960s, but saw Christopher from time to time while on visits to the States. He produced a book about Classic Athens, doing both the photographs and the text, and Christopher (always generous with time and advice for friends) went through the text with him. The book is dedicated to Christopher.

The years in Caskey's company were often wild and troubled, often fun, but also plagued by bouts of alcoholic excess. They were nonetheless not the infertile period that they seemed to some of Christopher's friends abroad, who waited year after year for a good novel to appear. Some of the less generous critics in England, who had disapproved of Christopher's "exile" during the war, gloated that the States had killed his talent. It was true that the gestation period for the novel *The World in the Evening* was the most difficult, and the result the least satisfactory, of Christopher's career, but his detractors ignored the fact that he had also produced the South American travel book and several Vedanta-orientated books and pamphlets during the post-war years.

A little later, Christopher met a rather shy teenager of great charm by the name of Don Bachardy. Years afterwards, in an interview with the Californian gay newspaper *The Advocate*, Bachardy gave a delightful but dramatically simplified account of their meeting at a party on St. Valentine's Day, 1953, when, he said, he approached Isherwood, who was standing by an open window. Both of them had had a few drinks, and they fell backwards out of the window. Some time later they joined up, and they have lived together ever since.

In fact, things developed much more slowly during that winter of 1952–53. Christopher met and became friends with both Don and his elder brother. Both boys were crazy about films, and came from a moderate, rather conventional family, their father being about Christopher's age. Initially, Christopher's feelings were a little ambivalent, but soon he began to realise that he had fallen in love. However, he was forty-eight and Don was eighteen, and California was not Ancient Greece. Don looked even younger than his age, and a few of Christopher's friends declared that this time he really had gone too far. Some of them have never been forgiven for their hasty decision. Evelyn Hooker found herself in a difficult position. She sympathised deeply with Christopher's feelings, but was highly alarmed at the possibility of legal proceedings instigated by malicious Los Angeles residents, of whom there has never been a lack. She felt that a scandal would be hard to bear for her husband, who was working with great devotion on a definitive edition of Dryden. She therefore asked Christopher if he could find somewhere else to live, if Don was to move in with him. Anyway, the summer-house was not really big enough for two people. Dr. Hooker continued to keep a lively interest in the relationship, nevertheless, and has remained a friend. Bill Caskey received an anonymous poison-pen letter telling him that he ought to go to the police to report Christopher and Don, but of course he did no such thing.

The situation was solved in the first instance by Marguerite Lamkin, Speed's sister. At the time, Marguerite was the young bride of the writer Harry Brown (author of A *Walk in the Sun*). Speed had joked that he knew something terrible would happen if he ever introduced Christopher to his sister, but on the contrary they got on very well, and Marguerite and Don quickly became firm friends. Don went to live with her and her husband, while Christopher rented a place a stone's throw away, as a temporary arrangement.

Christopher had written to Edward Upward in a letter dated January 29, 1953:

My watchword to you for 1953 is Forward. After an examen de minuit scene in which reason really tottered on her throne, I said to myself Enough, and gave orders for a frontal attack on the material with everything we had. Throwing all sinuous approaches to the winds, we advanced straight to the end of the novel and arrived there the day before yesterday. . . .

My novel is very vulgar reactionary pornographic trash. But who cares? All that matters to me is the knowledge that I'm not yet totally impotent.

The revised version of *The World in the Evening* was sent to the publishers in August. Methuen seemed very enthusiastic about it, whereas Random House was warm but critical, so Christopher agreed to do some further re-writing. The novel in its final form is his longest and his least successful. It traces the fortunes of Stephen Monk, a wealthy lapsed Quaker in his mid-thirties, who sets out on a voyage of personal reappraisal in the early years of the Second World War, after discovering his second wife (partly based on Bill Caskey) *flagrante delicto* with another man in a dolls' house (a detail born from a visit to Norma Shearer's beach-home in Santa Monica, where Christopher had seen a huge doll's house). Stephen Monk flees California to stay with an honorary saintly Quaker aunt in Pennsylvania, who has taken in an intelligent young German woman refugee. He recalls his life with his first wife, a famous novelist (partly based on Katherine Mansfield and Virginia Woolf), who had married him when he was very young. He talks to his deceased spouse constantly during the book.

Stephen is given the ideal opportunity for reflection when he is (subconsciously) willingly run over by a truck and is forced to convalesce. He remembers his relationship with a younger man, whom he used dishonestly. A couple of wholesome queers in the Pennsylvania village provide an excuse for a discussion of homosexuality. After his recovery, Stephen obtains a divorce from his second wife, though later they meet again amicably, each destined to a new and cleaner life, Stephen in an ambulance unit in North Africa.

Many people felt that *The World in the Evening* confirmed their worst fears about the effect of Hollywood upon good novelists. There is little of the old Isherwood sparkle, and some passages do tend to read like dialogue from a B movie. Of course, many people in real life *speak* as fictional characters do in a B movie, but in this case the characters are complex beings capable, surely, of much more. However, the real problem with *The World in the Evening* is its central character, Stephen. The device of using him as a first person narrator does not work at all. For some of the time, he is recognisable Isherwood derivative, doing Isherwood things. At other times, he is utterly different—a victim of the author's loathing for bisexuals. The reader is confused about the stance he should take *vis-à-vis* Stephen, yet does not find the enigma satisfying enough to warrant any great effort on his part. Isherwood fails to convey the essential heterosexual lust which Stephen is meant to feel towards his second wife (possibly because it is a sensation outside his own experience), while his portrayal of the young homosexual couple is such that they often seem silly and, occasionally, embarrassingly cute.

Immediately after sending off the manuscript, Christopher once more confessed his true feelings about the book, writing to Edward Upward on August 31:

> It is terribly slipshod, and vulgar and sentimental at times in a Hollywoodish way, and there is a great deal of sex, including some homosexual scenes which will shock many people, I dare say, worse than anything I've written—though not in the least pornographic. . . . All of it has been rewritten three times—some of it more.

Edward confirmed Christopher's fears about the novel; but this time Christopher had sent him the manuscript *after* sending it to the publishers, so that it was rather too late to do anything about it. Over the next year, various reports of the negative reaction to the book filtered through. In a letter dated September 21, 1954, Somerset Maugham wrote to his friend Strong:

> I waited to thank you for sending me Christopher's book till I had read it. I have done so. There is a lot of cleverness there, parts that are charming & true, but on the whole I find it disappointing. I can't quite make out why. I think perhaps there is an awkwardness in the construction which is irritating. I don't find the characters very interesting. Elizabeth is

almost a caricature of the portentous, second rate female novelist. She does not move but exasperates. And Stephen is
surely a poor fish.

Perhaps I shouldn't have felt so let down if I had not so
greatly admired and cherished the Christopher of twenty
years ago. What damage Gerald Heard did to our English literature when he induced thru you these talented writers to
desert their native country for America!

And in a long review in the magazine *Encounter*, Angus Wilson
wrote:

[The] failure in central purpose is particularly sad because
The World in the Evening shows no decline in Mr. Isherwood's powers; indeed, in the understanding of certain
human relationships and, above all, in technical control both
of range and organisation, it shows, I think, a very considerable advance. Nevertheless he has tried to stick out his spiritual neck a great deal further than it will stretch, and, by
doing so, he has, I'm afraid "asked for it". . . . A great deal
of the novel is highly entertaining, much of it is percipient,
some of it very moving, but it is not important at the level to
which it aspires.*

During 1954 Christopher did another stint of film-work at
MGM. *Diane*, a costume piece about Diane de Poitiers for Edwin
H. Knopf, was the only film in which Christopher had a completely
free hand to write what he liked. He revelled in the opportunity,
stealing from Balzac, Dumas and other French historical fiction,
garnished with lots of poignards, poison and purple velvet. However, he was not so fortunate about casting. He wanted a European
cast, preferably with Ingrid Bergman in the title role, and Julie
Harris as Catherine de Médicis (wife of Henry II of France). The
studio said that Bergman was quite out of the question, though
not all that long afterwards she proved them wrong by winning
an Oscar for *Anastasia*. Julie Harris said she would be enchanted
to do *Diane*, but when she went to the studio for an audition
she was turned down. In the end, Lana Turner played Diane and

* Angus Wilson, "The Old and the New Isherwood," *Encounter*, III, No. 2
(August 1954).

Marisa Pavan was given the role of Catherine. Pedro Armendariz played Francis I (a role for which Christopher had selected John Williams). Christopher later admitted that Pavan and Armendariz looked perfect in their parts, but there were great problems with their diction during the shooting of the film. Isherwood anyway disliked the American twang in the film, as it did not fit in with his conception of the film as High Camp, which one of the characters in *The World in the Evening* had defined in these terms:

> . . . the whole emotional basis of the Ballet, for example, and of course of Baroque art. You see, true High Camp always has an underlying seriousness. You can't camp about something you don't take seriously. You're not making fun of it; you're making fun out of it. You're expressing what's basically serious to you in terms of fun and artifice and elegance. Baroque art is largely camp about religion. The Ballet is camp about love.

Work on *Diane* meant that Christopher was unable to accept an offer from Henry Cornelius to do a screenplay for a filmed version of *I Am a Camera*. That was a double pity, as Christopher would have liked to have had control over his material, and the job would almost certainly have given him the chance of a period in England. However, that in itself would have presented problems, as he would not have wished to go to Britain without Don, who was then in the middle of college and threatened by the draft. Therefore, John Collier did the script.

Julie Harris—at the time working on a movie of John Steinbeck's *East of Eden,* and seeing a lot of Chris and Don—accepted the role of Sally Bowles, which she had already immortalised on stage. Laurence Harvey played Christopher and Shelley Winters was a rather curious Natalia Landauer. Henry Cornelius had been in Berlin with Max Reinhardt at the time of the story, so he was familiar with the terrain. However, he decided that the relationship between Christopher and Sally was not plausible on film. The audience, he said, would never buy two young, healthy people of the opposite sex going through a film as *friends,* so in the film they get married.

The film was well received by the public, but some of the reviews were scathing. Alan Brien, then writing for the *Evening Standard*, wrote uncompromisingly: "It has a distinct and unforgettable taste like a caviar sandwich dipped in sugar and cream" (October 13, 1955); while Harold Conway of the *Daily Sketch* rapped Cornelius and Collier over the knuckles for the liberties they had taken with the original story-line: "The screen version exchanges subtlety for horseplay, an awkwardly-contrived happy-ending for the astringent charm of the original" (October 13, 1955). In a letter to John Lehmann (September 14, 1955), Christopher said that he and John Van Druten thought it "disgusting, ooh-la-la near pornographic trash."

By the winter of 1954–55, Christopher and Don had moved into an apartment and took their first major trip together, to Mexico. They went by car with friends called Ben and Jo Masselink, driving down the coast through Tijuana, and inland to Mexico City, returning via El Paso. The holiday started well, and Christopher was elated to see an iguana. However, disaster struck in Mexico City in the form of sickness, which laid out both Don and Chris (as he was now invariably called by his American acquaintances, with very few exceptions like Evelyn Hooker). When they were finally able to get away from the city, Christopher shook his fist at it and shouted "Good-bye, Death Valley!"

The trip to Mexico with Don resulted in the germination of a new novel in Christopher's head. On May 20, 1955, he wrote to Edward Upward:

Very dimly but with increasing excitement I receive adumbrations of a quite different sort of novel—a fantasy: realistic throughout but nevertheless queer (I don't mean *queer*). I shall tell you more of this later. It has some relation to my recent trip to Mexico. A journey which is not a journey, or perhaps after all it *is* a journey. Something of the inferno, something of Journey to the Border [a novel by Upward], and of course Kafka, but more cheerful, even hilarious—hilarious-hideous, maybe. Very suggestive—to give you a final hint, is the thought that (according to Wall St) we are entering a new period of peaceprosperityexpandingeconomypermanentboom, in which tragedy is unmodern.

It was to be called *Down There on a Visit* (a reference to Huys-man's *Là-Bas*). It was completely written before eventually being shelved; only the title was retained—for another novel.

They still saw Marguerite (Lamkin) Brown several times a week, usually over a splendid meal, the menus of which she preserved for posterity, though she later cursed herself for not filling her diary with notes from the table conversations. On January 22, 1955, she gave a large party for their mutual friend, Tennessee Williams, and at the beginning of February she went to New York with Williams to work with him on *Cat on a Hot Tin Roof*. Christopher and Don travelled to Philadelphia in March to see the play. William Faulkner was also at a celebration party there. The meals continued back in Los Angeles the following week, with Gore Vidal in town. Birthday-parties were always a good excuse for a slap-up do, and the succession of feasts at least partly explain why Christopher thought it necessary to spend time in the gym keeping himself in shape. Another good friend of both Christopher and Marguerite was Truman Capote. Unhappily, later that year Marguerite's marriage broke up.

While the shooting of *Diane* progressed during 1955 Christopher was working on a new screenplay—a life of Buddha. An original script had been written by Robert Hardy Andrews, which Christopher used as a basis from which to fabricate his own highly inventive version. He took several liberties with the Buddhist legend, in order to make the story more feasible dramatically. He introduced a pretender to the throne, who had every reason to try to fulfil the prophecy that the young crown prince would renounce his heritage and become a monk. Despite these and other flights of fancy, the film was originally intended to be very authentic, shot in India, with Asian actors.

The project fell through, though it was resuscitated in 1960 when Ram Gopal, the Burmese-Indian dancer, told the *Evening Standard* that he was going to the Himalayas for two months' seclusion and meditation to prepare for the role of the young Buddha. The film was to be called *The Wayfarer*, but nothing more seems to have come of it.

In the summer of 1955 Christopher and Don moved to Malibu (29938 Pacific Coast Highway), then in October they left for a trip to Europe, taking an Italian boat from New York. Don had never been to Europe before, so it was largely a sight-seeing tour. They stopped off at Tangier to see Paul Bowles, and here Christopher tried kif for the first time. Up until then he had stayed clear of drugs, primly refusing to try hash when neighbours of his a few years before had offered him some of their home-grown weed. In Tangier Christopher took a large dose of kif and had a very unpleasant and frightening reaction, which is partly fictionalised in the story "A Visit to Anselm Oakes," which appears in *Exhumations*. Oakes is, of course, based not on Paul Bowles but on Aleister Crowley.

For the first time in his life Christopher visited Italy, until now studiously avoided as the place that all Englishwomen loved. Italy was enjoying a marvellous Indian summer when they arrived there. They hired a car, and drove through Tuscany. In Milan, they met up with Christopher's friend King Vidor, who was making his epic version of *War and Peace*. They visited the set, and made a home movie of it. To Vidor's annoyance, and the visitors' delight, the Italian extras hired for the big scenes failed to take their work seriously, fell off bridges, generally fooled around and roared with laughter. Later, Christopher and Don went to Venice, arriving in thick fog. They stayed in a vast suite in a grand hotel, and when in the morning Christopher went to the window and saw the canal in glorious Guardi-like sunlight he burst into tears.

After a short tour of the Rhineland and France they went to England for the usual round of friends and close family, Don having to brave their critical eyes, and the inevitable behind-the-back comparisons with those who had gone before him.

In London, Christopher tried some mescaline, which he had bought perfectly legally in New York, on Aldous Huxley's recommendation. The pharmacist had never heard of it, but was able to order some; a prescription was not necessary. Huxley had recorded the interesting effects of the drugs on his perception, taken under very scientific conditions, and observed minutely. Christopher took the mescaline in a much more slapdash way, and the result was frankly disappointing. Under its influence, he walked into Westminster Abbey, to see if God was there. He wasn't. Subsequently, Christopher never really dabbled with hard or medium drugs, but very happily fell into the growing American habit of the sixties and seventies of a shared joint of hash with friends after dinner. In this he was always moderate, and also lessened his drinking, as he found that with increasing middle age he could get drunk on very small amounts of alcohol.

Quite shortly after their arrival back in the States Don went down with hepatitis and had to go to hospital. Then Christopher started showing symptoms of the same disease. However, the attacks were fairly mild and they were well past the illness by the summer of 1956. Nevertheless, they were both forbidden alcohol for a year.

Christopher and Don's relationship was growing continually in its understanding, and as a measure of security, Christopher bought a house—for the first time in his life—at 434 Sycamore Road, Santa Monica. It was in a street at the bottom of the Canyon, near the beach, with a patio in front, full of subtropical plants, a banana tree, a magnolia and a Spanish bayonet. They lived there for three years before fleeing up the hill out of the way of the screaming children of their neighbours. The nature of the Canyon had changed considerably. Many of the great European émigré community had returned to their old countries, or died, or just moved out of the area, while they were replaced in the main by young families who were looking for sun and a comfortable life, replete with the conservatism and intellectual mediocrity of those dedicated to the goals of the rat race of the modern world.

Don started going to art school five days a week. His burgeoning artistic talent and dedication delighted Christopher, and helped Don to establish his identity and some form of parity in the relationship *vis-à-vis* the outside world. It was not always easy, especially in the early years, to be viewed by people as Mrs. Isherwood, as he once told a Gay Pride gathering.

The first draft of the new Mexican novel was finished in November, by which time Christopher was back in the film studios, this time at 20th Century-Fox, working on a version of Romain Rolland's *Jean-Christophe* for Jerry Wald. One day Ivan Moffat introduced Christopher to a young English writer who was a great fan of his and wanted to meet him: Gavin Lambert. Lambert was currently working on a script for D. H. Lawrence's *Sons and Lovers*. They soon became very good friends, and later Lambert became interested in the teachings of Krishnamurti, who had many devotees in California, including Iris Tree. Thus Gavin and Christopher shared a common interest in the spiritual, as well as in the cinema and in people.

Lambert was a compact young man, with rather birdlike features, someone who did not give himself easily in conversation with strangers, but who could be very amusing when with friends. He lived in the Canyon until the sixties, and became its most successful chronicler in his book *The Slide Area*. Another volume of his, *Inside Daisy Clover*, enjoyed some popularity both in print and as a film. Later, he moved to Tangier, swelling the literary community of that extraordinary North African town that included Paul and Jane Bowles, Alec Waugh and William Burroughs. He returned to California several times, however, for both work and pleasure. Christopher appointed him literary executor in the event of Bachardy and Isherwood dying simultaneously.

Another temporary British resident in the area, from the end of 1955 to early 1957, was Stephen Spender's second wife, Natasha, a pianist. She had developed a close friendship with Raymond Chandler, and in January 1956, when she was staying with Edward and Evelyn Hooker, Chandler came to dinner on the same occasion as Gerald Heard and Christopher. Chandler wrote that he liked Christopher and felt at ease with him, but Christopher found the evening very tense, as he felt on edge with Chandler, whom he believed to be anti-homosexual.

Normally affable and socially easy, Christopher could bristle when confronted with someone whose political or moral stance he found antagonistic. He was especially sensitive about homosexuality and personal loyalties, and although he lost most of the aggressiveness that showed itself on some occasions prior to meeting Don, he nevertheless sometimes lost control. On one notable occasion, he hit an underground film-maker, who sued him, but it was settled out of court. Usually people who sinned against his strict personal code of behaviour were just excommunicated and condemned to oblivion.

In 1957 Dell Publishing Company in New York brought out an anthology of *Great English Short Stories*, edited by Christopher. He chose thirteen writers: Joseph Conrad, G. K. Chester-

ton, George Moore, H. G. Wells, E. M. Forster, Rudyard Kipling, D. H. Lawrence, Katherine Mansfield, Ethel Mayne, Robert Graves, W. Somerset Maugham, V. S. Pritchett and William Plomer. Originally there were to be two more, but Dylan Thomas's executors would not give permission to reprint his story, and the Trustee of the Conan Doyle Estate made it a condition of his agreement that Isherwood's comments on the story be submitted to him for approval, which Christopher rejected as an unacceptable form of literary censorship. His London agents, Curtis Brown, offered the anthology around British publishers, but they all rejected it, saying that the selection was too ordinary.

In October 1957 Don and Christopher set off on a trip which was originally intended as a sort of pilgrimage to places connected with Gauguin, Katherine Mansfield and D. H. Lawrence. However, they dropped Tahiti, Australia and New Zealand from their route, going instead on a sweep across the Pacific via Hawaii to Japan, Hong Kong, Bali, Bangkok and India, returning to America via England. Hong Kong was so obviously picturesque that Christopher wondered how his younger self had found it so hideous nineteen years before. Naturally, the highlight of the trip was India, where they visited the headquarters of the Ramakrishna Monastery. Christopher was struck by the contrast of the squalors of the Indian environment, and the quiet, simple cleanliness of the monastery. He had intended to write a travel book about the journey, with Don doing the illustrations, but this did not materialise. Indeed, he wrote nothing whatsoever directly connected with this trip, apart from the entries in his yet unpublished diaries.

However, he did accept a request from the Vedanta Society to write a biography of Ramakrishna, which he began at a good pace with a long introduction, explaining his own personal involvement with Vedanta, but then realised that this gave the book a wrong emphasis. The work was not thrown away, however, but appeared as a separate booklet, *An Approach to Vedanta* (1963). The completion of the biography was deferred for several years.

Meanwhile, the Mexican novel was still uppermost in Christopher's mind, but towards the end of 1958 he became disen-

chanted with the work in progress, writing on September 16 to
Edward Upward:

> I have rewritten 72 pages to date. I think the detail of it is
> good in places and will amuse you, and there is far less "saw-
> dust" than in World. My motto has been "best trust the
> hate-filled moments," to paraphrase Masefield. But I am still
> sick with fear that [it] isn't really about anything at all. Just
> oddity for oddity's sake. I long to send you what I have writ-
> ten but I mustn't.

By December, the work seemed to be breaking up into two separate books, and then suddenly it was brushed aside and another
book, which was to become the novel finally published as *Down
There on a Visit*, took shape. It was to be in four parts, dealing
with four different periods in Christopher's life—from 1928 to
1952. During the spring of 1959 he worked on the first episode,
"Mr. Lancaster," which was based on his visit to Basil Fry in
Bremen. Christopher sent it to John Lehmann, who published it
as a separate story in the *London Magazine*. It was somewhat revised before appearing again in the finished novel. By June Christopher was working on the second section, "Ambrose," which
drew on his experiences in the Greek island of St. Nicholas with
Francis Turville-Petre in 1932. Acknowledging Upward's favourable comments on "Mr. Lancaster," Christopher wrote to him on
June 17, 1959:

> It is so easy, in the dull toxic half-light of middle age, to get
> depressed about one's work and to imagine one's powers are
> failing. On the contrary, I have to keep telling myself: *gemir,
> pleurer, prier, c'est egalement lache*—and never forget that 55
> to 70 has been a truly creative period for many artists.

Don's energy and activity were a constant encouragement to
Christopher to keep a youthful attitude towards his work. Don
had sold his first picture in 1958, and in 1959 worked on a fashion
magazine. Christopher noticed that he had a kind of "comic-
glamorous" feeling for women which he was able to convey in his
work. Portraiture became Don's forte, and over the coming years
he produced a series of line portraits of many famous sitters, originally signed not by the artist but by the sitter. This was partly to

show that the drawing was done from life and not from a photograph, but also gave them an added personal interest. Often he was able to delve down into the harder or sadder inner personality; one of his most famous drawings is of Bette Davis, with a ferocious mouth. On seeing the finished work, she exclaimed: "Oh yes! That's the old bag!" Naturally, he did many portraits of Christopher, some of which reflect a moodily reflective or depressed side of Isherwood which is rarely visible in public, and never in interviews.

Don had moved with Christopher to a new house, where they have remained together ever since. This was a bungalow on the south ridge of the Canyon, with a beautiful view of the sea as well as of the Canyon itself. They decorated it with pictures by their friends, an increasing number of artists entering their circle of friends and acquaintances. Don had a studio fixed up at the back of the car port and became fairly successful with his portraits in New York.

Christopher himself settled down to a fairly domestic existence, which did not change much for the next twenty years. Methodical and ordered, he would usually rise early for breakfast, which was light but sometimes featured healthful items such as tiger's milk. Then he would write, or work on his diaries, going down to the beach in the late morning for a swim before lunch. Quite often, he would go to a gymnasium for a workout, liking the camaraderie and mixture of ages and types found in the gym. In the evening he and Don would go to the cinema, or else to dinner at friends'; small dinner parties were usually preferred to big parties, because of their more intimate and brilliant conversation.

At the end of March 1960 Christopher finished "Ambrose" and sent it off to Stephen Spender for possible publication in *Encounter*. Spender cabled back that it was marvellous, but then he procrastinated, sending a letter to the effect that the magazine would not be able to publish it after all. Christopher was rather hurt, and wondered whether someone in the *Encounter* office had been shocked by the story. "Waldemar," the third section of the book, was completed in the early summer.

Meanwhile, Christopher accepted some work as guest lecturer at colleges, notably the Los Angeles State College and the University of California at Santa Barbara, in the latter case taking over a post relinquished by Aldous Huxley. He found the experience a rewarding one. Many of the students carried full-time jobs to finance their studies, and were eager to learn and discuss. He was pleasantly surprised that there seemed to be no restriction on speech. This lecturing work was particularly welcome as there was a depletion of finances following the move to the new house, and there was no free-lance work available from the film studios since the writers were out on strike. As ever, Christopher took an interest in the political issues of the day, at this time concentrating on the abolition of capital punishment in California following the Chessman case, in which Aldous Huxley had also shown great interest.

On June 15 Kathleen died, at the age of ninety-one. Richard was with her when she passed away, her last words being, "Oh, for peace, for peace. . . ." The funeral was held at High Lane Church; then, after cremation, her ashes were buried in accordance with her wishes in a grassy bank outside Wyberslegh Hall, close beside those of her favourite cats. Christopher knew that on many occasions during her life, he had been unjust, hard and impatient with her, yet could take comfort from the fact that she had been gratified by his literary success. She had been able to live out her last years at her beloved Wyberslegh, in the company of her other son. In his early years, Christopher had sometimes viewed her as a threatening presence, overpowering and to be escaped from. His escape had been total, so that recently she was no challenge to his full independence. As this realisation dawned on him, so his attitude towards her mellowed, and continued to improve with hindsight after her death.

Christopher saw a great deal of Charles Laughton during 1960. Laughton and his wife, Elsa Lanchester, had bought the house next to Christopher and Don's, and Laughton and Isherwood worked together on a theatrical version of the dialogues of Plato, based on the life of Socrates. Laughton had translated an Italian play on the subject, but that proved of little help. They were searching for a more informal, improvised format. Unfortunately Laughton went down with gall-bladder trouble in the middle of the work on the scheme, and had a heart-attack. During the work, Laughton had initially proved to be a poor sight-reader, but soon he had the material under control. They laughed a great deal, and would frequently break off from the serious work to indulge in comic readings and buffoonery. On one occasion, Laughton read from the Book of Job, in which God sounded like a Nazi Gauleiter, and Job a stage Jew. Sometimes, however, there were clashes. Christopher told Laughton's biographer:

> Elsa, in the kindness of her heart, used to try and warn me not to be victimized by Charles, and I always replied that, after all, I'm a monster, and quite able to take care of myself with other monsters—such as Charles undoubtedly was. And as I told her, monsters are very loyal to each other in their own peculiar way. And she wasn't to be afraid that either was going to eat the other.*

Christopher was fascinated by Laughton, a complex man painfully aware of his physical inelegance but the master—as is well known—of an amazing voice and theatrical ability. Laughton always had problems in accepting his own homosexuality. In fact, he did not tell his wife about his inclinations until after their marriage, when he nearly got into trouble over an affair with a youth. Elsa Lanchester bore this with the generous self-sacrifice of true love, and at the time of the Plato dialogues Laughton was again involved with a young man. Illness, despair and a trip to the Far East kept Laughton from finishing his project with Christopher. He died in December 1962.

In August 1960 Christopher finished the rough draft of the fourth and final part of *Down There on a Visit*, entitled "Paul." On December 19 he was able to write to John Lehmann:

> Yes, the novel is finished, and indeed largely revised. However, the last longest and most horrendous section, nearly as long as The Memorial, isn't! Heaven alone knows what it is like, let alone what you will think of it; I can only tell you that I feel far fewer misgivings than I did about Whirled in the Evenink. This, for better or worse, is *me*.

Down There on a Visit was the swan-song of Isherwood's affair with his dummy narrator. Finding the right tone for the Chris-

* Charles Highman, *Charles Laughton.*

topher Isherwood character in the book was his gravest problem, but he resolved it triumphantly. "Christopher" is no longer a mere observer (though he maintains a brilliant faculty to sum up people in a few perceptive and often damning phrases); he is a participator, playing off the other characters against each other and at the same time revealing many facets of himself, as he had developed over the years. The book is not all fact, but Isherwood has never believed that only fact is true. In the opening pages of "Mr. Lancaster" he summed up his current perspective on the old Christopher:

> . . . before I slip into the convention of calling this young man "I," let me consider him as a separate being, a stranger almost, setting out on this adventure in a taxi to the docks. For, of course, he *is* almost a stranger to me. I have revised his opinions, changed his accent and his mannerisms, unlearned or exaggerated his prejudices and his habits. We still share the same skeleton, but its outer covering has altered so much that I doubt if he would recognise me on the street. We have in common the label of our name, and a continuity of consciousness; there has been no break in the sequence of daily statements that I am I. But *what* I am has refashioned itself throughout the days and years, until now almost all that remains constant is the mere awareness of being conscious. And that awareness belongs to everybody; it isn't a particular person.

The Christopher of "Mr. Lancaster" is a self-conscious young rebel, fuming against the older generation, and in particular Mr. Lancaster. By the time he reaches the island of St. Gregory in "Ambrose," Christopher has sunk into torpor and indecision, drowning his uncertainty in alcohol and sunshine. In "Waldemar" he has gained a new hardness and self-avowed calculation:

> How do I appear to my friends and acquaintances?
> To judge from the jokes they make about me, they see a rather complex creature, part despot, part diplomat. I'm told that I hold myself like a drill sergeant or a strict landlady; I am supposed to have an overpowering will. Hugh Weston [Wystan Auden] compared it once to a fire hose before

which everybody has to retreat. Then again they say I'm so sly; I pretend to be nobody in particular, just one of the gang, when all the time I have the arrogance of Lawrence of Arabia and the subtlety of Talleyrand. Oh, yes—and I'm utterly ruthless and completely cynical. But I do make them laugh.

The last throwaway line is very important, for even if Christopher has rarely been the monster he sometimes makes himself out to be, he has always had the ability to dispel unpleasantness, and often win things his way, by reducing his adversary to laughter.

The reader should be very wary about accepting Isherwood's self-portraits and reflections as wholly accurate impressions. For one thing, a sizeable chunk of *Down There on a Visit* is pure fiction, though the person with enough inside knowledge of Isherwood's life will be tempted to swallow it all as fact, as he encounters familiar landmarks. Even at this stage Isherwood was not honest about Christopher's involvement (sometimes sexual) with the other characters. The "Waldemar" section is the most misleading of them all. Although culled roughly from Christopher and Heinz's experiences, Waldemar is most certainly not Heinz (or any of Christopher's other German friends), and his fiancée is pure invention.

The Christopher of "Paul" is suddenly much older, full of responsibilities and groping awkwardly towards spirituality. America shows itself to have been the major turning-point of his life.

When *Down There on a Visit* was first published in 1962 several critics commented either favourably or unfavourably on what they considered to be the sexual preoccupation of the book. Theirs was a mistaken emphasis, for the book is not about sexual deviation any more than any other Isherwood books are. It is, on the contrary, a study of a maturing individual moving through a world of people who are unable to communicate with each other. The theme is profoundly sad, but the treatment is often very funny. Of all the reviews, maybe Stuart Hampshire's was the most perceptive:

> From Mr. Norris onwards he has sustained the story of a hero who is obstinately loyal to the values of private life and of personal relations, as they have been represented by Mr. Forster: of friendship and truthfulness. These values, the way

of life that they require, have been constantly threatened by the noise and rumour of political barbarians without the gates, gates which enclose a very small area marked "private: no politicians, no public poses." The hero's defensive tactics —and the substance of his heroism—have been evasion; he keeps on the move; for he is perpetually on a visit, and has never stayed long enough to compromise, and to settle down with the enemy. He recounts four of his visits here; for the hero is always a writer before he is anything else.*

* *Encounter*, XIX, No. 5 (November 1962).

13

Don Bachardy took art courses at the Slade School of Fine Art in London from February to July 1961. Christopher also spent quite a lot of time in England for the first six months of that year. Old friends noticed that Christopher's accent, which had acquired a pronounced North American twang when he first went to the States, had begun to soften back into melodious English tones, though it was still punctuated with occasional New World slang, such as "Wow," "Gee" and "Great." Favourite vocal mannerisms also included an almost French "very good," and the phrase "the thing is. . . ."

Christopher went to visit his mentor E. M. Forster at Cambridge, and found him sad and old. Then aged eighty-two, Morgan Forster lived quietly at the university, but said he felt out of things, and couldn't work any more. He wistfully told Christopher that he hoped that he would "pop off quickly."

There seemed some possibility of work for Christopher on a film script of Graham Greene's *England Made Me*, but the project fell through. Curiously, the two writer cousins had extremely little contact. Christopher sometimes wondered if Graham Greene disapproved of his homosexuality. Equally abortive was a proposal that Auden should collaborate with Isherwood on a musical version of the Berlin stories.

Following a show in London, Don received several commissions, which meant that he had to stay on in England for a while after his studies ended. He and Christopher went to the South of France for a holiday, then Christopher returned alone to California, where he started his courses at Santa Barbara. These covered Kingsley Amis' *Lucky Jim*, William Golding's *Lord of the Flies*, Shelagh Delaney's *A Taste of Honey* and John Osborne's *Look Back in Anger*. He had offered to teach American literature as well, but the university authorities preferred that he limit himself to contemporary British works. The American literary establishment continued to consider him British, despite his obtaining American citizenship in 1946, and his election as member of the United States National Institute of Arts and Letters in 1949. In 1976 *Time* magazine was still calling him a British writer.

The germ of a new novel was stirring, based on a father-son relationship. This interested him deeply, even though he had only juvenile memories of his own father, and had never had children of his own. However, he often declared that he *felt* like a father to some of the boys with whom he had been involved. The fact that these relationships were also sexual was not incompatible with his outlook. Some of his strongest memories of his father were sexual, and he often had fantasies of an incestuous relationship with a mythical brother. Nothing seems to have come off the drawing-board, however, and by March 1962 he was talking of resuscitating the Mexican material again.

Teaching at college used up a lot of his time and energy. During the spring he ran a Creative Writing Class, and was startled by the language of some of the students' pieces. When he read them out loud, he was nervous that people outside would hear and get him fired. And he was appalled at the way students tore each other's work to pieces unmercifully when it was read out in class. In later courses he took his pupils individually for a walk round the games fields or made other arrangements to discuss their work privately.

A magazine offered him a handsome fee to review a new novel by a distinguished novelist, but he turned it down: by the second chapter he realised that the book bored him terribly, and he did not wish to say so in print. This is a good example of his strict reviewing ethic, a code which he felt had been broken by one well-known novelist who having asked Christopher whether he would like *Down There on a Visit* reviewed, then produced an adverse criticism. Morgan Forster also did not like the book very much, but he said so in a private letter to Christopher, not in print. Meanwhile, Christopher himself provided a glowing review for Edward Upward's *In the Thirties*. He often found himself approached to write short comments for the blurbs of his friends' books, though in the case of John Lehmann's *I Am My Brother*, he had felt that he should refuse as he himself figured so prominently in the book.

During the summer Christopher went up to San Francisco, and Don prepared for another exhibition of his work. The novel was in a bad way, and at times Christopher suffered from depression. On September 9, 1962, he wrote to Edward Upward:

Melancholia is the occupational disease of us oldies. Senile melancholia is quite different from the romantic melancholia of the young. I am rather lucky, in that a doctor told me long ago that I suffer from pyloric spasm, a flap in the vagus nerve at the entrance to the stomach; so, whenever I find myself thinking "what's the use?" I firmly remind myself of the physical cause. Or I try to. It is very insidious. The Hindu concept of dharma helps: one employs one's talents because one has them, not in obedience to some external Power but because of the obligation which the talents impose. I find I can make this argument stick, most of the time. Though it is dangerously apt to turn into a sort of stoic masochism: *fais energiquement ta longue et lourde tâche*. Tâche suggests a taskmaster, so you become a groaning slave; whereas dharma can only be obeyed by an act of free will. It does seem to me too that all occupations are symbolic, or rather that their fruits are quite other than they appear to be. It isn't really the finished novel that matters but something that happens to [you] while you are writing it. But still, the question arises, what about what happens to the reader while he is reading it? So you can't get mystical and say it doesn't matter if the novel ever gets finished at all.

Out of the creative turmoil appeared a new work, entitled *An Englishwoman*, the story of an Englishwoman who has married an American GI but then finds herself isolated and floundering in California. There was to be a narrator character, who would be a lecturer who taught her son, and who is embroiled in family conflict by the boy. However, during the winter of 1962–63, the book turned out differently, and A *Single Man* was born. The female lead character had been reduced to a secondary role, while the limelight was focused on the lecturer, George, a fifty-eight-year-old homosexual. He was so longer the narrator, but was closely observed by the reader on one day of his life. Christopher sent the manuscript to Edward Upward for his approval in July 1963, and it was published the following year.

George is seen going through the deliberate, everyday actions of a man on the borderline of old age, staring at himself in the mirror, sitting on the john, painfully recalling the death of his lover, with whom he had shared the house which he still inhabits. He lives out Mortmereish aggression fantasies as he hurtles automatically down the freeway to his college. He is a charming, soggy liberal, quietly militant about homosexual rights in thought if not in word, and is probably considered an amusing and harmless old thing by his students, whose youth and beauty passively stir his desire and make his day more enjoyable. He prides himself on being in better shape than his peers when he has a workout at the gym, and is capable of spontaneous fun when one of his students turns up in a gay bar. But he ends his day alone in bed, drunk and with no consolation but a handkerchief, and with the knowledge that one night, perhaps tonight, he will die.

A *Single Man* is Isherwood's masterpiece, but will probably never be his most popular work. Indeed, at the time of writing, it is not even in print! Inevitably, much of the attention gained by the novel at the time of publication was because of its treatment of homosexuality. But it is not a novel *about* homosexuality; it is a study of an individual, who, as usual in Isherwood's fiction, is partly Christopher and partly a composite, and of his life-style as a solitary man with one toe in the grave. It is a story of survival life-playing by a man who has lost both youth and the one person who could give him true personal happiness. By chance, this individual belongs to a minority, that of homosexuals. But he belongs to several other minorities who are just as important. He is one of the living, as opposed to the dead. He is an educated man in a philistine world. He has independent means, and is thus isolated from the full fury of the rat-race. He is still rooted in his English past, as opposed to the overwhelmingly American Americans around him, whatever their names and ethnic origins. George is aware of the political significance of minorities, but he is not blinded to their true nature by sentimentality or guilt. As he tells his students in class one day:

"Now, for example, people with freckles aren't thought of as a minority by the non-freckled. They aren't a minority in the sense we're talking about. And why aren't they? Because a minority is only thought of as a minority when it constitutes some kind of threat to the majority, real or imaginary. And no threat is ever *quite* imaginary . . . minorities are people; *people*, not angels. Sure, they're like us—but not exactly like us; that's the all-too-familiar state of liberal hysteria, in which you begin to kid yourself you honestly cannot see any difference between a Negro and a Swede. . . . So, let's face it, minorities are people who probably look and act and think differently from us, and have faults that we don't have. We may dislike the way they look and act, and we may hate their faults. And it's *better* if we admit to disliking and hating them, than if we try to smear our feelings over with pseudo-liberal sentimentality. If we're frank about our feelings, we have a safety valve, we're actually less likely to start persecuting."

During the war, the minority with whom Christopher was most directly concerned in his everyday life was the exiled European Jews. Yet even though he identified with their struggle, and was referred to as an Honorary Jew, he could never be a Jew. Since then, the all-important minority for him has been the homosexual one, and he has become increasingly active in liberalising movements in support of male homosexuality. He is proud of being one of a minority, and has said on several occasions in interviews that, should the homosexuals ever become a majority, he would become heterosexual. However psychologically unconvincing this might sound, one should not ignore the sincerity of the intent behind it. It is not dissimilar to Graham Greene's affirmation that in a capitalist society he would be a communist, and in a communist society a capitalist.

A *Single Man* gives only the minimum necessary description of the functioning of the homosexual subculture, as it now only forms a small part of George's life. Christopher was not unfamiliar with the haunts of the gay world, however, nor with its new literature. In the summer of 1963, when the first clean draft of *A Single Man* was ready, he was reading William Burrough's *The Naked Lunch*, and had been instrumental in seeing John Rechy's *City of Night* (1963) into publication. In fact, Rechy had become quite a good friend, though relations later soured temporarily over what some people considered to be a tasteless portrait of Christopher and Don in a subsequent Rechy novel called *Numbers*. However, Rechy himself maintained that it was meant neither to be disloyal nor recognisable. Rechy felt himself in some ways a protégé of Christopher's, and retained a great admiration both for the man and his work.

Christopher's teaching experiences were of course very important background material for the novel. In April and May 1963, he gave some significant lectures at the University of California at Berkeley, entitled "The Autobiography of My Books." Originally, there should have been two lectures, but so little ground had been covered at the end of the first that an extra lecture was scheduled, as well as a later opportunity for students to talk to him quietly in a faculty office. The date of one of the lectures was changed because James Baldwin was billed for the same time, and both Christopher and the students wanted to go and hear him.

Christopher's lectures gave him the opportunity of trying out on a young and critical public something which had become an increasingly attractive prospect for himself: a deeply researched reappraisal of his own works and the background to them, which might take several years, or indeed the rest of his life. Parts of the Berkeley lectures were very amusing. Christopher is a born actor and loves to manipulate an audience—in the nicest of ways. As yet, the lectures have not been published, though they are preserved on tape. They give good insight into the early works, but are much hastier in their treatment of the later ones because of the shortage of time.

Christopher was sure that some of his readers would consider him something of a Dr. Jekyll and Mr. Hyde, as it looked as if publication of *A Single Man* might coincide with his biography of Ramakrishna, which was sent chapter by chapter to Swami Madhavananda, head of the Ramakrishna Order in India, for approval and correction. In fact the book did not appear in volume form until 1965. It was very much a labour of duty, dedicated to Swami Prabhavananda, who was highly conscious of the work that Christopher had done, and continued to do, for the Vedanta Society of Southern California and beyond. Yet the book is of value in that it makes the Indian physical and religious environment accessible to the average Westerner, and has the advantage of being devoted to a man who was a fascinating eccentric.

During the summer of 1963 Christopher had a car accident, his little Volkswagen colliding with several large American automobiles, which resulted in a broken rib and a huge repair bill. And a few months later, he was taken in by the cops for drunken driving, but fortunately did not lose his licence.

On November 22 Aldous Huxley died of cancer, which proved a great loss to all his friends, though his departure from the world was overshadowed for the general public by the assassination, on the same day, of President John Kennedy. Huxley was cremated the following day without any ceremony, but on November 24 a few intimates, including Christopher, assembled at Mulholland Highway to make a commemorative walk along the trail that Huxley took daily until incapacitated by his fatal illness. Later, a memorial volume was produced, to which Christopher contributed. In it, Christopher recalled his visit to Huxley at the Cedars of Lebanon Hospital on November 5:

Aldous looked like a withered old man, grey-faced, with dull black eyes. He spoke in a low, hoarse voice which was hard to understand. I had to sit directly facing him because it hurt him to turn his head. And yet—seeing what I saw and knowing what I knew—I could still almost forget about his condition while we talked, because his mind was functioning so well. I was nervous at first and talked at random. I mentioned Africa, and Aldous said that all the new African nations would soon be governed by their armies. I mentioned V. V.

Rozanov's *Solitaria,* which I had just been reading. Aldous promptly quoted a passage from it, in which Rozanov says that "the private life is above everything . . . just sitting at home and even picking your nose, and looking at the sunset." I told him a silly story—not at all the kind of story I would normally have told him—about Our Lord and the Blessed Virgin playing golf. He laughed at it, quite heartily.

Christopher was pleased that Julian Huxley, who edited the volume, liked his piece.

In December, and January of the following year, Christopher was in India with Swami Prabhavananda for the centenary celebrations of Vivekananda's birth. The celebrations lasted a whole year, and the two visitors from California took part in mass meetings at Belur Math, the Vedantist headquarters. Christopher was not sure how much of his speech the Bengalis understood, but it was important for him to be there. Two of Christopher's friends from the center in Hollywood were also present at the time, taking their final vows, so he was able to observe and talk with them about their feelings, although he was not allowed to sit in on the actual ordination, which always takes place in private.

It was on the plane back to America that Christopher at last came to realise what he should do with his Mexican material in order to mould it into a workable novel. Part of the Mexican material was a dialogue, a confrontation. For a long time Christopher had been thinking about the concept of two people meeting on neutral territory between their two worlds, rather like Jesus of Nazareth and Satan meeting in the wilderness. A line of Byron's, from "The Vision of Judgment," stuck in his mind: "Between His Darkness and His Brightness there passed a mutual glance of great politeness," referring to the encounter of Lucifer and Michael.

In the "Mexican" *Down There on a Visit,* which involves a Denny Fouts character, an American comes down just south of the Mexican border, where he meets a man who is permanently exiled, because he would be arrested if he stepped on American soil. The "clean" American is appalled at the squalor of his new friend's life, and says that he can save him, since he has very good connections back home, including a brother in the FBI. The exile laughs in his face, as *he* was going to suggest that the visitor settle down, to escape the load of his respectable Washington existence, his wife and his responsibilities. On reflection, Christopher realised, the confrontation would be more effective if one of the protagonists were a monk. The venue was therefore changed from Mexico to India, and now the seed of A *Meeting by the River* had been sown.

Back in California, Christopher tidied up some odds and ends. Methuen had asked him to do a volume of miscellanea. This he agreed to, the collection later being assembled under the title *Exhumations*. On February 25, 1964, Christopher wrote to John Lehmann (who had just been awarded a CBE, Commander of the British Empire):

> . . . the usual emptying of the wastepaper basket. I shall probably add a few unpublished things, including maybe my poem, On His Queerness. And I have two other books shadowing themselves forth: a sort of autobiographical one, and another short novel, based on these very recent experiences in India.
>
> In the immediate future, there are two prospects, both movie-writing. One is the screenplay of The Loved One, *if* Tony Richardson agrees to direct it. The other is the screenplay of Stevenson's The Beach of Falesa—which, as you probably know, Dylan Thomas already did a script on. Richard Burton wants to play the heavy. But first we all hold our breaths to see how his Hamlet does in New York. (Alas, I finally didn't get down to see him in Mexico; we had our talk here in Los Angeles when he was on his way through, right after my return trip.)

Tony Richardson did agree to direct *The Loved One*, based on the novel by Evelyn Waugh. Jessica Mitford, author of *The American Way of Death*, had been approached to write a script for it, but she turned it down—though she did have some contact with the film, making several suggestions. Terry Southern and Christopher worked on the script and were present on the set during the shooting, for last-minute dialogue changes. Christopher found the film a very amusing piece of work, and started a rewarding working relationship and friendship with Tony Richardson. In fact, Terry Southern was mainly responsible for the screenplay, though Christopher wrote the scene in the chapel, when a wedding is transformed into a funeral. Christopher was not entirely satisfied with the book, though, feeling it to be snobbish about California. He considered the hero a boring heel. Richardson was on the crest of a wave, having had a tremendous commercial success with *Tom Jones* (1963). The cast of *The Loved One* included John Gielgud, Rod Steiger, Dana Andrews and James Coburn. Christopher himself appeared fleetingly in the film, as an extra in a crowd scene, frowning ferociously. The film was quite a laugh, but, inevitably, a travesty of Waugh's brilliant book.

Shortly afterwards, Isherwood and Richardson were due to work together again, on Carson McCullers' *Reflections in a Golden Eye*. Christopher produced a screenplay, on which he much enjoyed writing, following the book very closely. Richardson, however, did not direct the film after all, though it was finally produced, with another script starring Marlon Brando, Elizabeth Taylor and Julie Harris.

In October 1964 Christopher started a third script for Richardson, from Marguerite Duras' novel *The Sailor from Gibraltar*. Tony Richardson and Don Magner both contributed to the final screenplay, and Woodfall Films assembled an impressive cast including Jean Moreau, Ian Bannen, Vanessa Redgrave, Orson Welles and Hugh Griffith.

While Christopher was working on the films Don prepared and held exhibitions in San Francisco and New York, and also made a trip to Egypt. Christopher's own movements were severely restricted by his work, particularly as he had accepted the position of Regent's Professor of English at the University of California at Los Angeles (UCLA) from February 1965 to the early summer, which required preparation and meant staying put.

Work progressed on *A Meeting by the River*, the second draft of which was completed in the early autumn of 1965. Christopher described the plot in a letter of October 22 to Marshall Bean, an East Coast correspondent with whom Christopher carried on an extensive correspondence mainly about death and spirituality at this time:

Briefly, there are two brothers—Patrick and Oliver. Patrick is very successful and a rather unusually imaginative and intelligent business man. Oliver is a social worker, admirable, energetic, capable and a bit of a puritan, who has spent his life in the Red Cross, the Friends Service Committee and suchlike. Suddenly Oliver meets a Hindu monk, goes to India, joins a monastery there and prepares to take his final vows. Patrick visits him. It now develops that the brothers have a strong emotional relationship, much love, much hate, and, in addition, Oliver as the younger brother can't help depending on Patrick's approval. He *wants* Patrick to tell him that it's all right for him to become a monk, and of course Patrick disapproves, and tells him so. And then Oliver tells Patrick that Patrick's way of life fills him with horror. Neither one will back down. Yet at the end, when Oliver has taken the final vows, the brothers *are* reconciled, because their love turns out to be stronger than their prejudices. They part again, agreeing, as it were, to think each other wrong, ridiculous and lovable.

Christopher was still not satisfied, however, and he started another draft of the novel. He was still working on it during the spring of 1966, by which time he was teaching twice a week at the University of California at Riverside, again as a Regent's professor. On March 28 he wrote to Edward Upward:

I think this new draft is a great improvement and I am keeping in mind your advice about heightening the tension between Patrick and Oliver and sustaining it until the last possible moment. I have now rewritten as far as the big showdown scene, after which the Californian boy Tom makes the drunken phone-call. . . .

Trying as much as possible to ignore the arthritis which had started plaguing him, Christopher managed to finish the third and final draft of the novel by June. He sent it to John Yale, one of the two Americans who had become swamis during Christopher's last visit to India. Yale was now living at the Vedanta Center outside Paris as Swami Vidyatmananda, and he gave Christopher useful information and criticism. The manuscript was then sent to

Edward Upward, and finally to Christopher's London publishers, Methuen.

The novel is in the form of a series of diary extracts by Oliver, who is just about to become a swami in an Indian monastic order, and in the form of letters from his elder brother Patrick to his mother, wife and his young lover, Tom. A crisis is reached when Tom telephones hysterically to the monastery, and Patrick confesses the affair to Oliver. Patrick expects and hopes that Oliver will tell him to remember his duty as a family man, and turn his back on the infatuated young man. Instead Oliver says that he believes it would be more honest to Patrick's feelings if he were to honour his duty by leaving his wife and giving her alimony, and following his heart with the young man. Patrick, being a Truly Weak Man, instead goes running back to his forgiving wife and children and ditches Tom. Oliver passes through a last-minute spiritual doubt, but because of his belief in, and love of, his deceased guru, he is able to go through with his final vows. The two brothers part lovingly.

The relationship between the brothers and their inevitable moment of confrontation and communication are the essential elements of the book. Both of them are aware of the past and present emotional and physical possibilities of an intense brotherly relationship, though neither of them admits it to the other. Oliver confesses to his diary:

> . . . *of course* I love him—I mean, I'm capable of it. Part of me probably loves him all the time. All of me certainly does, sometimes. When I was going through my Freudian phase, I used to wonder if I wasn't actually in love with him, romantically and even physically. I'm quite sure now that that's not true, at least not any longer. It isn't nearly as simple as that—considering what I've been through lately, I almost wish it were. Now and then I suspect that Patrick thinks it is—when he sort of flirts with me. But I'm afraid the truth is less interesting. Patrick's flirting is just a nervous habit he's got into, he tries it on all ages and both sexes. It doesn't mean anything and I suppose it's usually harmless, except that it has probably fooled a few people and made them unhappy later.

What I love about Patrick, and always have, is his joy, his

boldness in demanding enjoyment for himself and the get-away-with-murder impudence with which he accepts the best as his absolute right. A gloomy old puritan like me is naturally attracted to a Patrick, however much he may resist the attraction, and in our case, being brothers, we're that much more closely involved.*

Patrick does indeed flirt with Oliver, by smiles or unashamedly exhibiting his powerful, well-provisioned body to him. But Patrick's own recognition of his incestuous longing is directed towards his temporary boy lovers of whom Tom is not the first and, the reader feels, will not be the last:

Tommy . . . I'm certain that *you* could be my brother—the kind of brother I now know I've been searching for all these years, without even quite daring to admit to myself what it was that I wanted. I suppose I was frightened off by the taboos which surround the idea of brotherhood in the family sense—oh yes, they encourage you to love your brother, but only as far as the limits they've set—beyond that, it's a deadly sin and a horror. What I want is a life beyond their taboos, in which two men learn to trust each other so completely that there's no fear and they experience and share everything together in the flesh and in the spirit. I don't believe such closeness is possible between a man and a woman—deep down they are natural enemies—and how many men ever find it together? Only a very few even glimpse the possibility of it, and only a very few out of that few dare to try to find it.†

Patrick veers away from his dream of an incestuous Whitmanesque utopia out of a fear which, in Isherwood's writing, accompanies selfishness in the conduct of bisexuals. Yet Isherwood cannot overtly condemn Patrick, because, as he wrote once in a letter to the present writer (dated April 29, 1971): "I myself am far more Patrick than Oliver—but I understand Oliver better than Patrick did!"

It is easy also to see *A Meeting by the River* as an allegory of a confrontation between sexuality and spirituality. Symbolically,

* *A Meeting by the River* (1967).
† Ibid.

neither side wins out, nor is either defeated. Both must continue to exist, and can learn something from each other. Yet if the book is really intended to deal with what the French would call a *grand sujet*, then it would need to be far longer than its actual format. The characters, both as people and as symbols, are not exhaustively portrayed, which helps give the work an air of delightfully worked slightness. The novel does not encompass the dramatic potential of a confrontation, and the material was to lend itself far more readily to a stage version.

In the autumn of 1966 Christopher flew to Europe on a television assignment, to make a film about the creation of the Christmas carol "Silent Night." He was able to contact Gottfried Reinhardt, who had gone back to Europe. Later he was able to visit London, staying with Stephen Spender, before going up to Cheshire to see Richard. He suggested to Richard that they should go over to Marple to see the sight of Marple Hall which had been demolished by the local council in 1959. Richard said that he could not bear to do so, memories flooding back from the last time they had been to see it together, in February 1956, and found only a gutted ruin visited by curious tourists. This time, therefore, Christopher went alone, in a taxi.

The entrance gates to the park had gone, and new houses had been built near the main road. In place of the big house stood the Marple Hall Grammar School, surrounded by games fields. As the taxi-driver waited impatiently, Christopher wandered round looking for some sign of the past, and finally came across a headstone of the terraced doorway inscribed "H.B. 1658," now lying in the grass. As he recalled in *Kathleen and Frank*:

> There was no grimness or sadness today. Christopher felt wonderfully joyful. For him, this certainly wasn't the end of an ancient enemy but it did seem to be the lifting of a curse. Whatever here had exorcised an evil power seemed appeased now and buried, like Heathcliff in Gimmerton churchyard. He summoned Emily Brontë to say goodbye for him to this place and its dead:

> "I lingered round them, under the benign sky, listened to the soft wind breathing through the grass and wondered how any-

one could ever imagine unquiet slumbers for the sleepers in that quiet earth."

Back in California on November 2 he wrote his television play, but by the New Year he was under way on a new book—about his origins, or, more specifically, about his parents. Now that the "evil power" had been appeased and buried, he felt able at last to work on the material.

The original conception was rather different from the finished book, *Kathleen and Frank*. It was to be written entirely in the present tense, skipping backwards and forwards in time, showing the influence of certain characteristics and acts of his parents upon Richard and himself. The book originally opened with an extract from a letter which Frank had written to Kathleen in 1902, telling her of a book he was reading about esoteric Buddhism.

> Then, after quoting this, I jump to the fall of last year, when I am visiting my Brother in England and we are sitting reading through this and other old letters. And my Brother Richard remarks that they make him see our Father in a quite different light—he has always felt rather hostile toward him but now begins to realise that he was a very sympathetic person!*

This method of revelation did not work satisfactorily, however, and for the final book he chose a simpler chronological time sequence, though still using some flashbacks and projections into the future. Meanwhile, he was correcting the proofs of *A Meeting by the River*, and writing the introduction to a book of lectures by Swami Prabhavananda.

The original publication date for *A Meeting by the River* had been April, but it did not appear until June 1. Christopher arrived in London during May to help with publicity. In an interview with the London *Evening Standard* (May 11, 1967) Christopher spoke of his new work in progress, and reaffirmed his desire to stay in America, unlike Wystan Auden who was spending increasingly longer periods in Europe.

> I think America needs me more than England. My involvement in civil liberties makes me feel that my thing is to be

---

* Letter to Marshall Bean, dated January 19, 1967.

there rather than here. In any case, America is the only home
I have ever had.

Christopher's new novel met with a mixed reception, and,
rather to his annoyance, he was to receive limelight not for that
book but for the resurrection of his Berlin stories, in the form of a
stage musical, *Cabaret*. The musical was born in 1966, "from the
book by Joe Masteroff, based on the play by John Van Druten
and stories by Christopher Isherwood," with music by John
Kander and lyrics by Fred Ebb. Edward Upward wrote to Christopher when the London version opened at the Palace Theatre on
February 28, with Judi Dench playing Sally Bowles, who had been
transformed into a very competent singer in a cabaret. He asked
Christopher what he thought of it, and on March 11, 1968, received a short and bitter reply: "As for Cabaret I try and keep as
far from it as possible. It's an ill bird that fouls the nest where the
golden eggs are laid. Especially when the nest is anyhow made entirely of sawdust and shit."

In February 1968 it had seemed almost certain that Christopher
would go to England to work on a television production of A
Christmas Carol, but that fell through. He also had an un-
confirmed commitment to adapt Frank Wedekind's two Lulu
plays, *Earth Spirit* and *Pandora's Box*, for possible production at
the Royal Court Theatre in London.

Much of his time for the next three years, however (both in the
United States and on visits to Britain), was spent toiling over
diaries and letters for *Kathleen and Frank*. By March he had
progressed as far as his own birth in the story.

Christopher also started work with Don Bachardy on a play
based on A *Meeting by the River*. As he wrote to Edward Upward
on November 30, 1968:

It is very instructive work, turning a novel into a play; I'm
learning all over again those truths we used to preach about
the dangers of describing your effects instead of creating
them. And then one falls in love with a bit of literary dialogue and has to admit painfully that it isn't dramatic dialogue. I think we shall at least get it a try out here and I believe it may reach England in due course. The great difficulty
here is that it demands two really good young English actors.

It looked as though the play might get its first production in England, in the autumn of 1969, at the Royal Court. The ballet dancer Christopher Gable agreed to play the role of Oliver; Christopher and Don had been keen to use him after seeing him in a televised version of the life of Delius. The production never came off, however, being yet another episode in the saga of disappointments which befell both the stage version of A *Meeting by the River* and its later screenplay.

The connection with the Royal Court Theatre was largely through Tony Richardson who, in the summer of 1969, was in Australia making a film about the boy outlaw Ned Kelly, with Mick Jagger in the title role. Christopher and Don went there to visit the set, travelling via Tahiti, Bora-Bora, Samoa and Auckland, New Zealand. In Samoa they were able to make their dreamed-of pilgrimage to Stevenson's grave, and were highly amused by the local guides who had them clambering up and down hillsides and making rude jokes about them. However, their arrival in Australia was inauspicious. The airline lost the passengers' baggage, whereupon one impatient traveller declared quite audibly "fucking inefficiency!" An airline official retorted: "Don't you use that kind of language in this country—we have ways of dealing with people who do!" Christopher thought this very sinister, and was ready to believe rumours that the Australian police were just dying to get Mick Jagger for drug use. Isherwood was impressed by Jagger, especially with his tenderness when Marianne Faithful turned up in rather a state. Chris and Don returned to California via Honolulu, where Chris looked up Jim Charlton.

In February 1970 Christopher and Don were back in Europe, revising the play of A *Meeting by the River*, and together they completed the *I, Claudius* script for Richardson. Their writing collaboration added a new aspect to their relationship. Christopher had also been doing some work on a forthcoming film version of *Cabaret*, and was already full of forebodings, though both he and Don were initially enthusiastic when they heard later that Liza Minnelli was to play the part of Sally.

Christopher visited France on a "whizz tour" with the painter David Hockney and his friend Peter Schlesinger, with whom they had become close friends in Southern California. Hockney had grown up in Bradford in Yorkshire, the son of quite poor but rather unusual parents who had encouraged his strong early interest in art. Christopher and David Hockney had immediately hit it off when they met in California, though Hockney was amused when Christopher declared absurdly that they had in common northern origins—industrial Bradford bearing no resemblance whatsoever to the gentility of Marple and Wyberslegh Halls. America had been a revelation to Hockney. He dyed his hair blond, became fascinated by the beach- and pool-boys of California, and in his late twenties was already an artistic guru in college classes, where he had met his extraordinarily handsome lover, Peter. Hockney painted an enormous portrait of Isherwood and Bachardy that is justly one of his most famous works (and graced Marguerite Littman's dining-room in London, where she had established herself on remarriage). Strictly speaking, it provides a far better likeness of Christopher than it does of Don, as Don was never in the right place at the right time for a sitting.

On the brief trip to France, Hockney snapped photographs all the time, and with characteristic energy rushed round various friends such as Tony Richardson and Natasha Spender, the latter charming her shivering guests by throwing one of her chairs on an open fire.

During 1971 Don and Christopher worked on a new film project based on Mary Shelley's novel *Frankenstein*. *Kathleen and Frank* was finished, and was published in the autumn. It was a long book, illustrated with several charming photographs (fewer in the British than the American edition), and deliberately without an index. Christopher refers to himself throughout in the third person, a technique which some people found irritating, but which he retained for *Christopher and His Kind*, a later autobiographical volume. The critic Glenway Westcott found the book "a masterpiece of the head and the heart." Others found it frankly boring. Christopher explained to a journalist from *The National Observer* (February 19, 1972): "I tried to see my parents as people in a novel, and it helped me tremendously—not just in the writing, but it made them interesting to me as people in a new way. Well, you see, just in being able to call them Kathleen and Frank and not mother and father, I discovered a tremendous psychological release." Certainly writing the book had been a drastic revelation to Christopher about his own background, and helped him to a better understanding of his former and present selves.

At the end of April 1972 good news came in the form of a production of the play of A *Meeting by the River*, at the Mark Taper Forum in Los Angeles, which had also housed an Isherwood version of Shaw's *The Adventures of the Black Girl in Her Search for God* in 1969. The new play was staged by the young writer and film director James Bridges who had become a very close friend of Christopher's. In the two-act play, the confrontation between the two brothers is more dramatically intense than in the book. The peripheral characters in the book are brought on-stage, and given a sharper reality. The mother becomes a forceful, bitter woman, tired of her children's antics. Tom and Patrick are shown embracing. Patrick is more blatantly flamboyant and irrepressible. His wife, also on-stage, accuses him of wanting an incestuous relationship with *her*, "a brother and sister who share every thought, who read each other's moods and who go to bed together. . . ." But the finale is out of hope, and all the characters in the play, from the mother to the swamis, join together in a crazy dance. Isherwood explained the new mood in the play:

> "A Meeting by the River" is a secret little book, but when I write for the stage I immediately become bold and want broad effects. My instinct is, if there's music, it ought to be louder! It's rather like painting with a broom.*

The film of *Cabaret* also materialised in 1972. Newspaper interviews show that Christopher was initially enthusiastic. Talking to the *Evening Standard* (February 4, 1972) about the choice of Michael York to play the Isherwood-based character, he said: "He is good type-casting for the role. They've even brushed his hair across his forehead like mine. And we've both got broken noses. He's a good-looking version of what I looked like."

Liza Minnelli was excellent publicity for the movie, appearing on the cover of both *Time* and *Newsweek*. But Christopher was disappointed and angry when he saw the film, largely because of the portrayal of the relationship between the Michael York and

* San Francisco *Sunday Examiner and Chronicle*, May 21, 1972.

Liza Minnelli characters and the way that Michael York's escapades with men were shown as temporary, immature aberrations, like bed-wetting. He was quite offensive to director Bob Fosse when he met him at a party.

In February 1973 Christopher and Don made a quick visit to England to do some work on their Frankenstein film, sadly unable to see most of their friends there, including Wystan Auden, who had accepted a residential post at Christ Church College, Oxford. However, they went over to Switzerland to visit Salka Viertel, who was living in Klosters, and Gore Vidal organised an impromptu champagne party when he discovered that it was the twentieth anniversary of Christopher and Don's relationship.

Frankenstein: The True Story was produced as a long television film by Universal Pictures Television Limited, directed by Jack Smight, and had a star-studded cast including John Gielgud, James Mason, Agnes Moorehead and Ralph Richardson, and featured the handsome young actor Michael Sarrazin as the Creature. Avon Books published a paperback edition of the television play the same year. It was filmed at Pinewood Studios, and was intended—by Christopher and Don—to go back to the original Mary Shelley story-line. Lasting about four hours, it won the prize for the best scenario at the International Festival of Fantastic and Science Fiction films in Paris in 1976. The Los Angeles *Times* called it "a total triumph." Even if the director and front-office boys did not respect each and every item of the Bachardy-Isherwood conception, nonetheless it was gratifying for Christopher that the multi-million-dollar project had brought a moment of success in an otherwise rather disappointing career as a scriptwriter.

In the summer of 1973, they worked on a screenplay of A *Meeting by the River*, but they were never able to get anyone interested in it.

On September 29, 1973, Christopher was shocked by the news of Wystan Auden's death. He wrote to Edward Upward, on October 9:

> I was absolutely incredulous at first. It was one of those shocks which one had neglected to prepare oneself for—I'd always taken it for granted that he'd survive to write all our epi-

taphs. It seemed curiously sad that he never got the Nobel Prize, because I think he had set his heart on it. Needless to say, the news reached me from the media—Reuters and the BBC. The latter, after a respectful pause of 10 seconds so I could indulge in private grief, asked for a "comment"—"how would you place him as a writer?" They really are grotesque.

Christopher was not informed about the moving memorial service which was held for Wystan at Westminster Abbey, and wondered if Chester Kallman had been responsible for this in a moment of ill-timed spite. Certainly, Kallman degenerated horribly in the few remaining months of his own life, mostly spent in Greece.

Christopher and all his friends felt Wystan's death most deeply, not only because he had been a remarkable friend, but also because he had been a great poet. All of them recognised that he was the one genius among them. For several days, Christopher re-read his deceased friend's work, then decided that the best tribute he could pay to Wystan was to carry on with his own writing.

Since the mid-sixties, Christopher had had no major novel project under way, and even now thought in terms only of re-working the diaries and memories of his past life, in autobiographical form. In 1973 his idea was to write a book about his early years in America based on the massive 300,000-word diary of the 1939–44 period. But as he progressed, he realised that too many things would need explaining, and that he would have to write another book beforehand, which would fill in the years between *Lions and Shadows* (ending 1929) and the beginning of his American period (1939). That book became *Christopher and His Kind*, published in America in 1976, and in Britain in 1977. The fundamental difference between this and his earlier books was that it would give full details of his homosexual exploits.

Christopher was rapidly becoming quite a cult figure in "gay" circles, though he loathed that adjective, much preferring the more brutal word "queer." He had never hidden his own homosexuality from his friends—indeed, they were obliged to accept it, if they were to become or remain friends—but it was really only in the 1970s that he became an outspoken propagandist for the respectability of homosexual relationships. He was interviewed on numerous occasions by gay magazines and newspapers on both sides of the Atlantic, and readily accepted speaking engagements on the subject. In December 1974, for example, Don and he travelled to New York by train to talk about homosexual literature to a convention of college teachers. Being such an evidently civilised, witty and unqueenly speaker, he became a popular spokesman for the cause.

Although a moderate in his manner as far as sexual matters were concerned, he was nonetheless quite radical in his thought, most especially in his defence of promiscuity. Many critics of homosexuals have lambasted them for excessive promiscuity and for spreading venereal disease. Christopher took the bull by the horns in defending promiscuity, even in situations such as his relationship with Don, claiming that a true loving relationship could only be evident when it had been tested by, and survived, sexual promiscuity by either or both partners. He also defended the validity of one-night stands, believing that some of man's greatest sexual experiences come in brief encounters, which need not necessarily be sordid, or even totally anonymous.

This candid public stance openly implied to the world many things about his relationship with Don. Initially, it had looked to some to merely be a replay of earlier affairs, based essentially on physical obsession, but over the years it became obvious that it was different. Christopher watched lovingly over the artistic and character development of the younger man, helping where he could, but not crushing Don's sensibility with his own forceful personality and his standing as a writer. He encouraged Don in his own branch of creativity, as well as working directly with him in the latter years. Don, in turn, provided moral support and a sense of stability, while accepting Christopher's outlook on other relationships. They shared the mundane necessities of everyday jobs, such as housework, and by preference chose new friendships that both could enjoy.

In the mid-1970s, a renaissance of interest in Christopher and fellow writers who had been prominent in the thirties took place. This could not have been a direct result of anything Christopher published, as it happened well before the publication of *Christopher and His Kind*. Possibly, it was inevitable that literary attention should move to their generation following the intensive coverage amongst scholars and in the media of their immediate predecessors, the Bloomsbury Group, whose biographies and studies dominated the literary pages and book stalls of the early 1970s. When the Auden generation revival began, Isherwood, Spender and Upward were still alive, and thus could enjoy the peculiar sensation of visiting an exhibition about themselves at the National Portrait Gallery in London, in June 1976. Everyone agreed that it was well set out, though Christopher was a little peeved that nowhere was it mentioned that so many of the leading figures of that literary generation had been homosexual or bisexual.

The summer of 1976 also brought the death of Swami Prabhavananda, after a quite lengthy period of frailty. Christopher was stoical about the death of his guru, and soon decided that his next book should trace the complex spiritual relationship between the two men, a work that would perhaps be a greater challenge to his ability to communicate to the general reader than had been any other.

Christopher and His Kind was moderately well received in the States, but caused more interest in Great Britain, where it even crept into the bottom of the Top Ten Best Sellers in hardback. It is a cleverly controlled book, with flashes of the old Isherwood humour, but with the urgency almost of a novel.

Most biographies have an obvious ending. This one happily does not. I started writing this book about an author whose work I admired, but finished up by writing about a friend. In the summer of 1976, when the main researches were finished, Isherwood drove me to the Santa Monica Greyhound Bus Station. We both chuckled nervously, remembering that this was the place we had first set eyes on each other. For want of anything better to say, I murmured that I hoped there wouldn't be *too* many shocks in the book. Characteristically he replied reproachfully, "Oh, but there *must* be!"

APPENDIX ONE

Selected list of identities of pseudonyms in *Lions and Shadows:*

Wystan Auden	Hugh Weston
John Barbirolli	Forno
Roger and Stella Burford	Roger and Polly East
Bill Lichtenberg	Bill Scott
André, Olive, Fowke and Sylvain Mangeot	The Cheurets
Kenneth Pickthorn	Mr. Gorse
G. B. Smith	Mr. Holmes
Stephen Spender	Stephen Savage
Edward Upward	Allen Chalmers
Vernon Watkins	Percival
Hector Wintle	Philip Linsley

APPENDIX TWO

Authorship of the Auden-Isherwood plays, courtesy of Edward Mendelson:

THE DOG BENEATH THE SKIN

I	i	Auden.
I	ii	Isherwood, song by Auden.
I	iii	Auden.
I	iv	Mostly Isherwood.
I	v	Auden.
II	i	About half Auden, half Isherwood.
II	ii	Mostly Auden.
II	iii	Modified from Auden's original by Isherwood.
II	iv	Auden.
II	v	Verse by Auden, dialogue of the feet by Isherwood.
III	i	Auden.
III	ii	Auden; Destructive Desmond sequence by Isherwood.
III	iii	Auden?
III	iv	Auden.
III	v	Auden, revised by Isherwood for published text.

THE ASCENT OF F6

I	i	Auden.
I	ii	Isherwood.
I	iii	Isherwood, verse by Auden.
II	i	Isherwood, except for the dialogue between Ransom and the Abbot.
II	ii	Isherwood, except for Ransom's soliloquy to the skull and his final speech.
II	iii	Isherwood.
II	iv	Auden.
II	v	Part Auden, part Isherwood.

ON THE FRONTIER

All the verse and part of the prose by Auden, remainder of prose by Isherwood.

THE MAJOR WORKS OF CHRISTOPHER ISHERWOOD

NOVELS
All the Conspirators, Jonathan Cape, 1928.
The Memorial, the Hogarth Press, 1932.
Mr. Norris Changes Trains, the Hogarth Press, 1935.
Goodbye to Berlin, the Hogarth Press, 1939.
Prater Violet, Methuen, 1946.
The World in the Evening, Methuen, 1954.
Down There on a Visit, Methuen, 1962.
A Single Man, Methuen, 1964.
A Meeting by the River, Methuen, 1967.

PLAYS (with W. H. Auden)
The Dog Beneath the Skin, Faber and Faber, 1935.
The Ascent of F6, Faber and Faber, 1936.
On the Frontier, Faber and Faber, 1938.

TRAVEL
Journey to a War (with W. H. Auden), Faber and Faber, 1939.
The Condor and the Cows, Methuen, 1949.

AUTOBIOGRAPHY
Lions and Shadows, the Hogarth Press, 1938.
Kathleen and Frank, Methuen, 1971.
Christopher and His Kind, Methuen, 1977.

BIOGRAPHY
Ramakrishna and His Disciples, Methuen, 1965.

PHILOSOPHY

Vedanta for the Western World, the Marcel Road Co., Hollywood, 1945.

Vedanta for Modern Man, Harper and Bros., New York, 1951.

An Approach to Vedanta, Vedanta Press, Hollywood, 1963.

Essentials of Vedanta, Vedanta Press, Hollywood, 1969.

ANTHOLOGY

Exhumations, Methuen, 1966.

TRANSLATIONS

The Intimate Journals of Charles Baudelaire, Blackamore Press, 1930.

The Song of God: Bhagavad-Gita (with Swami Prabhavananda), Vedanta Press, Hollywood, 1944.

Shankara's Crest-Jewel of Discrimination (with Swami Prabhavananda), Vedanta Press, Hollywood, 1946.

How to Know God: The Yoga Aphorisms of Patanjali (with Swami Prabhavananda), Vedanta Press, Hollywood, 1962.

INDEX